Interpreting the Environment at Museums and Historic Sites

INTERPRETING HISTORY

AASLH

About the Series

The American Association for State and Local History publishes the *Interpreting History* series in order to provide expert, in-depth guidance in interpretation for history professionals at museums and historic sites. The books are intended to help practitioners expand their interpretation to be more inclusive of the range of American history.

Books in this series help readers:

- quickly learn about the questions surrounding a specific topic,
- introduce them to the challenges of interpreting this part of history, and
- highlight best practice examples of how interpretation has been done by different organizations.

They enable institutions to place their interpretative efforts into a larger context, despite each having a specific and often localized mission. These books serve as quick references to practical considerations, further research, and historical information.

Titles in the Series

Interpreting the Environment at Museums and Historic Sites

Debra A. Reid and David D. Vail

ROWMAN & LITTLEFIELD
Lanham • Boulder • New York • London

Published by Rowman & Littlefield
An imprint of The Rowman & Littlefield Publishing Group, Inc.
4501 Forbes Boulevard, Suite 200, Lanham, Maryland 20706
www.rowman.com

6 Tinworth Street, London SE 11 5AL, United Kingdom

British Library Cataloguing in Publication Information Available

Library of Congress Cataloging-in-Publication Data

ISBN 978-1-5381-1548-0 (cloth : alk. paper)
ISBN 978-1-5381-1549-7 (pbk. : alk. paper)
ISBN 978-1-5381-1550-3 (electronic)

∞™ The paper used in this publication meets the minimum requirements of American National
Standard for Information Sciences—Permanence of Paper for Printed Library Materials, ANSI/
NISO Z39.48-1992.

Printed in the United States of America

Contents

Foreword

Whenever we began a project Father would always emphasize to my sister, my brother, and me an adage, "If it isn't broke . . . improve it!"

It became a standard of mine in approaching any type of task and employment, and I regularly look to see if others are thinking in a like manner. Too often I witness interpretive sites, programs, and writings moving in a different mode and relying on an older saying, "If it ain't broke, don't fix it," and becoming stale, outdated, and far too redundant as a consequence.

Dr. Debra Reid and Dr. David Vail have moved away from offering just another book on interpretive techniques with *Interpreting the Environment*. This book offers an improvement in what many may feel "does not need fixing."

Far from being another primer on interpretive techniques that is generic or too field-specific, this book approaches the subject in an agglomerated manner. Using their joint experiences in interpretation—cultural, environment, ecological, and historical—they approach the subject of interpretation with an appreciation that numerous panoramas must be explored to better and fully comprehend the importance and stimulate any subject interpreted to the public. No, it is more than a primer. It is a volume that makes us aware of the already-present connection between the collective fields of interpretation and how we must recognize and use these disciplines to better understand who we are historically and environmentally and how we should continue to provoke ourselves and future generations.

Without understanding the history and the environmental background of subjects we fail to comprehend the entire story of our surroundings and our heritage. Each contributes to a better understanding as to "why" situations occurred and how humankind was influenced and affected by what was around them and whether those factors were given attention or ignored.

As an example, in understanding the flood of Great Johnstown, Pennsylvania, in 1889, we can reflect better on the natural elements and fallible human actions that contributed to one of the worst natural disasters in U.S. history. Moreover, we can ask what was done to improve those issues in that area after that flood. We also can ask why so many "improvements" failed, contributing to the massive floods in both 1936 and 1977.

By understanding our heritage and collective past through multiple disciplines we better understand the land around us, the prehistory we regularly uncover, and the influences that contributed to the whys and wherefores of our world.

Dr. Reid and Dr. Vail furnish a panoptic contribution of interpretive methodologies that will better ensure that interpretive programming and support will provide better understanding of the continued mixing of all disciplines of cultural, historical, economical, and environmental representations that create a better understanding of our heritage to ourselves and our audiences. Nothing stands alone.

As a historian and a professional historic interpretive specialist, I welcome the insightful and professional standards that Dr. Reid and Dr. Vail have contributed to the field of interpersonal interpretation. It is excellent to have a text that illustrates and informs what so many have expressed for so long. It is a large step in creating improved interpretive programming and thought for all of us in these fields.

Interpreting the Environment is a volume that is relevant for any interpretive site and training. It has universal offerings for any theme and program design and should be a publication in any library devoted to telling the stories of our world and heritage.

John C. F. Luzader
Principal
Living Museums of the West
NAI Master
NAI Fellow

Preface

There is grandeur in this view of life, with its several powers, having been originally
breathed into a few forms or into one; and that, whilst this planet has gone cycling on
according to the fixed law of gravity, from so simple a beginning endless forms most
beautiful and most wonderful have been, and are being, evolved.

CHARLES DARWIN, *ON THE ORIGIN OF SPECIES*[1]

Interpreting the Environment at Museums and Historic Sites is for anyone who wants to better understand the environment that surrounds us and sustains us. It is for everyone who wants to discover the human perspective on the environments in which we live. It is for everyone who wants to share those human perspectives about nature and the environment with others.

Interpreting the Environment conceptualizes nature and wilderness as something that humans influence. It conceptualizes farms, mines, and Main Streets as things that humans built. Wilderness spaces and natural places conserved for use as tourist destinations and recreation areas attest to human manipulation of the environment, whereas farms, mines, and Main Streets indicate the layers of influence that humans exert on the environment in their effort to get water, grow food, travel and trade, and build things. This book supports documentation of all these spaces, preserved and interpreted at nature and forest preserves, conservation and park and recreation districts, and in museums and historic sites.

Interpreting the Environment supports a multidisciplinary approach—more science in the history, and more history in the science—to create the most authentic stories. Incorporating more human influence in nature centers and more science in historic sites conveys more accurately the biosphere that we inhabit and that others influenced before us. Incorporating the sciences, history, and the humanities ensures a deep and broad body of evidence about ecological and historical changes over time. Every place, from sea to mountain range and prairie, from rural route and Main Street to city center, has equal status as evidence. Every entity from metroparks to national parks and museums to ecotourism destinations share responsibility for telling the story. Multidisciplinary environment-centric interpretation should appeal to a wide audience.[2]

Good work already exists. Many dig deep into the local history and the natural history of a place. We explore ever-expanding circles of interconnection between one place and other places. We tell these stories, depending on disciplinary distinctions, by emphasizing either nature or history in their interpretation of the environment. The time is right to explore the theory and methods that have worked for so many institutions and to articulate some best practices that can help you interpret the environment.

The process starts by learning as much as you can about the environment that your museum or historic site occupies. The landscape might be the largest three-dimensional object in the collection, but do we perceive it as such? How many of us catalog the landscape and the flora and fauna in the same way that we catalog our decorative arts and other historical artifacts? Consider doing so. The exercise will help us itemize "nature" (i.e., the biology, geography, soil substrate, and climate of a place). With this evidence, we can begin to determine the physical properties that drew humans to a place or that kept them at a distance. We can also begin to conceptualize the stories that help make places meaningful.

The process continues by determining the relationships between humans and nature in a place. Every object in a collection can contribute to the exploration. Photographs provide a snapshot of a place in the past. Paintings convey perceptions of places. Furniture and other decorative arts stand as by-products of natural resources such as wood, iron, sand, clay, or precious metals extracted from, or transported to, a place. Museum collections, from the most expansive landscapes and impressive structures to the tiniest precious stone or silver-plated utensil, help document human-environment engagement. Each attests to the human quest to survive and thrive and can prompt conversations about the costs of human survival to the environment.

The Chief Aim of Interpretation: Provocation

Early naturalists and conservationists relied on words to express their concerns about human influences on the environment long before the environmental movement of the 1960s. Naturalist, geographer, and explorer Alexander von Humboldt wrote about negative environmental effects of deforestation and monoculture in Venezuela and other parts of South and Central America between 1799 and 1804. Diplomat Charles Perkins Marsh explained the connection between environmental degradation and the fall of the Roman Empire in *Man and Nature*, published in 1864. By 1875, ecology gained cache as a biological science that explored symbiotic relationships between flora and fauna in situ and in flux.[3]

As ecology came into its own as a science, conservationists drew on diverse forms of expression—photography, drawing, and painting—to persuade U.S. congressmen to designate Yellowstone as the first national park in 1872. Park designation helped protect lands from development, but debate continued about how to balance private access with the public good of preservation. During the 1940s, the National Park Service Trust Fund Board commissioned writer Freeman Tilden to advocate for parks as cultural spaces (not exclusively wild places) that needed sustained support. Tilden's 1940s publication, *The Fifth Essence: An Invitation to Share in Our Eternal Heritage*, resulted. He further stressed the mutual dependency between parks and people in *The National Parks: What They Mean to You and Me*

(1951). After World War II, and during the Cold War, the nation's parks were cast as the last vestige of the frontier, which many believed shaped the destiny of the United States. Furthermore, the parks protected unique historical assets that U.S. citizens needed to retain their rural identity. Tilden, knowing that parks could not speak for themselves, followed up with the book that conveyed the power of sharing the human-nature relationship, *Interpreting our Heritage* (1957). The six principles of interpretation that he outlined in this short book remain influential in structuring park and recreation and public history interpretation.

Tilden's fourth principle of interpretation, "The chief aim of Interpretation is not instruction, but provocation," emphasized the need to mobilize the public to care about "places where firsthand experience with the objects of Nature's and Man's handiwork can be had." Some have tried to improve on Tilden's principles, but *Interpreting the Environment* embraces his approach because Tilden advocated for interpretation as a process of discovery that led to advocacy. Specifically, he hoped that interpretation would mobilize the public to appreciate and protect "our preserved natural and man-made treasurers." As he explained, "Nature and Man are inseparable companions: They are one. If you vandalize a beautiful thing, you vandalize yourself. And this is what true interpretation can inject into the consciousness."[4]

We belabor Tilden here because his 1957 call to action was both a timeless call to use interpretation to effect change and a product of its time. Tilden wrote it in the context of Cold War nationalism and the nuclear age and for an audience appreciative of natural and cultural heritage. His work changed the way we reveal meanings and relationships about places. Others publishing at the same time changed the ways we think about human-nature relationships. William Vogt alerted readers to the ways that insecticides can destroy ecosystems and put humans and their environment at risk in his 1948 book, *Road to Survival*. Aldo Leopold explained the moral obligation that humans bear for the land in *A Sand County Almanac*, published in 1949. Rachel Carson completed her trilogy on the sea with *The Edge of the Sea* in 1955, making clear the connections among humans, coastal, and ocean health. These cautionary tales and calls for public stewardship of natural spaces, stood in contrast to unbridled geographic expansion and extraction of natural resources and agricultural land use. Tilden viewed interpretation as a means to an end, helping the public become better environmental stewards.[5]

Since Leopold, Carson, and Tilden, interpretation and environmentalism have gained traction. The American Society for Environmental History (ASEH) formed in 1977, twenty years after Tilden's first edition of *Interpreting our Heritage* appeared. The ASEH supported historical—objective—analysis of the human-nature continuum. Award-winning environmental historian William Cronon explained that those who studied the human-nature continuum believed that they could help change the world. His article, "The Uses of Environmental History," singled out policy makers, activists, and the general public as beneficiaries. He believed his readers should embrace their approach to studying the environment. "Seeing the past as a story to be told rather than as a problem to be solved" was an asset, and the lessons from the past could have profound influence to effect positive change.[6]

The messages that students of the environment convey have real urgency. A warmer climate, a shrinking supply of nonrenewable resources, and polluted waterways and oceans indicate the ways that humans have affected the environment on a global scale. *Interpreting the Environment* draws its first breath during the Anthropocene, a new epoch distinguished by irrefutable evidence of human imposition on the globe. It draws on decades of good work in environmental history and interpretation to lay out a road map to add the environment to museums and historic site interpretation. These real concerns provide a launch pad to discuss environmental topics, from the elemental (e.g., the environment collected, preserved, and interpreted at a museum or historic site, nature preserve, or conservation district) through the controversial (e.g., climate change, pollution, nonrenewable resources, and fossil fuels).

The environment writ large provides a solid foundation for interpreting different perspectives and experiences in one place over time. The landscape itself, and the artifacts made from natural resources (i.e., wood and stone), from flora and fauna harvested from the land (i.e., leather shoes, straw hats, woolen blankets), and from synthetic substances devised to reduce dependency on natural resources (i.e., plastics from petroleum), all document human-environment relationships.

Interpreting the Environment provides a toolkit (the IE Toolkit) that we can use to decide what topics to emphasize and what strategies to take to realize the chief aim of interpretation, provocation, as Tilden explained it. The stories of human-nature relationships can increase public investment with larger environmental issues, issues that affect the planet's survival. Museums and historic sites have the ability to introduce the public to this colossal subject and to provide a platform for them to move beyond appreciation of nature toward recognition of their individual roles in preserving their place and taking action to become better stewards of it.

Humans . . . Land . . . Nature . . . Conservation . . . Exploitation

Interpreting the Environment recognizes the public investment in conservation of natural areas. The most impressive natural landscapes became the first national parks. Municipalities, counties, states, and private nonprofit organizations also collected and preserved land by designating it as part of a forest preserve, a conservation district, or a nature area. Class, race, gender, and ethnicity factored into the history of the places. Tensions might continue to fester over access to and control of these places. Balancing public access with private use poses real challenges, but a land ethic statement justifies sustainable management.

Pollution . . . Environmental Degradation . . . Fossil-Fuel Dependency . . . Global Warming

Some might categorize these as imaginary enemies. *Interpreting the Environment* approaches them as real threats and worthy of engagement.

Composting . . . Green Certification . . . Reduce, Reuse, Recycle . . . Sustainability

Some consider these as futile efforts to reverse entropy. *Interpreting the Environment* approaches them as natural acts that stewards of cultural patrimony should perform and pursue.

Place in the Field

Interpreting the Environment is designed to serve a large audience. State and local history institutions have collections (e.g., landscapes, buildings, objects, and archives) to tell stories about the environment. Park and recreation districts, forest preserves, and conservation districts with historic properties have the facilities to interpret cultural heritage as well as recreational spaces. Communities manage nature trails and host cemetery walks. Special interest groups reclaim railway lines and clean up rivers and walkways.

A natural alliance should exist between keepers of state and local history and environmental historians who have spent the past forty years interpreting environmental issues in historic context. Several organizations serve institutions that interpret the environment and have a vested interest in successful ventures. These include the American Association for State and Local History, the National Council for Public History, the National Association for Interpretation, and the Association for Living History, Farm and Agricultural Museums. Regional affiliates to the American Alliance of Museums are well positioned to tackle environmental topics from numerous perspectives because they serve museums broadly defined, not just history-based institutions. Other special interest organizations exist to support the cause. This includes the National Trust for Historic Preservation and the National Park Service, which advocates for the preservation of buildings and landscapes, and the American Society for Environmental History, which supports the study of the environment in historical context.

Good work on sustainable practice has appeared recently, including books such as Cheryl M. Hargrove's *Cultural Heritage Tourism: Five Steps for Success and Sustainability* (2017), Sarah Sutton's *Environmental Sustainability at Historic Sites and Museums* (2015), Rachel Wolgemuth's *Cemetery Tours and Programming* (2016), and the third edition of Rudy J. Favretti and Joy Putman Favretti's *Landscapes and Gardens for Historic Buildings: A Handbook for Reproducing and Creating Authentic Landscapes* (2017). *The Public Historian*, the journal published by the National Council on Public History, has featured environmental stewardship and the role of public history in advocating for sustainability in one special issue, a white paper, and in working groups at annual conferences. The articles in journals such as *Environmental History* and regional and state publications become the basis for developing place specific interpretation. Finally, numerous publications of the National Association for Interpretation (NAI) inform interpretive theory and method addressed in *Interpreting the Environment.*

For decades, the NAI has served a growing number of park rangers employed in municipal, county, state, and national parks and park-and-recreation facilities. NAI based its long and distinguished career on the principles of interpretation as proposed by Freeman Tilden. Tilden did not frame his approach around humanist thinking, but his principles indicate clearly that the content must be structured in ways that engage the public. For decades, members of NAI have lobbied for more support of cultural heritage interpretation. Individuals have built consulting careers around cultural heritage interpretation workshops. NAI certification programs include one focused on cultural heritage. Momentum still tracks toward natural history and natural resources. Why? Because NAI publications still take an "environmental thinking" approach to interpreting the natural environment.

Interpreting the Environment synthesizes good work from these professional organizations, but it takes a different tact. It emphasizes the environment as an actor in a larger historical story. It also serves as a call-to-act, informed by multiple disciplines. The book:

- proposes a methodology that recognizes disciplinary approaches of the physical sciences, history, and the humanities.
- advocates for including historical thinking as a skill that furthers environmental education and interpretation.
- shares best practices of science, technology, engineering, and math (STEM) to the power of H (or STEALTH) approach suitable for use in park and recreation facilities, nature preserves, conservation areas, and forest preserve districts as well as in museums and historic sites.
- links interpretation to sustainable practices and environmental stewardship.

Throughout, *Interpreting the Environment* emphasizes connections between the actions of people and the long-lasting consequences to the environment. This aligns with current debates about climate change as a figment of the imagination, a natural environmental cycle, or a consequence of human agency. Today, nature as we know it hangs in the balance. *Interpreting the Environment* explores the numerous points of entry each site can take to engage visitors with these provocative and timely subjects.

Layout of the Book

William Cronon summarized the methodological approach of environmental historians in "A Place for Stories: Nature, History, and Narrative" (1992):

> Environmental historians . . . add a theoretical vocabulary in which plants, animals, soils, climates, and other nonhuman entities become the coactors and codeterminants of a history not just of people but of the earth itself. . . . [T]he importance of the natural world, its objective effects on people, and the concrete ways people affect it in turn are . . . the very heart of our intellectual project.[7]

The first part of *Interpreting the Environment* introduces readers to environmental history, historical thinking, and environmental education guidelines and interpretive potential. The second part is structured around the ways that humans manipulate the environment—creating working environments, getting water, generating and harnessing power, growing food, traveling and trading, building things, and preserving and conserving natural landscapes. Chapters in this part include case studies that showcase local, state, or regional history infused with environmental issues.

The first chapter organizes the work of environmental historians into subjects immediately useful to thinking about the environment in museum and historic site contexts. Environmental historians have changed the ways we think about Chicago (Cronon, *Nature's Metropolis*), Illinois Country, and the Great Lakes (White, *The Middle Ground*), the Kansas prairie (Least

Heat-Moon, *PrairyErth*), the Comanche Empire (Hämäläinen), and the Dust Bowl (which remains a provocative topic for many historians).[8] Each of these, and many others, helps us envision local histories that incorporate the natural world as co-actor and co-determinate. Historians come to different conclusions about the human influence on the environment. Reconceptualizing local history as a study of human-nature interaction provides opportunities to engage communities in discussions about hot topics such as waste management, environmental sustainability, and biodiversity; about environmental inequality and ecofeminism; and about renewable energy historically and today, including solar and wind, in contrast to fossil fuels.

Chapter 2 summarizes differences in the ways scientists and humanists think about the environment. It distinguishes between the ways that each approach researches, analyzes evidence, and uses knowledge. Then it explores how a multidisciplinary approach (humanities infused with science) can increase public engagement with environmental issues and do so in an objective way. A humanities skill, historical thinking, facilitates close reading of period literature about the history of a place. It also supports analysis of period evidence of flora, fauna, soils, and other natural resources of that place in the past. Historical thinking provides a means to help us avoid presentism and to recognize the scientific, cultural, and social mindsets expressed by those who generated the evidence in the first place. A case study of *Bison bison* shows how science, social science, and humanities help interpret faunal-human engagement in one region across millennia.

The third chapter addresses environmental literacy and public engagement with environmental topics relevant to your museum or historic site. It describes an exercise in cataloging collections that can help us rethink historical artifacts as evidence of human exploitation of natural resources. It explains how to build mission-relevant collections that document the environment. It aligns K–12 guidelines for environmental education with strategies to develop provocative interpretation.

Chapters in the second part of *Interpreting the Environment* explore seven subjects that most museums and historic sites can explore with their collections. Each chapter incorporates case studies of research and interpretation that presents the environment as co-actor and co-determinate.

The book concludes with two resources that identify main themes and resources to consult to build provocative interpretation about the environment. A bibliographic essay helps readers manage a growing literature on environmental history and the public history of the environmental movement. A timeline of relevant policy and significant ideas in environmental history round out the resources. These materials should help you identify relevant stories. These, in combination with the other chapters, will help you document stories about the environment and develop interpretation that stimulates further exploration of and engagement with the environment.

Notes

1. Charles Darwin, *On the Origin of Species by Means of Natural Selection, or The Preservation of Favoured Races in the Struggle for Life* (London: John Murray, Albemarle Street, 1859), 490.

2. Definitions help establish parameters but also indicate opportunities. The *Oxford English Dictionary* (*OED*) defines "environment" as "the area surrounding a place or thing" and "the physical surroundings or conditions in which a person or other organism lives, develops, etc., or in which a thing exists." These few words raise numerous opportunities for elaboration and interpretation. The *OED*'s definition of "nature," implies more limitations: "the phenomena of the physical world collectively; esp. plants, animals, and other features and products of the earth itself, as opposed to humans and human creations." Yes, human actions affect nature at the microscopic and megalithic scale.

3. For biographical information on Humboldt, see Andrea Wulf, *The Invention of Nature: Alexander von Humboldt's New World* (New York: Knopf, 2015). Andrea Wulf also explored the role of botany in empire-building and in the construction of botanical gardens in *The Brother Gardeners: Botany, Empire and the Birth of an Obsession* (New York: Vintage, 2010) and focused on U.S. nation builders and their obsession with plant collecting and cultivation in *Founding Gardeners: The Revolutionary Generation, Nature, and the Shaping of the American Nation* (New York: Knopf, 2011). David Lowenthal, *George Perkins Marsh: Prophet of Conservation* (Seattle: University of Washington Press, 2015).

4. Freeman Tilden, *Interpreting our Heritage*, 3rd ed. (Chapel Hill: University of North Carolina Press, 1977), 32–39, first quote, 33; second and third quote, 38.

5. Civil servant William Vogt cautioned readers against indiscriminate use of insecticides in *Road to Survival* (New York: William Sloane Associates, 1948). For more on Vogt, see Charles C. Mann's comparative history about Vogt and Norman Borlaug, *The Wizard and the Prophet: Two Remarkable Scientists and Their Dueling Visions to Shape Tomorrow's World* (New York: Alfred A. Knopf, 2018). Wildlife ecologist Aldo Leopold articulated the concept of a land ethic based in humans-flora-fauna interactions in *A Sand County Almanac and Sketches Here and There* (New York: Oxford University Press, 1949). For more on Leopold's influence, see Richard L. Knight and Suzanne Riedel, eds., *Aldo Leopold and the Ecological Conscience* (New York: Oxford University Press, 2002). Rachel Carson's three books on the sea included *Under the Sea-Wind: A Naturalist's Picture of Ocean Life* (New York: Simon & Schuster, 1941), *The Sea Around Us* (Oxford: Oxford University Press, 1952), and *The Edge of the Sea* (New York: Houghton-Mifflin, 1955). For more on Carson, see Linda Lear, *Rachel Carson: Witness for Nature* (New York: Houghton-Mifflin, 1998; rev. ed. 2015) and William Souder, *On a Farther Shore: The Life and Legacy of Rachel Carson* (New York: Crown Publishers, 2012).

6. William Cronon, "The Uses of Environmental History," *Environmental History Review*, vol. 17, no. 3 (Autumn, 1993), 1–22, quote 17.

7. William Cronon, "A Place for Stories: Nature, History, and Narrative," *Journal of American History*, vol. 78, no. 4 (March 1992), 1347–1376, quote 1349.

8. See the bibliographic essay for selected humanist readings on the environment, broadly defined.

Acknowledgments

Exciting things happen when humanists talk to scientists about a particular place. The ripple effects that result from such interactions keep us informed across disciplinary divides and committed to collaboration. Reaching beyond one disciplinary eddy or whirlpool helps us see the possibilities that exist when approaching subjects from broader vantage points.

Those who study the environment find common ground on many subjects. Special interest networks link people and support kinship communities across disciplines. Those who study vernacular architecture find like-minded colleagues among cultural geographers, architectural historians, and historians of landscape architecture. Those who study environmental history find like-minded colleagues among those who study earth science, public policy, or agricultural history. Finding kindred spirits may result from chance encounters between individuals pursuing connections between place and people.

We co-authors share some support networks but not all. We find our perspectives informed by different historical organizations. David interacts with humanities council staff in Kansas and Nebraska, each committed to local engagement with constituents concerned about their environments. He also engages with environmental historians through the American Society for Environmental History and with historians of agricultural science and technology. Debra has twenty more years of experience engaging with museum and historic-site service organizations, including the Association for Living History, Farm and Agricultural Museums (ALHFAM) and the American Association for State and Local History (AASLH), but she has been a member of the Vernacular Architecture Forum almost as long and has studied historical and cultural geography even longer. We both view professional interest groups that we participate in and serve not as indoctrination centers but as networks that support think tanks. The intersection of our professional circles drew us both to the Agricultural History Society conference in Springfield, Illinois, in 2011. Seven years later, we appreciate this opportunity afforded by Charles Harmon, editor, Rowman & Littlefield, and Bob Beatty and John Marks, AASLH, to put our heads together and write *Interpreting the Environment at Museums and Historic Sites.*

Our conversations since 2011 kept us both committed to researching and sharing environmental history. We both know that staff in museums and historic sites play a pivotal role in helping spread the word. We intend this book to help people invested in and committed to learning more about the environment and using the lessons learned to develop their own provocative public programming.

Each of us had formative experiences that reinforced our interests in multidisciplinary study of the environment.

Debra fell in love with cultural geography in fifth grade. She regaled her father with details about the lives of ten-year-old Pacific Islanders and their coconut palm trees as we hauled hay from field to barn. Their stories captivated Debra's imagination, perhaps because they stood in stark contrast to the stories her father told about his experiences in the U.S. Navy, deployed to the South Pacific during World War II. The textbook, a product of the Cold-War era may have contained bias, but that did not register at the time. The human-nature exchange captivated Debra, probably because she also hugged trees on the family farm, played on a dirt pile rather than a sand pile, and roamed the woods daily, totally comfortable in the spaces that gave cattle shade and water. The lessons learned in fifth grade remained vivid as her parents watched her traipse off to earn degrees in historic preservation, history museum studies, cultural geography, and history, all of which sustained her study of people and their relationships to the places they inhabit, despite her physical removal because of job choices from these spaces that informed her worldview.

David found his love for history in the Oregon woods, Cascade Mountains, and annual family trips to Crater Lake National Park. The time he spent with his father and grandfather traversing farming, ranching, and wilderness terrains sparked a love of environmental history and agricultural history that had as much to do with adventures on the land as thinking about the history of place and peoples. Multiple visits to museums and historical societies continued to guide David's passion for the past, but his many trips with family showed that discovery, primary sources, and historical artifacts can be mountains, rivers, and grasslands as much as they can be farm ledgers, threshers, and policy statements.

We consider *Interpreting the Environment* our opportunity to expand the circles of those invested in studying the environment and using the lessons learned to teach about the precarious future of the human-nature continuum. Specifically, we advocate for a broad-based effort to ensure the long-term stewardship of place and the survival of people in those places.

Debra A. Reid
Dearborn, Michigan
February 2019

David D. Vail
Kearney, Nebraska
February 2019

Part I

A PRIMER ON THE ENVIRONMENT, CULTURAL HERITAGE, AND HISTORY INTERPRETATION

CHAPTER 1

Exploring Environmental History

In Wildness Is the Preservation of the World.

HENRY DAVID THOREAU[1]

FOR MANY OF US, our interest in the environment and our desire to interpret it began through personal observations and adventures in parks, nature centers, and recreation areas. Yet, the dynamic biological relationships that create landscapes, affect animal populations, and inspire artists, scientists, and adventurers remain hidden to most of us. As a consequence, "the environment" lies just below the surface in our exhibitions, displays, and historic sites. There are many reasons for this oversight. In certain ways, the environment is so common and fundamental that it is quite easy to overlook the layers of culture, technology, economy, and ecology that build a landscape or remake it. Or, it is easier to discuss "the environment" as a neatly packaged single category and not as complex multifaceted things within and beyond our control. The environment is the elephant in the room for us and for our visitors. Just as surprises abound on our favorite hiking trails, the field of environmental history—the themes, the approaches, the complexities, and the controversies—can inspire us to think differently about our histories and to deploy our collections to tell new stories.

Mapping the Trails

Environmental history is part of the IE Toolkit. Understanding "the environment" starts with reading how others have interpreted it at different times in the past and in different contexts. Close reading of secondary sources helps envision ways to incorporate the environment into exhibits, historic site plans, preservation briefs, and interactive outreach programming. Secondary readings help us identify different arguments about cause and effect and change over time. We can then test these findings in the context of museums and historic sites in specific places and interpreting specific times. This will help us realize our goal to connect visitors to their interconnected, nonhuman world.

Environmental History: Part of the IE Toolkit (Batteries Included)

Tool 1: Arriving Is Different than Leaving

Most museums or historic sites have this goal in mind: We want visitors to leave with new interpretations and perspectives that they did not carry in. New interpretive trails, however, can pose challenges and opportunities. Environmental history offers much to help. What we learn can help us and our visitors recognize stereotypes or partisan perspectives and their influence on landscapes, plant life, and animal communities. Its intellectual roots and its activist expressions make environmental history a useful approach to engage in conversations about policies and personal views that manifest in the biosphere (i.e., the ecological system that incorporates all animate and inanimate things). Past and present, personal and professional can all merge together, offering visitors new opportunities to reconsider how they see environments, how they feel about conservation practices, and how they appreciate the commercial or the intrinsic value of local natural resources. Complexity abounds and environmental history can help us see how the past adds context to understand current issues.

Tool 2: Connections Count

At its heart, interpreting the environment starts by identifying a series of connections between multiple layers of a landscape. Environmental history helps us see these layers and can make clear the past actions that helped create the layers. As historian Louis Warren suggests, to interpret the environment historically means exploring "the changing connections between people and nature, a project that has been dominated by questioning, abrading, interrogating, and otherwise troubling the boundary between nature and culture."[2] This history is "complex, confusing, and for that reason all the more intriguing."[3] Historians draw on other disciplines to profile biological interactions among animals (human and nonhuman), plants, microbes, diseases, soil, and the list goes on. These relationships and interconnections changed over time, and historians help explain what caused change and what benefits or collateral damage occurred as a consequence.

Tool 3: Participation Provides New Perspectives

Historians of the environment actively engage with their subject matter. Historian Donald Worster suggests that "the environmental historian must learn to speak some new languages as well as ask some new questions. . . . [They] must begin by reconstructing past landscapes, learning what they were and how they functioned before human societies entered and rearranged them."[4] This involves studying the three-dimensional evidence, the landscape and its environments, walking paths that others have trod, and considering the vantage points of those who created the sources that historians reference. Such engagement with evidence can lead to new interpretations of the past. Yet, environmental historians also avoid letting presentism affect their interpretation of the historic evidence at hand. The hands-on and minds-on approach to studying historic landscapes and environments transfers easily to participatory programming that gets visitors to museums and historic sites outside and engaging with multiple senses, experiencing their surroundings and reading the layers of evidence before them.

This kind of participatory learning can take many forms. The case studies in *Interpreting Environment* offer observations and perspectives that can help instruct your approaches, but a couple of concepts are key. First, culture is fluid and so is nature. As historian William Cronon points out, in "rate and scale . . . the relationship between nature and culture should always be viewed as a problem in comparative dynamics, not statics."[5] Both are shaped by individual as well as collective actions. Environmental history gives a "sense" of a mobile, uncertain, and unpredictable past. Second, visitors are part of a much larger mosaic that is biological, ecological, and historical. Historian James Sherow's concept of biosystems can assist here. Humans and nonhumans, he writes, are part of the "biosystems in which they live; the difference between them and other species arise only in the degree to which humans are aware of their place in their environments . . . human beings are a conscious part of environments. In an important way environments are becoming aware of themselves."[6] A biosystems approach, then, can encourage archivists, museum docents, and visitors to see primary sources and artifacts in new ways—to begin to see interconnections and complex relationships where they least expected it. By adding biosystems to our interpretive programing, we can help visitors "acquire a new way of seeing history [a history not just about humans], and in that vision, a route toward a better understanding of ourselves."[7]

Tool 4: Digitizing Natural Things

Central to interpreting the environment is visitors' access. The rapidly expanding advances in digital technologies and new forms of study such as digital humanities make this "tool" fundamental in archival preservation, museum interpretation, and historic site engagement. Environmental history offers much for institution digitization plans. From seaborn maps that identify layers of settlement and ownership and historic specimens of soil and insects to remote telepresence technologies in use at various national parks or historic sites, digitizing environmental artifacts or capturing ecological processes through maker spaces (i.e., public spaces for designing, building, and learning) can offer a kind of ecological heritage visualization and crowd-sourcing activity that, in the words of Neil Gershenfeld, director of Massachusetts Institute of Technology's (MIT) Center for Bits and Atoms, connects "the programmability of the digital worlds we've invented" that is applied "to the physical world we inhabit."[8]

The Batteries

Finally, most toolkits need a power source to get work started and to keep it moving. Interdisciplinary approaches propel environmental history. Drawing on many sources may seem overwhelming at first, but from such diverse vantage points, a more complete impression of a place results. The rest of this chapter explores environmental history that can help you comprehend the environments that you steward and realize the potential they hold for interpretation.

Thinking about Wilderness and Getting Others to Do the Same

Section (C) "A wilderness, in contrast with those areas where man and his own works dominate the landscape, is hereby recognized as an area where the earth and its community of life are untrammeled by man, where man himself is a visitor who does not remain. An area of wilderness is further defined to mean in this Act an area of undeveloped Federal land retaining its primeval character and influence, without permanent improvements or human habitation, which is protected and managed so as to preserve its natural conditions."

THE WILDERNESS ACT, 1964[9]

Few visitors to museums, historic sites, or national parks in the United States have read *Section C* of the 1964 Wilderness Act. Congress passed the legislation during an era of environmental activism that demanded reforms around cleaner air, waterways, pollution superfund sites, and proliferation of agricultural chemicals. Scientists such as ecologist Aldo Leopold and biologist Rachel Carson inspired the era's policies and practices. They drew on early twentieth-century debates by forester Gifford Pinchot, naturalist John Muir, agriculturalist Seaman A. Knapp, U.S. president Theodore Roosevelt, and others over the conservation and preservation of natural resources.[10]

The cultural concepts of "conservation," "preservation," and "wilderness" inspired powerful scientific discoveries and forged potent political views on how to think about and what do with the natural resources of the United States throughout the twentieth century. One crucial moment is when President Roosevelt spoke to a council of governors in 1908 about the values of being "conservation-minded." In his speech, he outlined the early framework of the 1916 Organic Act that President Woodrow Wilson signed into law, creating the National Park Service.[11]

"The wise use of all of our natural resources," Roosevelt bellowed to the nation's governors, "which are our national resources as well, is the great material question of today. I have asked you to come together now because the enormous consumption of these resources, and the threat of imminent exhaustion of some of them, due to reckless and wasteful use, . . . calls for common effort, common action." Roosevelt insisted that every state consider the environment—the natural surroundings, resources, and landscapes—because it carried cultural as well as intrinsic value:

> The time has come for a change [from unrestricted individualism]. As a people we have the right and the duty, second to none other but the right and duty of obeying the moral law, of requiring and doing justice, to protect ourselves and our children against the wasteful development of our natural resources, whether that waste is caused by the actual destruction of such resources by making them impossible of development hereafter.[12]

The National Park Service (NPS) is one of the first organizations in the United States to connect the environment to the public at large. Stephen T. Mather's lobbying in the early 1900s emphasized these values by arguing for preserved places that all visitors from all walks of life could find restoration. For Mather and many others, parks became synonymous with restoration and tourism. As Carol Shull and Dwight Pitcaithley suggest, Mather "saw them [national parks] as extensions of local parks, places where the American public could and should go to recharge their batteries, places where they should expect to find hotels and roads and other amenities that would accommodate their visit without too much hardship." The "wilderness" in the park system, at certain moments, conformed to preservationist views of John Muir as expressed in *My First Summer in the Sierra* (1911) and in *The Yosemite* (1912), and at other moments, contested them for wise use of natural places and their resources. Decades later, other authors weighed in on environmental stewardship, including Wallace Stegner in *Angle of Repose* (1971), Wendell Berry in *The Unsettling of America: Culture and Agriculture* (1996), Edward Abbey in *Desert Solitaire: A Season in the Wilderness* (1968), and Terry Tempest Williams in *Refuge: An Unnatural History of Family and Place* (1991). Horace Albright expanded the NPS mission to begin to recognize that historical landscapes were both natural and built environments, in keeping with Muir's perspective. With support of President Franklin Delano Roosevelt during the 1930s, Albright helped guide the NPS toward establishing the framework for the Historic Sites Act of 1935. This ultimately served as the central guiding legislation for the National Historic Preservation Act of 1966.[13]

The Wilderness Act of 1964 defined "wilderness" as places where "the earth and its community of life are untrammeled by man, where man himself is a visitor who does not remain."[14] In fact, the Bureau of Land Management (BLM), U.S. Forest Service (USFS), and NPS constructed "wilderness" and "natural" places and then preserved and maintained them. Wilderness areas carry evidence of human and nonhuman occupations, geological forces, regional development, and politics, to name a few. Even the biological make-up of parks—their plants, animals, soils, hydrological pathways, or mountain trails—result from complex connections between the cultural, the constructed, and the natural. Most Americans have come to know "wilderness" as a concept that mixes the environmental with the commercial. Parks such as Arizona's Grand Canyon National Park, Oregon's Crater Lake National Park, California's Yellowstone National Park and Yosemite National Park, or Hawaii's Volcanoes National Park interpret historic as well as elemental forces. They also cater to visitor needs, providing campgrounds with modern plumbing or hotels on the outskirts of mountains that allow them access, exercise, and escape.

Historians have long traced this cultural making and remaking of wilderness. William Cronon addresses this in his pioneering essay "The Trouble with Wilderness; or, Getting Back to the Wrong Nature" in *Uncommon Ground: Rethinking the Human Place in Nature* (1996) as do Richard Sellars in *Preserving Nature in the National Parks: A History* (1997), Paul Sutter in *Driven Wild: How the Fight against Automobiles Launched the Modern Wilderness Movement* (2002), and Hal Rothman in *Devil's Bargains: Tourism in the Twentieth-Century American West* (1998). These studies of humans, their technologies, and their influence on nature provide a first step toward understanding wilderness spaces as historic artifacts. The next step entails combining the lessons from the books with personal experiences of hiking through a crater, or scaling the crags, or observing the predictable rise of geyser Old Faithful, or the majestic hydrology of Niagara Falls. Well-read rangers and museum docents add to the sense of adventure. Tilden wanted national parks to be ecological hands-on classrooms where

Don't Kill Our Wildlife. Works Progress Administration poster. Federal Art Project. 1936–1940. Library of Congress Prints and Photographs Division, Washington, D.C.

Hawai'i Volcanoes National Park, 2013. The 13th national park, created in 1916 by President Woodrow Wilson. David D. Vail.

stewardship became the take-away. Environmental historians are Tilden's accomplices. Their work adds depth to any interaction with places conserved or commodified.[15]

Cultural and Environmental Costs of Preservation

Topics such as the human-nature continuum, debates around conservation and preservation, or the complexities of "wilderness" resonate beyond academics or policy makers. Historic sites and museums, archives, and other public institutions face similar concerns when preserving and interpreting their environments. Who and what to profile? What stories to tell? Which environment/landscape do we return to? Do we even accept the 1964 wilderness definition? Perhaps even more important: How do we connect these ideas, policies, and debates to a general public to get them engaged with the past, hoping to encourage their interest, enthusiasm, and participation in the issues of now? "Somewhere between the vast extremes of modern landscapes and empty ones," as historian Rebecca Conard writes:

> historic preservationists, environmentalists, and land managers work to protect, preserve, restore, and rehabilitate as much of the past as they can. For the most part, practitioners in all three camps work with their own kind. Even so, there is more and more talk about the need to cooperate. Entrenched ideas about what should be preserved or restored, however make collaboration arduous.[16]

Carriage on road through Golden Gate Canyon, Yellowstone National Park, circa 1892. Image from the Collections of The Henry Ford. Gift of Ford Motor Company.

For example, visiting a national park such as Yellowstone offers a direct view of beautiful environments, a sense of ecological relationships between plants, animals, and the landscape, but it also means engaging in long-standing debates over wise use of these places—which includes the adverse effects of consumerism and the tourist industry. Other factors also affected these spaces. Understanding these other forces starts by considering corrosive stereotypes that helped make and remake Yellowstone including dispossessing American Indians of their lands and eliminating certain plant and animal species to curate a park based on persistent U.S. cultural ideas. As Mark David Spence argues in *Dispossessing the Wilderness: Indian Removal and the Making of the National Parks* (1998),

> generations of preservationists, government officials, and park visitors have accepted and defended the uninhabited wilderness preserved in national park remnants of *a priori* Nature (with a very capital *N*). Such a conception of wilderness forgets that native peoples shaped these environments for millennia and thus parks like Yellowstone, Yosemite, and Glacier are more representative of old fantasies about a continent awaiting "discovery" than actual conditions at the time of Columbus's voyage or Lewis and Clark's adventure.[17]

Environmental history can redefine how local landscapes are considered, preserved, and protected. Educational programs or preservation boards might consult how locally built places can also be places for environmental thinking. As David Glassberg explores in *Public History and the Environment* (2004), historical landscapes "are the products of human interaction with the natural environment over time . . . . Landscapes not only bear the imprint of past economic forces, technologies and cultural ideals; they also reflect a period's prevailing racial, class, ethnic, and gender relationships"[18] Interpreting the environment requires thinking about these connections between human and nonhuman interactions in the creation of parks, agriculture as implemented in a living history context, agritourism to sustain a family farm, or local boosters who sustain rural Main Street storefronts.

The Public Historian, the journal of the National Council on Public History, focused its November 2016 issue on "A Centennial History of the National Park Service." Historian William Stoutamire focused on Arizona's Walnut Canyon National Monument, where all of these forces around "wilderness" collide. Built and natural places become intensely blurred when goals of "pothunters, boosters, and preservationists on the local stage" all influence preservation priorities. The agenda becomes muddied with cultural memories, social stereotypes, natural environments and reconstructions.[19] Few would "discount the importance of protecting these sites in the early twentieth century," Stoutamire observes, "however problematic some of the original arguments for preservation may be when viewed through a twenty-first-century lens." Stoutamire argues for "more inclusive narratives" that can result from "consciously rethinking the traditional and often exclusive definitions of community, heritage, and identity, which were first established in these formative years." The depth of understanding comes from understanding the history as well as the people who inhabited a place over time, and the combination may ensure "the continued success of the National Park Service as it moves forward to its second century."[20] Historical scholarship helps staff in museums, historic sites, or any ecotourism attraction identify past controversies and current significance of the places they steward.

Reaping at Firestone Farm, July 2018. The Henry Ford, Dearborn, Michigan. Photograph by Ryan Jelso.

Professional Experts, Neighborhood Scientists, and Backyard Environmentalists

Environmental history takes seriously the records of biologists, ecologists, botanists, agrostologists (grass scientists), weed scientists, and agricultural scientists. Each shaped the scope and breadth of environmental learning and discoveries historically, and they continue to do so today. But they are only part of the story. Familiar narratives around conservation science included as many unfamiliar contributions from hunters that practiced amature science. Farmers and ranchers employed their own techniques to prevent soil loss during the dust storms of the 1930s and their own toxicity experiments to better understand the risks of agricultural chemicals in the 1950s. To make concepts such as ecosystems, interconnectedness, and toxicity accessible beyond the work of scholars, you could start with Aldo Leopold and Rachel Carson. Both scientists wrote key books to shape mid-twentieth century ideas around natural resources, policies on agricultural production, and land use. Beginning with Leopold's ecological journals collected in *Round River: From the Journals of Aldo Leopold* (1972), a blending of humanities and STEM as well as citizen science reside in the passages that argue for conservation as "a state of harmony between men and land. . . . Harmony with land is like harmony with a friend; you cannot cherish his right hand and chop off his left. That is to say, you cannot love game and hate predators; you cannot conserve the waters and waste the ranges; you cannot build the forest and mine the farm. The land is one organism."[21]

Leopold's other works, such as *A Sand County Almanac and Sketches Here and There* (1949), carry some fundamental ideas for the kind of environmental thinking that museums and historic sites need to do, especially to grapple with exhibits and artifacts that connect conservation, preservation, and agricultural production. Throughout the 1930s and 1940s, Leopold stressed interconnectedness of human and nonhuman environments. Large-scale agriculture that developed on the Plains in the early twentieth century contributed to the Dust Bowl in the 1930s. The kinds of "immediate and visible economic gain for themselves" had to change, Leopold argued. "A land-use ethic based wholly on economic self-interest" endangered more than it produced. Instead:

> A thing is right only when it tends to preserve the integrity, stability, and beauty of the community, and the community includes the soil, waters, fauna, and flora, as well as people . . . cease being intimidated by the argument that a right action is impossible because it does not yield maximum profits, or that a wrong action is to be condoned because it pays.[22]

A little more than a decade later, in 1962, biologist Rachel Carson published *Silent Spring*, a book that sparked a national environmental movement. Carson revealed a growing dilemma on the U.S. landscape: the ubiquity of pesticides in U.S. life. In the United States after World War II, chemical companies deployed poisons as "unseen defenders" against noxious weeds and insects. The argument went something like this: the same chemical dusts that protected U.S. forces from deadly diseases could save U.S. fields as insecticides wafted from field to field. Many Americans, including those living in rural communities, however, worried increasingly about the risks and hazards of such potent protection. Carson crystalized these hazards and risks in urgent terms.

> [We have put] poisonous and biologically potent chemicals indiscriminately into the hands of persons largely or wholly ignorant of their potential for harm and allowed them to be used with little or no advance investigation of their effects on soil, water, wildlife, and man himself. Future generations are unlikely to condone our lack of prudent concern for the integrity of the natural world that supports all life.[23]

Carson argued against the entire approach. The "chemical barrage" could never protect plants. Instead, controlling nature destroyed life. As Carson explained:

> The control of nature is a phrase conceived in arrogance, born of the Neanderthal age of biology and philosophy, when it was supposed that nature exists for the convenience of man. . . . It is our alarming misfortune that so primitive a science has armed itself with the most modern and terrible weapons, and that in turning them against the insects it has also turned them against the earth.[24]

Several historians document the transfer of chemicals from wartime use to standard household and agricultural applications. Michelle Mart explains this in *Pesticides, A Love Story: America's Enduring Embrace of Dangerous Chemicals* (2015): "The first brilliant glow of DDT symbolized modernity, scientific prowess, and the idea that the environment was a resource to be harnessed." Edmund Russell, Pete Daniel, and others indicate that many slowly acknowledged risks associated with toxicity, and dismissed the seriousness of toxicity for various reasons.[25]

Historians who study chemical use and human and environmental consequences include extensive lists of sources. These can help readers connect to primary sources created by a host of experts—U.S. Department of Agriculture (USDA) scientists, land-grant college agriculturalists, and practitioners. These sources exist because of citizen science, collaborations launched by "scientists and volunteers, particularly (but not exclusively) to expand opportunities for scientific data collection and to provide access to scientific information for community members."[26]

What do toxicology reports, aerial spraying manuals, or data tables that report on trends in pesticide use in the United States tell us? Plenty, it turns out. Importantly, agricultural science records emphasize local knowledge or "practitioner approaches" along with more professional laboratory science expertise.[27] Use was, in fact, not as indiscriminate as perceived by outsiders, and risk was not dismissed as readily.

A growing number of books explore the conversations that occurred among early adopters, their concerns, and some solutions they pursued. Frederick Rowe Davis explores this in *Banned: A History of Pesticides and the Science of Toxicology* (2014). Brian Frehner writes about drillers concerns, among other things, in *Finding Oil: The Nature of Petroleum Geology, 1859–1920* (2011). David D. Vail documents debates about risk, health, and agricultural pesticide applications in *Chemical Lands: Pesticides, Aerial Spraying, and Health in North America's Grasslands since 1945* (2018). Jeremy Vetter, in *Field Life: Science in the American*

West during the Railroad Era (2016), explores changes in wilderness areas that resulted from railroad rights of way, among other topics.[28]

Archival collections at land-grant universities offer an abundance of primary sources that reveal the science, people, and politics around the historical implications of uncertainty, risk, and hazards—three central themes that come with nearly any environmental story. For example, how did farmers, scientists, and rural community members survive the drought, Great Depression, and dust storms throughout the 1930s? Extension reports, field books, and personal diaries tell tales of local farming innovations to stop soil erosion and dust storms—practices that would become central strategies of future protection against environmental hazards, especially drought.[29]

Citizen science can also be found in federal sources such as the popular USDA *Yearbook of Agriculture*. Meant to be an accessible publication for farmers and agricultural scientists, this annual volume connected viewpoints, experiments, and studies on the latest agricultural science advances from the laboratory and the field, merging professional discoveries with practitioner experiences. As the 1940 volume "Farmers in a Changing World" states in its opening pages:

> A certain unity of viewpoint will be evident throughout most of the [yearbooks], but there are also a good many differences. The yearbook does not represent official policy; it makes no claim to final wisdom; it simply explores agricultural problems, and the reader will sometimes find official policies treated with skepticism, controversial viewpoints defended, and things discussed that do not enter into any policy. It would have been possible to avoid such differences. But the great merit of democracy . . . is that it not only permits but encourages the expression of different viewpoints. We think this is essential if social and economic problems are to be dealt with intelligently.[30]

The USDA *Yearbook of Agriculture* combined scientific knowledge and technological advancement for the "common American." These yearbooks, thus, constitute an important collection of firsthand sources to interpret environment and agriculture together. The 1938 *Yearbook*, "Soil and Men," for example, guided readers on how to keep soils healthy, prevent wind erosion, and perform local experiments to reduce soil blowing from dust storms. Other volumes such as the 1941 *Yearbook*, "Climate and Man," explored the variety of scientific studies of drought, wind erosion, and climatic changes. This volume highlighted various concerns of the agricultural community and scientific community over long-range patterns that could hurt future crop production. Other years, such as the 1943–1947 "Science and Technology" *Yearbook* or the 1953 "Plant Diseases" *Yearbook*, highlight how agriculture advances linked to scientific efforts around regional threats from insects and weeds. Other *Yearbooks*, such as the 1966 volume "Protecting our Food" or the 1977 volume "Gardening for Fun," combine the professional with the vocational expanding on the "farmer-scientist" to "feed the world." And these scientific discoveries and ecological relationships occurred in personal gardens as often as agricultural fields.[31] Historical topics that consider urban gardening, agricultural science, or climate change can benefit from these kinds of sources.

Citizen advocacy is also key to the history of environmental activism. Historians outline how mainstream environmentalism incorporated activists' agendas at every level, from scientists, writers, and policy makers to neighborhood organizers and elementary school students. Adam Rome explains, in "Giving Earth a Chance," how concerns about wilderness, conservation, preservation, and ecological consciousness informed the Earth Day movement in 1970. Rome argued that the "willingness of newly affluent Americans to insist on environmental quality, the increased destructiveness of modern industry, and the popularization of ecological ideas—make clear why environmentalism was a postwar phenomenon, not why it became a force in the sixties . . ."[32] Rome's book, *The Genius of Earth Day* (2014), offers insights that museums and historic sites can use to build public programming about the longer arch of environmental thinking, and the moment-by-moment events of Earth Day that still resonate. "Earth Day: Selected Resources," compiled by the Library of Congress's Science Reference staff conveys the rich primary and secondary source material that can help visitors engage with archival material that first expressed grassroots organizers' and mainstream activists' environmental ideas.[33]

Both forms are included in Wisconsin senator Gaylord Nelson's speech in Denver, Colorado to inaugurate the First Earth Day. In his remarks, Nelson captures Leopold's ecological consciousness and Carson's interconnectedness, but he also connects the call of protest to larger, fundamental arguments of equality:

> Our goal is not just an environment of clean air and water and scenic beauty. The objective is an environment of decency, quality, and mutual respect for all other human beings and

Late 1940s crop dusting in the Midwest. Courtesy of Morse Department of Special Collections, Kansas State University Libraries.

all other living creatures. Our goal is a new American ethic that sets new standards for progress, emphasizing human dignity and wellbeing rather than an endless parade of technology that produces more gadgets, more waste, more pollution . . . Establishing quality on a par with quantity is going to require new national politics that quite frankly will interfere with what many have considered their right to use and abuse the air, the water, the land, just because that is what we have always done.[34]

Cultural Identity and the Environment

It bears mentioning the ways that people build their identities in relation to the environment. They create boundaries between them and others, using natural features or imposing imaginary lines across landscapes. They also wax nostalgic about home places, even if isolated and remote. Literary critic and historian Thomas Carlyle explained in an 1828 issue of the *Edinburgh Review* that Robert Burns' work romanticized "affections which spring from a native soil" without balancing that against the "insular home feeling" that local environments could impose.[35]

During the late-nineteenth century, open-air museums developed as collections of buildings selected and arranged to acknowledge cultural distinctions but stress a common national identity. These museums became popular destinations for those who saw themselves in the exhibitions, but they also reinforced exclusion of others without attachment to a native soil featured in the exhibitions.[36]

Historian Roderick Frazier Nash first surveyed connections between perceptions of nature and human identity in *Wilderness and the American Mind* in 1967. It stressed the ways that forced removal of American Indians paved the way for a nation of immigrants to impose their insular home-feeling, as Carlyle phrased it, on someone else's land.[37]

Other humanists critique literature, art, film, and other creative works as environmental statements. Since the Association for the Study of Literature and the Environment (ASLE) began in 1992, a new field—environmental humanities—and a new approach to analysis—ecocriticism—have emerged. This can help us put creative works into historical context. The journal published by the ASLE, *Interdisciplinary Studies in Literature and the Environment*, provides a good introduction to the range of topics addressed. Films produced during the Dust Bowl, the Nuclear Age, and the Environmental Movement offer much to contemplate. Robin L. Murray and Joseph K. Heumann have assessed several genres, putting films into context and teasing out the deeper meaning of cinematography. Their work includes *Gunfight at the Eco-Corral, Monstrous Nature*, and *Eco-Cinema in the City*.[38]

Ecofeminism and Environmental Justice

Environmental history can expand other narratives about gender, race, and class so we comprehend conflict centered on places. Authors often approach their subject with an activist agenda, informed by ecofeminism and environmental justice. After all, environmental advocacy has much to do with women's advocacy, both before and after Carson's *Silent Spring* appeared in 1962. Early studies such as Alice Hamilton's *Industrial Toxicology* (1934), Ellen

Swallow Richards' *The Chemistry of Cooking and Cleaning* (1882), and *Food Materials and Their Adulteration* (1885), Susan Fenimore Cooper's *Rural Hours* (1850), and Anna Botsford Comstock's *Handbook of Nature Study* (1911) emphasized an environmental worldview that addressed public health challenges. Ornithology is part of this influence and serves as a key connection that shaped Carson's work. Other authors complicated the scientific and cultural ideas of conservation, including Mabel Osgood Wright's study, *Birdcraft: A Field Book of Two Hundred Song, Game, and Water Birds* (1895), Neltje Blanchan's *The Bird Book: Bird Neighbors and Birds that Hunt and are Hunted* (1932), and Florence Merriam Bailey's *Birds Through An Opera Glass* (1889). These books confirmed that conservation neither resided exclusively within the work of notable male scientists nor kept only to ideas of U.S. wilderness. Bird watching and nature writing could inspire the amateur as well as the professional. Carson's growth as an author, scientist, and political stalwart as well as her legacy was a direct product of these earlier works and networks.[39]

Ecofeminism as well as environmental justice appear in both Carson's and Terry Tempest Williams's writings. Both offer useful perspectives to connect as well as rethink how environment, individuals, preservation, conservation, wilderness, science, and technology can be understood as acting in one place over time. Both also provide the much-needed frameworks to tell new stories about people and perspectives that often get left out.

Environmental historian Carolyn Merchant has long explored the interplay between gender, race, and class as important lenses to interpret the environment: "How these three categories are constructed socially and culturally, how and why they change over time, and why they are important add to the complexity of history. They help us to envision the possibility of a socially just world that could be a better place in which to live."[40] These considerations can help museums and historic sites rethink the artifacts they collect and the stories they tell. As Merchant points out:

> Environmental historians have reflected on the place of racial awareness in the field and have begun the process of writing an environmental history of race. They have explored the negative connections between wilderness and race, cities and race, toxic wastes and race, and their reversal in environmental justice and have analyzed the ideology and practice of environmental racism.[41]

To be sure, ideas that crystallize in ecofeminist approaches or narratives of environmental justice can assist in building public history, community history, and historic preservation that sustain an environmental thinking. This condition "offers a more balanced and complete picture of past human interactions with nature and advances its theoretical frameworks."[42]

Another part of ecofeminism theory is moving beyond these general approaches described previously to consider distinctive forms, experiences, and symbols that connect the domination of women to the domination of nature. Karen J. Warren's essay "The Power and Promise of Ecological Feminism" is a good starting point to understand this strand of environmental activism.[43] Ecofeminism reveals a different form of interconnectedness—that between oppressive beliefs, values, attitudes, and assumptions in historical approaches toward women and that of the environment. This theory can help challenge the dualisms often inherent in environmental interpretations by also confronting them in race, class, and gender histories. Again, Warren provides important insight for us:

> Ecofeminism refocuses environmental ethics on what nature might mean, morally speaking, for humans, and on how the relational attitudes of humans to others—humans as well as non-humans—sculpt both what it is to be human and the nature and ground of human responsibilities to the non-human environment. Part of what this refocusing does is to take seriously the voices of women and other oppressed persons in the construction of that ethic.[44]

Environmental justice also offers a narrative that both confronts and compliments traditional historical interpretations about landscapes, cities, natural resources, and wilderness. It challenges destruction of environmental resources, cultural views of consumption, practices of waste, and socioeconomic factors that allow oppression, racism, and genocide to coalesce in neighborhoods or communities. The First National People of Color Environmental Leadership Summit met in Washington, D.C., in October 1991 to deliver a declaration of environmental justice. Participants articulated seventeen principles that linked exploitation of natural resources to racist and sexist policies and that attributed ecological destruction and environmental degradation to greed, bias, and hate. Environmental justice affirmed respect for nature, the interdependence of all species, and respect for humanity. Museums and historic sites can add racial, gender, and class dynamics to their interpretation by using these environmental justice principles to assess the treatment of their own environment over time.[45]

Ecotourism

Interpreting the environment also has a commercial side. Different from traditional funding models for archives and museums, ecotourism pursues environmental thinking in programing for profit and nonprofits alike. The Nature Conservancy adopts the definition of ecotourism articulated by the World Conservation Union:

> Environmentally responsible travel to natural areas, in order to enjoy and appreciate nature (and accompanying cultural features, both past and present) that promote conservation, have a low visitor impact and provide for beneficially active socio-economic involvement of local peoples. Ecotourism is distinguished by its emphasis on conservation, education, traveler responsibility and active community participation.[46]

Specific benefits of this approach include:

- Conscientious, low-impact visitor behavior.
- Sensitivity towards, and appreciation of, local cultures and biodiversity.
- Support for local conservation efforts.
- Sustainable benefits to local communities.

WE, THE PEOPLE OF COLOR, gathered together at this multinational People of Color Environmental Leadership Summit, to begin to build a national and international movement of all peoples of color to fight the destruction and taking of our lands and communities, do hereby re-establish our spiritual interdependence to the sacredness of our Mother Earth; to respect and celebrate each of our cultures, languages and beliefs about the natural world and our roles in healing ourselves; to ensure environmental justice; to promote economic alternatives which would contribute to the development of environmentally safe livelihoods; and, to secure our political, economic and cultural liberation that has been denied for over 500 years of colonization and oppression, resulting in the poisoning of our communities and land and the genocide of our peoples, do affirm and adopt these Principles of Environmental Justice:

The Principles of Environmental Justice (EJ)

1) **Environmental Justice** affirms the sacredness of Mother Earth, ecological unity and the interdependence of all species, and the right to be free from ecological destruction.

2) **Environmental Justice** demands that public policy be based on mutual respect and justice for all peoples, free from any form of discrimination or bias.

3) **Environmental Justice** mandates the right to ethical, balanced and responsible uses of land and renewable resources in the interest of a sustainable planet for humans and other living things.

4) **Environmental Justice** calls for universal protection from nuclear testing, extraction, production and disposal of toxic/hazardous wastes and poisons and nuclear testing that threaten the fundamental right to clean air, land, water, and food.

5) **Environmental Justice** affirms the fundamental right to political, economic, cultural and environmental self-determination of all peoples.

6) **Environmental Justice** demands the cessation of the production of all toxins, hazardous wastes, and radioactive materials, and that all past and current producers be held strictly accountable to the people for detoxification and the containment at the point of production.

7) **Environmental Justice** demands the right to participate as equal partners at every level of decision-making, including needs assessment, planning, implementation, enforcement and evaluation.

8) **Environmental Justice** affirms the right of all workers to a safe and healthy work environment without being forced to choose between an unsafe livelihood and unemployment. It also affirms the right of those who work at home to be free from environmental hazards.

9) **Environmental Justice** protects the right of victims of environmental injustice to receive full compensation and reparations for damages as well as quality health care.

10) **Environmental Justice** considers governmental acts of environmental injustice a violation of international law, the Universal Declaration On Human Rights, and the United Nations Convention on Genocide.

11) **Environmental Justice** must recognize a special legal and natural relationship of Native Peoples to the U.S. government through treaties, agreements, compacts, and covenants affirming sovereignty and self-determination.

12) **Environmental Justice** affirms the need for urban and rural ecological policies to clean up and rebuild our cities and rural areas in balance with nature, honoring the cultural integrity of all our communities, and provided fair access for all to the full range of resources.

13) **Environmental Justice** calls for the strict enforcement of principles of informed consent, and a halt to the testing of experimental reproductive and medical procedures and vaccinations on people of color.

14) **Environmental Justice** opposes the destructive operations of multi-national corporations.

15) **Environmental Justice** opposes military occupation, repression and exploitation of lands, peoples and cultures, and other life forms.

16) **Environmental Justice** calls for the education of present and future generations which emphasizes social and environmental issues, based on our experience and an appreciation of our diverse cultural perspectives.

17) **Environmental Justice** requires that we, as individuals, make personal and consumer choices to consume as little of Mother Earth's resources and to produce as little waste as possible; and make the conscious decision to challenge and reprioritize our lifestyles to ensure the health of the natural world for present and future generations.

More info on environmental justice and environmental racism can be found online at www.ejnet.org/ej/

Delegates to the First National People of Color Environmental Leadership Summit held on October 24-27, 1991, in Washington DC, drafted and adopted these 17 principles of Environmental Justice. Since then, the Principles have served as a defining document for the growing grassroots movement for environmental justice.

The Principles of Environmental Justice. Adopted by delegates to the First National People of Color Environmental Leadership Summit, October 24–27, 1991. Available at https://www.nrdc.org/sites/default/files/ej-principles.pdf.

- Local participation in decision-making.
- Educational components for both the traveler and local communities.

Other organizations such as the Center for Great Plains Studies at the University of Nebraska–Lincoln pursues a consortium model that blends public and private support to offer a form of conservation that "that works with, instead of against, business, landowners, and communities is a way forward in preserving our rural communities and dwindling wild places. For many locations around the globe, nature-based tourism has provided a way to enrich human communities while protecting cultural heritage and natural areas."[47] In Nebraska, a state with significant production acreage, the Center for Great Plains Studies combines commercial outreach with ecological research and education. This Great Plains ecotourism coalition "includes both nonprofit and for-profit members and is coordinated by staff at the Center for Great Plains Studies. Its mission is to market the region, share information, and connect nature-based entrepreneurs with one another, creating opportunities for collaboration, learning and cooperation."[48] Both organizations warn of the tensions that come with this approach. More interest in natural or preserved areas can assist with increased interest and value by visitors toward the environment, but it can also cause severe damage to the integrity of ecosystems as well as local cultures. But ecotourism might be a hybrid model that promotes a kind of environmental thinking to deepen "the national consciousness of the economic and aesthetic value of their natural environment."[49]

Conclusion

Environmental history ought to play a fundamental role in shaping museum and historic site interpretation. Connecting histories of scientific experimentation or environmental activism can ensure immersive experiences for visitors. Humanities councils, local museums, university archives, historic preservation committees, and local nonprofits can benefit by incorporating environmental thinking in their grant applications, community outreach programming, and preservation approaches. New revelations and relationships can emerge when public history and environmental history blend, because together, both offer a new approach to acquisitions, preservation, and storytelling that comes from an interconnected past. Aldo Leopold's land ethic still guides here: "When we see land as a community to which we belong, we may begin to use it with love and respect. . . . We can only be ethical in relation to something we can see, understand, feel, love, or otherwise have faith in."[50]

Notes

1. Quote excerpted from Henry David Thoreau, "Walking," in *Nature Writing: The Tradition in English*, eds. Robert Finch and John Elder (New York: W. W. Norton: 2002), 181–87.

2. Louis S. Warren, "Paths Toward Home: Landmarks of the Field in Environmental History," *A Companion to American Environmental History* ed., Douglas Cazaux Sackman (West Sussex, UK: Wiley-Blackwell Publishing, 2014), 5.

3. Warren, "Paths Toward Home."

4. Donald Worster, "Doing Environmental History," in *The Ends of the Earth: Perspectives on Modern Environmental History*, ed. Donald Worster (New York: Cambridge University Press, 1988), 294.

5. William Cronon, "The Uses of Environmental History," *Environmental History Review*, vol. 17, no. 3 (autumn 1993), 13–14.

6. James Sherow, "Introduction: An Evening on Konza Prairie," in *A Sense of the American West: An Anthology of Environmental History*, ed. James Sherow (Albuquerque: University of New Mexico Press, 1998), 12.

7. Sherow, "Introduction," 21.

8. Neil Gershenfeld, *Fab: The Coming Revolution on Your Desktop: From Personal Computers to Personal Fabrication* (New York: Basic Books, 2005), 17. See also Jentery Sayers, Devon Elliott, Kari Kraus, Bethany Nowviskie, and William J. Turkel, "Between Bits and Atoms: Physical Computing and Desktop Fabrication in the Humanities," in *A New Companion to Digital Humanities*, ed. Susan Schreibman, Ray Siemens, and John Unsworth (New York: Wiley & Sons, 2016), 15–17. For works on the value of artifacts, see Debra A. Reid, "Tangible Agricultural History: An Artifact's-Eye View of the Field," *Agricultural History*, vol. 86, no. 3 (2012): 57–76; Darwin P. Kelsey, "Outdoor Museums and Historical Agriculture," *Agricultural History*, 46 (1972): 105–28; Reid, "Agricultural Artifacts: Early Curators, Their Philosophy and Their Collections," *ALHFAM Proceedings 2010*, vol. 33 (North Bloomfield, OH: ALHFAM, 2011), 30–52

9. "The Wilderness Act," Public Law 88-577 (16 U.S. C. 1131-1136), 88th Congress, Second Session (September 3, 1964). Available at: https://wilderness.nps.gov/document/wilderness-Act.pdf. Accessed February 21, 2018.

10. This essary does not provide a comprehensive overview of all topics addressed by environmental historians. See the bibliographic essay for more topics and suggested readings. Rather, it addresses some key topics, including perceptions of wilderness as well as economic, political, and social debates about conservation, natural resource exploitation, and pesticide use.

11. See the bibliographic essay for an overview of literature on preservation and conservation, the National Park Service, and environmentalism.

12. Theodore Roosevelt, "Opening Address by the President," *Proceedings of a Conference of Governors in the White House*, ed. Newton C. Blanchard (Washington, D.C.: Government Printing Office, 1909), 3, 5–10, 12.

13. Carol Shull and Dwight T. Pitcaithley, "Melding the Environment and Public History: The Evolution and Maturation of the National Park Service," in *Public History and the Environment*, eds. Martin V. Melosi and Philip V. Scarpino (Malabar, FL: Krieger Publishing Company, 2005), 58–59. See also Robert R. Archibald, *A Place to Remember: Using History to Build Community* (Walnut Creek, CA: AltaMira Press, 1999).

14. "The Wilderness Act of 1964," Public Law 88-577 (16 U.S.C. 1131-1136), 88th Congress, Second Session, September 3, 1964, Section 2c.

15. Cronon, "The Uses of Environmental History," 13; See also Cronon, "Introduction: In Search of Nature," and "The Trouble with Wilderness," in *Uncommon Ground: Rethinking the Human Place in Nature* (New York: W. W. Norton, 1996).

16. Rebecca Conard, "Spading Common Ground: Reconciling the Built and Natural Environments," in *Public History and the Environment*, ed., Martin V. Melosi and Philip Scarpino (Malabar, FL: Krieger Publishing Company), 4–5. See also Peter H. Brink and H. Grant Dehart, "Findings and Recommendation," in *Past Meets Future: Saving America's Historic Environments*, ed. Antoinette J. Lee (Washington, D.C.: The Preservation Press, 1992; A. S. Leopold, et al. (Advisory Board on Wildlife Management), *Wildlife Management in the National Parks* (U.S. Department of Interior, National Park Service, 1963); Denise D. Meringolo, *Museums, Monuments, and National Parks: Toward a New Geneadogy of Public History* (Amherst: University of Massachusetts Press, 2012); Melody Webb, "Cultural Landscapes in the National Park Service," *The Public Historian*, vol. 9, no. 2 (1987), 77–89; Edward T. McMahon and A. Elizabeth Watson, "In Search of Collaboration: Historic Preservation and the Environmental Movement," *Information, No. 71* (Washington, D.C.: National Trust for Historic Preservation, 1992); Thomas A. Woods, "Nature Within History: Using Environmental History to Interpret Historic Sites," *History News*, vol. 52, no. 3 (1997), 5–8; Mark Fiege, "Toward a History of Environmental History in the National Parks," *The George Wright Forum*, vol. 28, no. 2 (2011), 128–47.

17. Mark David Spence, *Dispossessing the Wilderness: Indian Removal and the Making of the National Parks* (New York: Oxford University Press, 1999), 5. See also Spence, "Crown of the Continent, Backbone of the World: The American Wilderness Ideal and Blackfeet Exclusion from Glacier National Park," *Environmental History*, vol. 1, no. 3 (July 1996), 29–49; Philip Burnham, *Indian Country, God's Country: Native Americans and the National Parks* (Washington, D.C.: Island Press, 2000); Robert H. Keller and Michael F. Turek, *American Indians and National Parks* (Tucson: University of Arizona Press, 1999); Derek Bouse, "Culture as Nature: How Native American Cultural Antiquities Become Part of the Natural World," *The Public Historian*, vol. 18, no. 4 (1996), 75–98; David Chidester and Edward T. Linenthal, eds., *American Sacred Space* (Bloomington: Indiana University Press, 1995); Donald Hardesty, "Ethnographic Landscapes: Transforming Nature into Culture," in *Preserving Cultural Landscapes in America*, ed. Arnold R. Alanen and Robert Z. Melnick (Baltimore MD: Johns Hopkins University Press, 2000), 169–85; Jacoby, *Crimes Against Nature.*

18. David Glassberg "Interpreting Landscapes" in *Public History and the Environment*, ed., Martin V. Melosi and Philip Scarpino (Malabar, FL: Krieger Publishing Company), 1, 27. See also Michael Sorkin, ed. *Variations on a Theme Park: The New American City and End of Public Space* (New York: Noonday Press, 1992); John Sears, *Sacred Places: American Tourist Attractions in the Nineteenth Century* (New York: Oxford University Press, 1989).

19. William F. Stoutamire, "Imagined Heritage: A Local History of Walnut Canyon National Monument," *The Public Historian*, vol. 38, no. 4 (November 2016), 17. See also David Glassberg, *Sense of History: The Place of the Past in American Life* (Amherst: University of Massachusetts Press, 2001); Rebecca S. Toupal and Heather Fauland, *Cultural Affiliations of the Flagstaff Area National Monuments: Sunset Crater Volcano Walnut Canyon, and Wupatki* (Tucson, AZ: Bureau of Applied Archaeology, Historic Preservation, and Nature Conservation, 2007); Joe E. Watkins, "The Antiquities Act at One-Hundred Years: A Native American Perspective," in *The Antiquities Act: A Century of American Archaeology, Historic Preservation, and Nature Conservation*, eds. David Harmon, Francis P. McManamon, and Dwight T. Pitcaithley (Tucson: University of Arizona Press, 2006), 187–97.

20. Stoutamire, "Imagined Heritage," 20.

21. Aldo Leopold, *Round River: From the Journals of Aldo Leopold* (New York: Oxford University Press, 1993), 145–146. See also Julianne Lutz Newton, *Aldo Leopold's Odyssey: Rediscovering the Author of A Sand County Almanac* (Washington, D.C.: Shearwater Book [Island Press], 2006); Richard L. Knight and Suzanne Riedel, eds., *Aldo Leopold and the Ecological Conscience* (New York: Oxford University Press, 2002); Susan Flader, *Thinking Like a Mountain: Aldo Leopold and the Evolution of an Ecological Attitude Toward Deer, Wolves and Forests* (Columbia: University of Missouri Press, 1974).

22. Aldo Leopold, "The Ecological Conscience," *Journal of Soil and Water Conservation*, vol. 3, no. 3 (July 1948): 109–12. For more on the Dust Bowl, see "Water and Drought" in the bibliographic essay.

23. Rachel Carson, *Silent Spring*. Fortieth Anniversary Edition. (New York: Houghton Mifflin Company, 2002), 12–13.

24. Carson, *Silent Spring*, 297. For some of the seminal works on Rachel Carson, *Silent Spring*, and environmentalism, see: Linda Lear, *Rachel Carson: Witness for Nature* (New York: Henry Holt and Company, 1997); William Souder, *On a Farther Shore: The Life and Legacy of Rachel Carson* (New York: Crown Publishers, 2014); James Whorton, *Before Silent Spring: Pesticides and Public Health in Pre-DDT America* (Princeton, NJ: Princeton University Press, 1974); Frank Graham, Jr., *Since Silent Spring* (Boston: Houghton Mifflin Company, 1970); Robert Gottlieb, *Forcing the Spring: The Transformation of the American Environmental Movement* (Washington, D.C.: Island Press, 1993); and Thomas Dunlap, *DDT, Silent Spring, and the Rise of Environmentalism* (Seattle: University of Washington Press, 2008).

25. Michelle Mart, *Pesticides, a Love Story: America's Enduring Embrace of Dangerous Chemicals* (Lawrence: University Press of Kansas, 2015), 4. For histories of toxicity, risk, and health, see Edmund Russell, *War and Nature: Fighting Humans and Insects with Chemicals from World War I to Silent Spring* (London: Cambridge University Press, 2001), and *Evolutionary History: Uniting History and Biology to Understand Life on Earth* (London: Cambridge University Press, 2011). Pete Daniel more narrowly focuses on a U.S. region and agricultural applications in *Toxic Drift: Pesticides and Health in the Post-World War II South* (Baton Rouge: Louisiana State University Press, in association with Smithsonian National Museum of American History, 2005). Thomas Dunlap focuses on one chemical and its ramifications in *DDT: Scientists, Citizens, and Public Policy* (Princeton, NJ: Princeton University Press, 1981). See also Nancy Langston, *Toxic Bodies: Hormone Disruptors and the Legacy of DES* [Diethylstilbestrol] (New Haven, CT: Yale University Press, 2010); Jody A. Roberts and Nancy Langston, "Toxic Bodies/Toxic Environments: An Interdisciplinary Forum," *Environmental History*, 13 (October 2008): 629–35; John Wargo, *Green Intelligence*; Arthur McEvoy, "Working Environments: An Ecological Approach to Industrial Health and Safety," *Technological and Culture*, 36, Supplement: Snapshots of a Discipline: Selected Proceedings from the Conference on Critical Problems and Research Frontiers in the History of Technology (April 1995): S145–S173; Angus MacIntyre, "Why Pesticides Received Extensive Use in America: A Political Economy of Pest Management to 1970," *National Resources Journal*, 27 (Summer 1987): 534–77.

26. The Cornell Lab of Ornithology, "Defining Citizen Science." Available at: http://www.birds.cornell.edu/citscitoolkit/about/definition. Accessed February 12, 2018.

27. See Frederick Rowe Davis, *Banned: A History of Pesticides and the Science of Toxicology* (New Haven, CT: Yale University Press, 2014), 207–08. See also Leonard P. Gianessi, *U.S. Pesticide*

Use Trends: 1966–1989 (Washington, D.C.: Resources for the Future, 1992); Gianessi and Nathan Reigner, in *Pesticide Use U.S. Crop Production: 2002* (Washington, D.C.: Croplife Foundation, 2006).

28. Frederick Rowe Davis, *Banned*; Brian Frehner, *Finding Oil: The Nature of Petroleum Geology, 1859–1920* (Lincoln: University of Nebraska Press, 2011), David D. Vail, *Chemical Lands: Pesticides, Aerial Spraying, and Health in North America's Grasslands since 1945* (Tuscaloosa: University of Alabama Press, 2018); Jeremy Vetter, *Field Life: Science in the American West during the Railroad Era* (Pittsburgh: University of Pittsburgh Press, 2016).

29. See examples such as the annual report of the Garden City branch of the Kansas Agricultural Experiment Station, published between 1932 and 1937. For a larger summary of Kansas State Agricultural Science archives during the Dust Bowl era, see David D. Vail, "Dry and Dusty Lands: Exploring the Dust Bowl through Kansas State Agricultural Experiment Station Reports, Photographs, and Posters," *Field Notes* for *Crossing Borders: An Interdisciplinary Journal of Undergraduate Scholarship* (2015): 1–3.

30. U.S. Department of Agriculture, "Farmers in a Changing World," *Yearbook of Agriculture 1940* (Washington, D.C.: Government Printing Office, 1940), 2.

31. Bob Bergland, "Foreword," *Gardening for Food and Fun: Yearbook of Agriculture 1977* (Washington, D.C.: Government Printing Office, 1977), xxxii.

32. Adam Rome, "Give Earth a Chance: The Environmental Movement and the Sixties," *Journal of American History*, vol. 90, no. 2 (September 2003), 525–554, and *The Genius of Earth Day: How a 1970 Teach-In Unexpectedly Made the First Green Generation* (New York: Hill and Wang, 2014). See also Brooks, *Before Earth Day*; Jeanne Nienaber Clarke and Hanna J. Cortner, *The State and Nature: Voices Heard, Voices Unheard in America's Environmental Dialogue* (Upper Saddle River, NJ: Prentice Hall, 2002); Frederick Rowe Davis, *The Man Who Saved Sea Turtles: Archie Carr and the Origins of Conservation Biology* (New York: Oxford University Press, 2007); Neil M. Maher, *Nature's New Deal: The Civilian Conservation Corps and the Roots of the American Environmental Movement* (New York: Oxford University Press, 2008).

33. Earth Day: Selected Resources, Science Reference Services, Library of Congress. Available at https://www.loc.gov/rr/scitech/SciRefGuides/earthday.html. Accessed September 2, 2018.

34. Gaylord Nelson, Speech, Denver, Colorado, April 22, 1970, "Turning Points in Wisconsin History," *Nelson, Gaylord Speeches and other Documents on Earth Day*, 1970. Available at: https://www.wisconsinhistory.org/turningpoints/search.asp?id=1671. Accessed February 19, 2018.

35. Thomas Carlyle, "Art. I.—*The Life of Robert Burns*. By J. G. Lockhart. L. L. B. Edinburgh, 1828," *Edinburgh Review*, vol. 48, no. 96 (December 1828), 267–312, quote, 288. Carlyle linked the concept of "native soil" in Burn's body of work to an "insular home feeling" and increased expressions of nationality and contrasted this with "attenuated cosmopolitanism" in other Scottish literature that failed to convey an emotional connection to place.

36. Sten Rentzhog, *Open Air Museums: The History and Future of a Visionary Idea* (Kristianstad, Sweden: Jamtli Förlag and Carlssons Förlag, 2007).

37. Roderick Frazier Nash, *Wilderness and the American Min*d 5th ed. (New Haven, CT: Yale University Press, 2014). Edmund Russell, *Evolutionary History: Uniting History and Biology to Understand Life on Earth* (Cambridge: Cambridge University Press, 2011), J. Baird Callicott, *In Defense of the Land Ethic: Essays in Environmental Philosophy* (New York: State University

of New York Press, 1989), and Donald Worster, *Nature's Economy: A History of Ecological Ideas*, 2nd ed. (Cambridge: Cambridge University Press, 1994).

38. For more information about the ASLE, see https://www.asle.org/. Accessed February 25, 2019. Robin L. Murray and Joseph K. Heumann, *Eco-Cinema in the City* (London: Taylor & Francis, 2017); *Ecology and Popular Film: Cinema on the Edge* (Albany: State University of New York, 2009); *Film and Everyday Eco-Disasters* (Lincoln: University of Nebraska Press, 2014); *Gunfight at the Eco-Corral: Western Cinema and the Environment* (Norman: University of Oklahoma Press, 2012); *Monstrous Nature: Environment and Horror on the Big Screen* (Lincoln: University of Nebraska Press, 2016).

39. See Robert K. Musil, *Rachel Carson and Her Sisters: Extraordinary Women Who Have Shaped America's Environment* (New Brunswick, NJ: Rutgers University Press, 2014.)

40. Carolyn Merchant, "Interpreting Environmental History," *Major Problems in American Environmental History* 3rd ed. (Boston: Wadsworth Cengage Learning, 2012), 25. See also Merchant, "Shades of Darkness: Race and Environmental History," *Environmental History*, vol. 8, no. 3 (2003): 380–394, and Merchant, "Gender and Environmental History," *Journal of American History*, vol. 76, no. 4 (1990): 117–21.

41. Merchant, *Major Problems*, 25.

42. Merchant, *Major Problems*, 25.

43. Karen J. Warren, "The Power and Promise of Ecological Feminism," in *Feminist Philosophies*, eds. Janet A. Kourany, James P. Sterba, Rosemarie Tong (Upper Saddle River, NJ: Prentice Hall Press, 1999), 452–53. See also Michael B. Smith, "Silence, Miss Carson! Science, Gender, and the Reception of *Silent Spring.*" *Feminist Studies*, vol. 27, no. 3 (2001): 733–52. Carolyn Merchant, *Ecological Revolutions: Nature, Gender, and Science in New England* (Chapel Hill: University of North Carolina Press, 1989); Connie Y. Chiang, "Race and Ethnicity in Environment" in *The Oxford Handbook of Environmental History*, ed. Andrew C. Isenberg, (New York: Oxford University Press, 2014), 573–99; Nancy C. Unger, "Women and Gender: Useful Categories of Analysis in Environmental History," in *The Oxford Handbook of Environmental History*, ed. Andrew C. Isenberg (New York: Oxford University Press, 2014), 600–643.

44. Warren, "The Power and Promise," 460.

45. For the seventeen points as articulated in 1991, see *The First National People of Color Environmental Leadership Summit*, October 24–27, 1991 (Washington, D.C.: Public Domain). Available at: https://www.nrdc.org/sites/default/files/ej-principles.pdf. Accessed February 19, 2018. For examples of the utility of environmental justice principles, see Steve Lerner, *Diamond: A Struggle for Environmental Justice in Louisiana's Chemical Corridor* (Boston: MIT Press, 2004), and Robert D. Bullard, eds., *The Quest for Environmental Justice: Human Rights and the Politics of Pollution* (San Francisco: Sierra Club Books, 2015).

46. The Nature Conservancy, "What does Ecotourism Mean, and Why Should You Care?" Available at: https://www.nature.org/greenliving/what-is-ecotourism.xml. Accessed February 21, 2018.

47. Center for Great Plains Studies, "Ecotourism," (Lincoln: University of Nebraska at Lincoln, 2018). Available at: https://www.unl.edu/plains/ecotourism. Accessed February 21, 2018. See also Katie Nieland, "Ecotourism: A Big, Interdisciplinary Idea," *Great Plains Research*, vol. 27, no. 1 (2017), 15–20; Steve Lerner, *Eco-Pioneers: Practical Visionaries Solving Today's Environmental Problems* (Boston: MIT Press, 1997); Paddy Woodworth, *Our Once and Future*

Planet: Restoring the World in the Climate Change Century (Chicago: University of Chicago Press, 2013).

48. "Ecotourism," Center for Great Plains Studies.
49. "Ecotourism," Center for Great Plains Studies.
50. Excerpted from Leopold, "The Land Ethic," in *A Sand County Almanac and Sketches Here and There*, 201–26.

CHAPTER 2

Thinking Historically about the Environment

Our engagement with primary sources is not the result of a profound love for dusty archives (or cold museum storages for the historians of material culture), but generates from the idea that what we find there is the "gem", or something that can become a new piece in the puzzle.[1]

GIORGIO RIELLO, "THINGS THAT SHAPE HISTORY," (2009)

A COMPLETE IE TOOLKIT INCLUDES an assortment of devices that do different things. A tape measure and carpenter's pencil helps you plan and prepare. A saw and a hammer move a construction project along or can dismantle what already exists. You cannot skimp if you want to get the job done. You need a wrench to tighten or loosen a bolt; a hammer or screwdriver will not do. Depending on bolt size, an adjustable wrench reduces risk because you can be prepared to adapt to the size of the fastener head. The most complete IE Toolkit needs a comparable assortment of tools and materials and the knowledge and skills to use them. With environmental history readings as the base of your toolkit, you can add the perspectives of science, history, and other humanities to your study of the environment.

Disciplinary Methodologies

Scientists document the physical, biological, and social world by collecting empirical evidence through observation and measurement. They hypothesize and experiment to test hypotheses. They practice inductive reasoning to posit general rules or to draw conclusions based on evidence. They test their conclusions by repeating experiments and critically analyzing results. They continue to hypothesize, observe, practice induction, verify, review, assess, and revise.[2]

Humanities approaches emphasize reflective assessment or critical theory or speculative analysis, each distinct from the empirical basis of sciences in which understanding grows from observation and experience. History, narrowly defined as the study of written records, emphasizes human expressions and individual creations rather than observable patterns of behavior. Other humanities disciplines include literature, philosophy and ethics, linguistics and language, religion and theology, visual arts and design, performing arts including theater, and musicology. Some of these rely more on evidence of human thought and what can be known, others further human creativity, and still others critique human action.[3]

A combination of disciplinary approaches contribute to collecting, preserving, and interpreting the environment. Preservationists draw on science and social science knowledge and skills but may also be influenced by humanities approaches as they practice landscape rehabilitation or reconstruction, wilderness preservation or conservation, or structure restoration. They comply with standards recommended by the U.S. Secretary of the Interior, specifically standards for four treatments of historic properties (e.g., preservation, rehabilitation, restoration, and reconstruction).[4]

Naturalists and environmental educators draw on physical and biological sciences for evidence to interpret the spaces they manage. They benefit from historical timelines relevant to their parks or nature centers and from biographies of people that preceded them in their jobs and that influenced the environments they manage. They draw on social sciences to understand the policies and economics that affect their parks, their visitors or students, their communities, and their jobs. They mobilize activists to protect it.

Obviously, many disciplines have a vested interest in the environment. Including these perspectives in any research project should result in a comprehensive report on the environment most relevant to your museum or historic site.

Science, Falsifiability—Historical Method, Advocacy

Scientists and historians have different audiences. Incorporating information from each requires reaching across the aisles to engage with others. It requires learning new theories, methods, and languages for describing things. It does not require abandoning historical for empirical methods, or vice versa. The goal should be the creation of a more complete and authentic account of places visited, inhabited, and imagined. The compilation of information should generate a list of questions to explore further. This is the dynamic nature of interpreting the environment.

It seems appropriate to launch an exploration of disciplinary thinking by learning how a scientist involved in living history interpretation perceives the environment. Barbara Corson, DVM and farmer, interprets the term "environment" as "the air, water, and minerals that, arranged in various ways, provide the scaffold on which life can occur."[5] Corson explains that "the environment is not static but influences itself via feedback mechanisms." As she explains, "the water in the Great Lakes in their present state provides resources for the plants, animals (including people), fungi, and microbes that are living there now. The Great Lakes also affect the climate, locally for sure and even globally." A scientist gains understanding by hypothesizing and testing the hypothesis. To that end, Corson ponders, What if "the water in the Great Lakes was spread over the continental United States[?] [I]t would (so I've heard) cover the land entirely to a depth of 1 foot. That would provide resources for an entirely different set of living things and would also create changes in the climate."[6]

Historians might perceive this as counterfactual, not the purview of historians. Scientists, however, ask these questions because they may contribute to understanding conditions more than one billion years ago when tectonic plates separated, or prior to the end of the last glacial age, twelve thousand years ago. Thinking about how scientists asks questions and form hypotheses can inspire us to do the same as a step toward increasing our understanding of the environment.

The National Science Foundation (NSF) explains that a valid hypothesis is "testable and falsifiable," and cites Karl Popper, a philosopher of science, for these standards. Popper proposed the criterion of falsifiability in his 1934 book, *Logik der Forschung: Zur Erkenntnistheorie der modernen Naturwissenschaft*, published in English in 1959 as *The Logic of Scientific Discovery*. In the preface to his 1959 English edition, Popper explained that "the growth of knowledge can be studied best by studying the growth of scientific knowledge." To facilitate the growth of scientific knowledge, he dismissed inductive reasoning and advocated for empirical science, a method that used experience to verify or falsify hypotheses. The process, Popper believed, would eliminate untenable hypotheses; only the fittest would survive.[7]

Popper may have focused on scientific knowledge, but he knew that scientists needed to use methods that philosophers and historians used too. Specifically, all needed to discuss ideas rationally, state problems clearly, and examine proposed solutions critically. Popper believed that empirical scientists needed to use historical method to document past experiences. Scientists (and philosophers), he explained, needed to "find out what other people have thought and said about the problem in hand: why they had to face it; how they formulated it; how they tried to solve it." Without this, rational discourse could not continue.[8]

Historians have been jockeying for position relative to scientists for centuries. By the mid-1700s, historians claimed autonomy over history, arguing that "everything that happens in history must be explained . . . according to specifically historical methods." They also argued that everything exists in historical context; everything is a product of its time and place. Change is the only constant. Beyond these two principles, historians could not agree. Some argued for objectivity, whereas others knew that their writing reflected the influences of their status and worldview. Historians accomplished their goals because they formed professional associations and gained status within academia. Their success, however, did not go unchallenged, particularly between the 1930s and 1950s when critics decried historicism as a tool of empire builders.[9]

Debates about the status of history compared to science continue. *Interpreting the Environment* respects methodological distinctions and argues for a multidisciplinary approach. It also embraces historical method as a tool to build awareness. This is the power of studying history. People can discover their personal place in time, as the History Relevance "Value of History Statement" explains, and with this knowledge, they can consider their actions in light of environmental justice principles and natural law.[10]

Avoiding Presentism; Developing a Mindset

Thinking historically involves being self-aware of differences between the past and the present. We develop this self-awareness through historical study and then application of that understanding to distinguish between our time and the past. The process of thinking historically continues through the highest levels of thinking, the creation of new understanding, specifically, our own understanding of the historic mindset and its application to the historic (and today's) environmental challenges.

Thinking historically reminds us to avoid presentism when analyzing the past. Presentism, defined as an "uncritical adherence to present-day attitudes," can blind us to the daily challenges that people faced in the past and the ways that they solved those problems. Presentism might cause us to imagine Plains Indians driving bison over a buffalo jump while riding horses and perhaps using bows and arrows to push the herds. This is a perfect example of the "tendency to interpret past events in terms of modern values and concepts." In fact, bison hunts before the 1700s did not involve horses. Prior to adopting horse culture, Plains Indians used other tactics to move herds over piskuns. That reality got lost, however, as American artists such as Alfred Jacob Miller romanticized the hunt.[11]

Overcoming presentism starts with developing a mindset more informed by evidence from the time being studied. Historic (i.e., written) evidence is an important place to start the process of constructing a historic mindset, but establishing a mindset appropriate to understanding the environment requires additional types of sources. The written evidence created by these other disciplines go a long way toward constructing the mindset about the place or specific location. The combination can help us comprehend the environment that we plan to interpret within the framework of the mindset informed by science, social science, and history (as well as other humanities).

Thinking Historically about Environmental Degradation

A letter from diplomat Charles Perkins Marsh to "Professor Baird" indicated frustration with scientific theory that dismissed human influences on the environment. Marsh wrote that "Whereas Ritter and Guyot think the earth made man, man in fact made the earth." Marsh used observation of his father's agricultural practices as evidence. "My father had a piece of thick woodland where the ground was always damp. Wild turnips grew there, and ginseng, and wild pepper sometimes. Well, sir, he cleared up that lot, and drained and cultivate it, and it became a good deal drier, and he raised good corn and grain on it." Then, Marsh challenged Baird to accept the fact that his father changed his local environment: "Now I am going to state that as a *fact* and I defy all you speculators about cause and effect to deny it." Marsh expanded this idea in his book, *Man and Nature Or Physical Geography as Modified by Human Nature*, published in 1864, arguing that, in fact, a degraded environment contributed to the fall of the Roman Empire, with the Romans responsible for their own demise. David Lowenthal considered Marsh's argument revolutionary—"in linking culture with nature, science with history, *Man and Nature* was the most influential text of its time next to Darwin's *On the Origin of Species*, published just five years earlier."[12]

The fact that Marsh was one of, if not the, first to introduce the concept that human action not only led to environmental degradation but also confirms the long history of concern. The topic informs curation and programming at the Marsh-Billings-Rockefeller National Historical Park in Woodstock, Vermont. This site includes the home built by the parents of George Perkins Marsh in 1805 and subsequently owned and inhabited by the Billings and Rockefeller families. The landscape includes a historic woodland, described as one of the oldest planned and continuously managed woodlands in America. Marsh's message, however, is relatively easy to transfer to other settings. The general public can monitor the consequences of their actions in their own backyards, where they can see, as Marsh's father did, the changes one person can make in their environment.[13]

Providing historic evidence encourages the public to engage with the sources and determine their veracity based on guided inquiry. They may study sources and then engage with interpreters to solve historical problems that the modern mindset cannot comprehend. An exhibit on the Trail of Tears at the Cherokee Heritage Center does this by asking questions with answers that range from bad to terrible, with no survival option (as was too often the case).

Thinking historically can be part of a multi-prong humanist approach that uses literature, theater, the arts, as well as history, to explore the environment. The combination increases strategies to interpret controversial topics about the environment. These include human forces that affect the climate, the water supply, the food supply, human survival, and the ability to cohabitate on planet Earth.

A Multidisciplinary Approach

Educational frameworks tend to emphasize the sciences: science, technology, engineering, and mathematics (STEM), STEM plus the arts (STEAM), and STEM plus invention and entrepreneurship (STEMIE). History is critical, too, but not obvious. Adding historical methods, and humanities subjects more generally, can lead to new understanding of STEM-STEAM-STEMIE subjects such as the environment.

First, history can contribute to STEM, STEAM, and STEMIE subjects. Historians can practice close reading of evidence, discerning the four corners of a document. Sources since debunked can document the mindset of an era, and this is essential to building as complete an inventory of human ideas about the environment at a given time in the past. Presentism might cause you to dismiss the historical source as useless because of falsifiability. Yet, the source can document thoughts of a time worthy for the lessons it can teach.

Second, history can demonstrate its relevance. In this day of instantaneous access to historical facts via Google and Wikipedia, "history" must become more active to survive. It can prove its utility by asking questions, developing hypotheses, testing them with evidence, and contributing new information about past human actions and their consequences to the environment. For example, most summaries of George W. Carver's significance impress with statistics. He developed more than 118 products from sweet potatoes and more than 300 from peanuts, both crops farmers could eat as well as sell. He also developed new products from cotton, soybeans, Alabama clay, and various natural resources as well as scrap wood and sawdust, vegetable biomass, and feathers. Yet, little is written about the specific experiments that Carver did or of the molecular level of his chemistry. His early work focused on soil improvement because a combination of open-range stock farming and soil exhaustion as a result of monoculture left fields with depleted soils. Carver recommended adding essential elements (nitrogen [N], phosphorus [P]), and potassium [K]) and biomass found naturally in manure to overcultivated Alabama farmland. This required radical changes in local agricultural traditions. Alabama farmers who cultivated crops other than cotton and who adopted new cultivation techniques could grow products that they could eat, and Carver's science made the crops marketable as well as.[14]

Carver's understanding of soil science added options to the limited choices that poor Alabama farmers had. He advocated for natural solutions and not chemical or synthetic applications to restore the agricultural environment. Ironically, his chemical experiments with agricultural commodities identified derivatives easily transformed into artificial foodstuffs and other synthetic by-products.

Sweet potato—Carbohydrate—Alternative starches/flours (sweet potato, etc.)

Peanuts—Protein—Nonmeat protein sources (peanut butter)

Soybean—Oil—Alternative milks (almond, soy, etc.)[15]

Adding environmental context and molecular details deepens our understanding of Carver's chemistry and indicates the relationship between his chemistry and the Alabama environment.

Third, too often museums and historic sites believe they can increase their relevance by adopting a STEM approach. In other words, they want to add science, technology, engineering, and math to their program delivery. This has merit, but it also may have unintended consequences. Adopting STEM-focused programming can appear to undermine the value of history. To counter this, historical method must add value. This can be done most readily by putting the history into context. Soil science provides an example. Soil experiments have varied little since the 1860s. Research at soil test plots and experimental farms systematically measured yields over time on quadrants treated with different types of fertilizers or treated with no fertilizer at all. Scientists measured crop yields and determined best practices historically, and they still do so today to avoid over-application and reduce nutrient run-off into waterways.[16]

Fourth, a multidisciplinary approach to interpreting STEM-STEAM-STEMI subjects must add "H" to the mix (STEM to the power of H). This can be done either by broadening the content implied by the STEM letters or by advocating for STEM-STEAM-STEMI to the power of H. Some might find this simply an exercise in semantics, but that is not the case. Instead, conceptualizing the study of the environment as an exercise in STEM to the power of H, or as a STEALTH activity, can facilitate multidisciplinary analysis of spaces and places.[17]

S = embrace the social science aspect of the sciences, including historical studies of scientists and social scientists, while incorporating relevant sciences.

T = technology, including tools and equipment, but also the social construction of technologies. Preservationists apply technological knowledge.

E = engineering, including the mathematical foundation of physical engineering and the theories of social engineering, and social sciences of economics, but also, of course, the big "E"—the environment—and ecology and ecosystems.

A = the arts, which includes visual arts and creative arts as a tool to observe and communicate about the environment, as well as algebra as a tool useful to documenting how long it takes to travel or how much it takes to haul quantities over spaces.

L = literature and language.

T = reinforcement of the need to take seriously the ways that technology (from hand tools to robotics) affected the environment over time but also the opportunity to use theater and other performing arts to convey new interpretations of the stories.

H = history and the broader humanities perspectives on the subject.

Case Study: American Bison (*Bison bison*)

Let's practice a STEM to the power of H (STEALTH) approach by exploring different disciplinary approaches to understanding an iconic American mammal, the American bison. We'll start the process at the most basic level of thinking, as Bloom's taxonomy ranked identification and recall. What is it? Scientists would identify the animal by its scientific name, *Bison bison*, and adding its family—*Bovidae*. What did it eat? It is herbivorous and an ungulate. Where did it live? Answering this question required higher levels of thinking skills, comparison of evidence, and new interpretations.

Scientists and social scientists each have knowledge and skills gained from guided instruction and field experience to inform their analysis of the three-dimensional evidence of American bison that they might encounter. A historian, strictly defined, leans toward written evidence, rather than artifacts, to analyze the past. For instance, a historian would answer "What is a 'buffalo'?" by searching for written records about the "buffalo," both in primary sources such as letters, diaries, and photographs and in published sources, including newspapers and magazines, and historiographic sources such as articles and monographs written by scholars based on an analysis of primary sources.

Ideally, scientists and social scientists move outside their comfort zone and draw on written evidence of the past, and historians move outside their comfort zone and analyze material evidence to come to fuller understandings of the environment. Museums and historic sites provide the perfect places to practice this cross-disciplinary activity.

Anthropologist Jeffery Hanson analyzed historical data, including eyewitness accounts from the 1700s and 1800s and ecological data to argue that bison herds in North Dakota ranged year-round between three grassland ecosystems, from the eastern tallgrass prairie, through a transition zone, to the mixed-grass prairie to the west. What herd structure did bison have? The animals ranged in larger herds of mature cows with young calves and young bulls and smaller herds of mature bulls. During the wet spring and early summer, as grasslands grew, the cow herds increased in size, but during drier seasons, the bison divided into smaller herds so they could sustain themselves on available forage. Herds that ranged along a forest edge or an aspen range tended to be smaller year-round. Hanson concluded that local environmental factors affected bison behavior, but so did "unpredictable stimulants . . . [such as] seasonal patterns of rainfall, drought, prairie fires, frequency of blizzards, over grazing of local ranges, and human hunting pressure." He also called for additional evidence in the form of archaeological excavations to test his conclusions.[18]

Biologists and ecologists contribute much to understanding bison behavior in North Dakota and beyond. So do archaeologists, anthropologists, and archaeo-botanists. It requires many experts to analyze residue of prehistoric and historic hunts, including stone tools and butchering marks on extant bones, as well as pollen and seeds that can help document flora common in the place at the time of the hunt. Pollen excavated at a piskun or buffalo jump site in southwest Texas, near Langtry, documents 2 jumps over 7,500 years. The jumps coincided with evidence of grasses that grew sufficient to attract bison herds and hunters, only twice since 10,000, with the most recent around 500 B.C.E. Otherwise, the landscape was too dry to support bison herds. In contrast, sites in the northern plains provide evidence of persistent use of piskuns over hundreds of years. The First Peoples Buffalo Jump State Park near Ulm, Montana, a National Historic Landmark, protects a mile-long cliff used as a piskun by Plains Indians for at least six hundred years to stampede herds of bison over the cliff to be dispatched by waiting hunters. Another piskun in Canada, Head-Smashed-In Buffalo Jump, near Fort MacLeod, Alberta, was designated a World Heritage Site by the United Nations Educational, Scientific, and Cultural Organization (UNESCO) in 1981.[19]

In North Dakota, historical descriptions combined with botanical specimens document native flora, which, with additional archaeological investigation, could revise interpretations of just how far Plains Indians had to range to ensure a food supply. Bison foraged on a variety of grasses, specifically big bluestem (*Andropogon gerardii*), the dominant grass in the tall-grass prairie, and Indian grass (*Sorghastrum nutans*), among others. These tall grasses thrived in eastern North Dakota, an area with a higher annual rainfall and moist subsoil when compared to central or western North Dakota. More drought-tolerant varieties such as blue grama (*Bouteloua gracilis*) and western wheatgrass (*Agropyron smithii*) grew dominant in the transition zone and a mixed-grass zone of more drought-tolerant grasses to the west. Yet, combining historical documents describing buffalo herd behavior and documenting their range with botanical evidence indicates that each zone included a variety of grasses and sedges that imply that buffalo could graze year-round in one more localized area, rather than migrating in waves across the state, and back, each season. During late spring and early summer, cool-season grasses such as porcupine grass (*Stipa spartea*) and western wheatgrass, and threadleaf sedge (*Carex filifolia*) sustained herds. During summer, warm-season grasses such as blue grama, buffalograss (*Buchloe dactyloides*), and little bluestem (*Andropogon scoparius*) sustained herds. Other factors affected herd range, including floods, droughts, blizzards, or prairie fire. More archaeological investigations will help prove the range that American bison and American Indians traversed to ensure their survival.[20]

Numerous Plains Indian nations depended on *Bison bison* for their food, clothing, and shelter. Near the confluence of the Missouri and Yellowstone rivers, seven Indian nations,

Lithograph, "Bos Americanus, Gmel., American Bison or Buffalo." Drawn from nature by J. J. Audubon. Printed and colored by J. T. Bowen, Philadelphia. 1845. Image from the Collections of The Henry Ford Museum.

especially the *Nakodabi* or Assiniboine nation, traded with the American Fur Company starting in 1828. Swiss-born painter Karl Bodmer accompanied an expedition during the early 1830s, and he documented a bison hunt on October 11, 1833, near the company's post, Fort Union. His artwork featured individuals, rituals, and routines, such as the bison hunt. These cultural practices disappeared rapidly after the 1830s because of a combination of overland trails, railroads, and permanent settlers. The bison hides traded at Fort Union became the robes that kept travelers warm during winter or the belts that transferred power from steam engines to line shafts in Eastern factories (Fig. 2.2).[21]

Photographs taken by William Henry Jackson for the U.S. Geological Survey in 1870 depicted the bison-hide shelter used by a large band of Eastern Shoshone affiliated with Washakie, a powerful statesman and warrior. The Eastern Shoshone represent a population in transition. Washakie, whose mother was Agaidŭka Shoshone and whose father was Flathead, found a home among the Eastern Shoshone of the Green River and Bear River region of Wyoming, Idaho, and Utah. The band hunted bison on the plains of Montana and Wyoming. Washakie gained credibility among white traders and bureaucrats in 1849 as they tried to reduce inter-tribal conflict to ensure safer passage for migrants across the northern Plains. Washakie effectively moved his band along the Green and Bear river basins into the high plains by the early 1860s. As Washakie's biographer, Henry E. Stramm explained, the geographic shift reduced encounters with white travelers (and Mormon settlers who now

Karl Bodmer, Indians hunting the bison. Lithographic print, published as Tableau 31 in Maximilian zu Wied-Neuwied, Maximilian Prince of Wied's Travels in the Interior of North America, during the years 1832–1834; Translation H. Evans Lloyd; Achermann & Company, London 1843–1844. Library of Congress Prints and Photographs Division, Washington, D.C.

homesteaded former Shoshone land) and ensured access to bison without violating territorial boundaries negotiated in the 1851 Treaty of Fort Laramie. Washakie secured lands formerly inhabited by the Crow people in 1868 when the Fort Bridger Treaty created the Shoshone and Bannock Indian Agency in the Wind River Valley in west central Wyoming. Jackson's photographs became stereopticon cards. Jackson's photographs, packaged as stereopticons, conveyed "Views of the Rocky Mountains" to large audiences. One published by E. and H. T. Anthony & Co. of New York, described the scene as "138. War Chief's Tent." (Fig. 2.3).[22]

Folk songs like "Buffalo Skinner," conveyed with more accuracy the numbing routine of killing and skinning thousands of bison a season and the tension between the boss and laborers, but it implied incorrectly that the bleached bones remained behind. Postcards depicted piles of bones, often perceived as the debris left behind after the hunt. A postcard of a sod house with piles of "buffalo" bones and skulls stacked in front, with the caption, "The Beginning of Better Things," hints at the commercial value of the bones. The bones bleached on the prairie but did not stay. After scavengers and bugs cleaned them of sinew and car-

Photograph of Shoshoni Indians, Skin Tepies [sic], 2687. Taken by William Henry Jackson, official photographer with the U.S. Geological Survey, Prof. F. V. Hayden in charge, 1870–1874. Subjects include Washakie and a band of Eastern Shoshoni near the Sweetwater River in the Wind River Mountains, Wyoming. Library of Congress Prints and Photographs Division, Washington, D.C.

tilage, residents and laborers collected the bones and processors bought them to ship east where bone crushers further processed them and ground them into meal used for a variety of purposes. Bone meal added phosphorus to fertilizers. A booming business in fertilizers existed as home and market gardeners and truck farmers as well as landscape architects who installed urban and suburban gardens, used it to enhance soil nutrition. Processors also charred the bones and produced bone black or bone char used to purify patent medicines and refine sugar. Processors also made bone ash, used to make bone china, to polish metals, and to facilitate separation of gold or silver from base metals.[23] A pile of bones in the yard amounted to cash in hand for certain prairie dwellers during the late nineteenth century.

Artistic depictions include paintings and sculpture that often romanticized the hunt. Charles M. Russell might even have used a paint with the natural black pigment, bone char, in his painting, "Buffalo Hunt (No. 7)." Russell also depicted American bison in three dimensions, as he did in his bronze sculpture, "Nature's Cattle." The American bison also appeared in a mass-produced sculpture—on official U.S. currency. The U.S. government authorized the adaptation of sculptures by James Earl Fraser into bas relief images of an American Indian and a *Bison bison* on the obverse and reverse of the 1913 "Indian Head

Postcard 524. "The Beginning of Better Things." Photographed and published by C. W. [Charles Wesley] Mathers, Edmonton, Alberta, 1893–1907. The postcard implies that collecting (and selling) *Bison bison* bones could lead to better things. Image courtesy of Peel's Prairie Provinces (peel.library. ualberta.ca), a digital initiative of the University of Alberta Libraries.

Nickel." This artifact offers opportunity to combine artistic expression with political science and economics (two social sciences). Understanding the nickel requires investigating the costs of securing the copper and the nickel used in the five-cent pieces. The images did not wear well, and this led to its rapid replacement in 1938, after twenty-five years of production.[24]

Popular culture featured bison. Examples include posters advertising "Buffalo" Bill's Wild West Show, or a postcard showing *Bison bison* that survived after the decimation of the Plains herds but that humans removed from that natural habitat, hitched to a chariot, and raced at the Calgary Stampede in 1912.

Efforts to preserve the American Bison became a national priority when President Theodore Roosevelt established the National Bison Range in 1908 in west central Montana. Donors purchased bison and established the herd. More than a century later, the Northern Plains National Heritage Area, created in 2009, exists to "preserve, promote, and develop the culture, natural and scenic resources of the Northern Plains region of central North Dakota along the Missouri River." Prehistoric and historic Indian peoples and American bison cohabitated in this area.[25]

Multidisciplinary approaches to studying the environment result in more informed interpretations of that environment. It is important to engage people with different disciplinary knowledge and skills as partners in the project. This should free us to engage with

The environment defies political boundaries and so did people on the northern plains. Bob Yokum and Edd Carr, from South Dakota, transported their *Bison bison* and chariot to participate in the Calgary Exhibition and Stampede in 1912. Image courtesy of Peel's Prairie Provinces (peel.library. ualberta.ca), a digital initiative of the University of Alberta Libraries.

others to create the most complete interpretation of the environment possible. It does not have to happen all at once, and public historians do not have to bear the full burden. Take action: form teams and get started.

Notes

1. Giorgio Riello, "Things that Shape History: Material Culture and Historical Narratives," in *History and Material Culture: A Student's Guide to Approaching Alternative Sources*, ed., Karen Harvey (London: Routledge, 2009), 38.
2. Scientists attend to the chemical, molecular, and geological aspects of their subjects, discerning the names and laws of nature. Biologists study living organisms, whereas ecologists study relationships among those organisms, the flora and fauna, and their interdependency in a place. Geologists study sediments, rock, and physical forces to document the Earth's history and to understand formation of natural resources such as coal, gas, minerals, and oil, among others.

   Social science approaches help us understand patterns of human behavior. These patterns become visible in society (sociology), in politics, in the law (political science), and in economics and consumer science or domestic science (i.e., home economics). Patterns are also visible in the built environment. Other disciplines, such as psychology, apply science methodologies to interpret behaviors of individuals and groups as well as their influence on their environment, be they rural, urban, or suburban.

3. Historians have debated their categorization as a social science or humanities since at least the 1890s because of different approaches taken. Those who study the written word, an articulation produced by an individual representing a particular frame of reference, identify with the humanities. Others argue for studies of society or culture through records that document people who left no individualized written evidence, and they identify with social sciences. Some categorize cultural anthropology or cultural geography, as well as political science and law as humanities subjects, but not all anthropologists, geographers, policy makers, or political scientists would agree, because their approach aligns more with science methodologies than humanities methodologies. Some humanities subjects, such as linguistics, depends on a blend of science, social science, and humanities methodologies.

4. *The Secretary of the Interior's Standards for the Treatment of Historic Properties* (2017), with details for each of the four treatments, plus guidelines for treatment of historic landscapes, and for environmental sustainability in historic structures. Available at: https://www.nps.gov/tps/standards.htm. Accessed June 15, 2018. Understanding environmental policy requires evidence about the place (natural sciences or geosciences), consideration of human or individual perceptions on the problem (humanities), the moral or ethical aspect of human action (humanities), the social behaviors that require regulation (social sciences), the political parties and institutions that affect the law (social sciences), and the institutions that enforce it (social sciences).

5. Barbara Corson shared these comments in an e-mail to Debra A. Reid on June 6, 2018, after pondering the discussion that occurred on Saturday, June 2, 2018, during Reid's session, "Interpreting the Environment," at the 2018 annual conference of the Association for Living History, Farm and Agricultural Museums.

6. Corson to Reid, e-mail, June 6, 2018.

7. Popper's 1934 German title translated as "Logic of Research: On the Epistemology of Modern Natural Science." See Popper, *The Logic of Scientific Discovery* (London: Routledge Classics, 2002), for the theory of knowledge, xix; for experience as a method, 16–17; and for falsifiability as a criterion of demarcation, 17–20.

8. Popper, for rational discussion, xix; for historical method, xx.

9. Frederick Beiser, "Historicism," in *The Oxford Handbook of Continental Philosophy*, eds., Michael Rosen and Brian Leiter (London: Oxford University Press, 2007), 155–179. Karl Popper, *The Poverty of Historicism* (London: Routledge and Kegan Paul, 1957).

10. "Value of History Statement, History Relevance. Available at: https://www.historyrelevance.com/value-history-statement. Accessed July 19, 2018. Geographer Yi-Fu Tuan called for more self-awareness when studying places and for more activism to effect change in his 1974 book, *Topophilia: A Study of Environmental Perception, Attitudes, and Values* (Englewood Cliffs, NJ: Prentice Hall, 1974). He urged geographers to understand their perceptions, attitudes, and values because, "without self-understanding we cannot hope for enduring solutions to environmental problems, which are fundamentally human problems." Tuan encouraged geographers to do good work in the world by resisting environmental destruction. Geographer Robert David Sack built on Tuan's ideas in his 1997 book, *Homo Geographicus: A Framework for Action, Awareness, and Moral Concern* (Baltimore, MD: Johns Hopkins University Press, 1997).

11. Alfred Jacob Miller, "Hunting Buffalo," watercolor on paper, 1858–1860, accession no. 37.1940.190. Walters Museum of Art, Baltimore, Maryland. Available at: http://art.thewalters.org/detail/16002/hunting-buffalo/. Accessed June 16, 2018.

12. Letter, Marsh to Baird, May 21–22, 1860, published in *Life and Letters of Charles Perkins Marsh*, compiled by Caroline Crane Marsh, vol. 1 (New York: C. Scribner's Sons, 1888), first quote 422–23. George Perkins Marsh, *Man and Nature: Or, Physical Geography as Modified by Human Action* (Seattle: University of Washington Press, 2003 [1864]). Marsh, on the title page of *Man and Nature*, paraphrased Horace Bushnell's sermon, "The Power of an Endless Life," published in *Sermons for the New Life* (New York: C. Scribner, 1858), 304–25, for the original passage, see 310; as paraphrased by Marsh: "Not all the winds, and storms, and earthquakes, and seas, and seasons of the world, have done so much to revolutionize the earth as Man, the power of an endless life, has done since the day he came forth upon it, and received dominion over it."

13. Marsh-Billings Rockefeller National Historical Park, in Woodstock, Vermont, interprets conservation stewardship and the contributions of George Perkins Marsh and Frederick Billings. Available at: https://www.nps.gov/mabi/index.htm. Accessible June 16, 2018.

14. George W. Carver, *How to Build up Worn Out Soils* (1905).

15. Ryan Jelso, associate curator for Digital Content, The Henry Ford, summarized these three examples on August 30, 2018, as part of a project with Debra Reid, Curator of Agriculture and the Environment, to revitalize the agriculture exhibit in the Henry Ford Museum of American Innovation.

16. The University of Illinois–Urbana Champaign maintains remnants of the Morrow Plot, the first agricultural experiment plot in the United States dedicated to documenting the effects of fertilizer on corn yields. The plots are listed on the National Register of Historic Places. Manure spreaders, produced by the millions by agricultural implement companies during the late nineteenth century, facilitated more even application of manure on farm fields. Agricultural scientists calculated manure and manure nutrient application rates by documenting the weight of manure spread on a tarp measuring 22 sq. ft. (either 3 feet × 7 feet 4 inches or 4 feet × 5 feet 6 inches) and calculating the total nitrogen (N), ammonium nitrogen (NH_4^+-N), phosphate (P_2O_5), and potash (K_2O) available in a manure load. Different livestock and bedding-to-manure ratios yield different quantities, but in general (and farmers knew) poultry manure measured three to ten times higher in nitrogen, ammonia nitrogen, phosphate, and potash than pig or beef manure. Farmers learned by doing, applying only what they needed to fields with different nutrient needs, historically and today. Agricultural extension services, operating out of each state's land-grant university, published bulletins explaining this to farmers. Today you can access these bulletins quickly with a search using keywords such as "calculating manure and nutrient applications."

17. Reid's colleague at Eastern Illinois University, Nora Pat Small, came up with the STEALTH acronym. See Debra A. Reid, *Interpreting Agriculture in Museums and Historic Sites* (Lanham, MD: Rowman & Littlefield, 2017), 7–8, and "Agriculture: Developing a Humanist Point of View," in *Interpreting Agriculture in Museums and Historic Sites*, 29–40.

18. Jeffery R. Hanson, "Bison Ecology in the Northern Plains and a Reconstruction of Bison Patterns for the North Dakota Region," *Plains Anthropologist*, vol. 29, no. 104 (May 1984): 102, citing D. W. Moodie and Arthur J. Ray, "Buffalo Migrations in the Canadian Plains," *Plains Anthropologist*, vol. 21, no. 71 (February 1976), 45–52.

19. For information on Bonfire Shelter, available at: http://www.texasbeyondhistory.net/bonfire/index.html. Accessed June 16, 2018; First Peoples Buffalo Jump State Park, available at: http://stateparks.mt.gov/first-peoples-buffalo-jump/ Accessed June 16, 2018; and for Head-Smashed-In Buffalo Jump, available at: https://headsmashedin.ca/. Accessed June 16, 2018.

20. Hanson, "Bison Ecology," 104–11.
21. David C. Hunt, William J. Orr, and W. H. Goetzmann, eds., *Karl Bodmer's America* (Omaha/Lincoln: Joslyn Art Museum/University of Nebraska Press, 1984).
22. Henry E. Stamm IV, *People of the Wind River: The Eastern Shoshones, 1825–1900* (Norman: University of Oklahoma Press, 1999). Views of the tent, one with the dark tent with light horizontal stripe on the right and labeled "138. War Chief's Tent," was taken near South Pass and Fort Stambaugh, near the Sweetwater River in the Wind River Mountains, in 1870. The other view has the dark tent on the left. These scenes captured opposite vistas beyond the hide shelters.
23. Piles of *Bison bison* bones and skulls in Rougeville, along the Rouge River near Detroit, along with offal from slaughter houses, became the basis for bone-meal fertilizer. The Detroit Public Library manages an oft-published photograph of two men and a pile of bones and skulls near Detroit. Identification handwritten on the back of the photographic matt reads: "C.D. 1892 Glueworks, office foot of 1st St., works at Rougeville, Mich." Available at: https://digitalcollections.detroitpubliclibrary.org/islandora/object/islandora%3A151477. Accessed June 16, 2018.
24. The painting and sculpture by Russell were part of the fiftieth "The Russell," an auction to benefit the C. M. Russell Museum, held March 17, 2018. See "Buffalo Hunt Oil Painting Selected for Live Auction," Live Art Today (March 14, 2018). Available at: https://fineartconnoisseur.com/2018/03/fine-art-auctions-buffalo-hunt-oil-painting-selected/. Accessed June 16, 2018. The C. M. Russell Museum reports results of "The Russell," available at: www.cmrussell.org. Accessed June 16, 2018.
25. "About the Range," National Bison Range, U.S. Fish and Wildlife Service, Department of the Interior. Available at: https://www.fws.gov/refuge/National_Bison_Range/about.html. Accessed September 2, 2018. For information about the Northern Plains Heritage Area, see the Feasibility Study (2007) available at: http://www.northernplainsheritage.org/. Accessed September 1, 2018. The mission is part of the Vision Statement, p. 59.

CHAPTER 3

Constructing Stories about Humans and the Environment

The ground itself, where we can read the information it affords, is . . . the fullest and the most certain of documents.

JOHN RICHARD GREEN, *THE MAKING OF ENGLAND* (1881), VII

Interpretation should aim to present a whole rather than a part.

FREEMAN TILDEN, *INTERPRETING OUR HERITAGE* (1977, 3RD ED.), 9

The earlier in time one goes, the more people were directly and intimately tied to their environment. . . . As culture became more complex, our removal from the natural world increased.

JAMES DEETZ, *IN SMALL THINGS FORGOTTEN* (1977), 21–22

THE IE TOOLKIT EXPANDS even more as we get to the heart of the subject—constructing stories about humans and the environment. You should be prepared with a good grounding in context and issues drawn from secondary readings, and you should feel comfortable having identified methods based in history and the sciences. The next step involves identifying primary evidence, analyzing it, and crafting stories or histories based on it. Consider how people have told stories about the environment in the past. Historian J. R. Green took into account the forests that armies had to navigate and the bogs and marshes that invaders encountered as he explained *The Making of England* up to 829 C. E. Green drew on the physical geography of a place and archaeological evidence that supplemented the written record to construct a whole human-environment interaction. Consider the advice that exists to construct these stories. Freeman Tilden implied that effective interpretation derived from understanding just such "a" whole, not "the" whole. As he explained, "It is far better that the visitor to a preserved area, natural, historic or prehistoric, should leave with one or more whole pictures in his mind, than with a mélange of information that leaves him in doubt as to the essence of the place, and even in doubt as to why the area has been preserved at all." A story constructed around "a" whole should "stir the imagination, leave an indelible impression, and lead the visitor to wish to know more about the subtle adaptations of organic life."[1]

Anthropologist James Deetz, who oversaw excavations at Plimoth Plantation, believed that, as the distance between humans and their environments increased, it became harder for them to conceptualize "a" whole environment (or any environment, for that matter). This increased the sense of urgency to interpret the environment. Deetz furthered the cause by conceptualizing artifacts as "the vast universe of objects used by mankind to cope with the physical world," and he defined "our world" as *that sector of our physical environment that we modify through culturally determined behavior.*" Deetz, writing in the years after the designation of Earth Day and creation of the Environmental Protection Agency, argued that humans might believe that they could overcome physical impediments with ease, but the environment still registered their actions and held that evidence in perpetuity.[2] Deetz's thought-provoking book, *In Small Things Forgotten*, appeared the same year as the third edition of Freeman Tilden's *Interpreting Our Heritage*. Another seminal 1970s book, *Interpretation of Historic Sites*, fell short of the mark when measured for its utility in furthering interpretation of the environment. That book did not incorporate the environment as one of the essential stories sites should tell, focusing instead on people and events. Perhaps the authors believed that Tilden's *Interpreting Our Heritage* covered interpretive strategies adequately so they did not expand on what historic landscapes and the built environment could teach. Whatever the reason, not including the environment as an essential story left historic sites on their own to realize the potential of their largest artifact—their landscapes and historic structures, their place, and their space. *Interpreting the Environment* picks up this torch and fans the flames toward the goal of invigorating interpretation of the environment at museums and historic sites.[3]

This chapter explains how to identify "a" whole story, inspired by the environment and worthy of telling. Doing so will help staff and visitors be more environmentally literate at a time when it matters most. It proposes a research methodology to document the local environment (both natural and human-made) and explains the steps to take to confirm relevant stories and align collections to tell those stories. It proposes collection development strategies that align artifactual evidence and interpretive planning strategies to build provocative environmental interpretation. Finally, it aligns K–12 guidelines for environmental education with strategies to develop provocative interpretation.

Research Methodology

Museums and historic sites preserve places and spaces, natural and built landscapes, historic structures, and pristine ecosystems. These places and spaces are the largest three-dimensional objects in museum collections, though many museums do not recognize them as such.

It is as important to document wilderness and natural spaces that humans imagine, explore, and try to conserve, as it is to document the places that humans demarcate on a map and transform by mowing, farming, excavating, or paving. Both spaces and places appear in the historical record and reflect human ambitions to survive and thrive. The by-product of those ambitions leave lasting imprints on the environment. They can be as remarkable as prehistoric drawings, perhaps made from bone char pigment drawn on a rock-face canvas or as ordinary as a stone wall piled up along a fence.

Museums and historic sites staff should dedicate adequate time to document the environment that they collect, preserve, and interpret. The process is straightforward, but it takes time. The returns warrant the investment.[4]

Secondary Sources

Research starts with reading secondary sources about your location, that focus either on the time period you interpret or on the community, state, or region. Start by compiling a reading list of secondary sources. You do not have to read everything because you are likely chomping at the bit to dig into archival sources. Pick ten monographs or articles that you believe can inform you. Form a reading circle among colleagues and schedule regular meetings. That will make the process more communal and will ensure that numerous perspectives inform the process. It will help increase collegial investment in the process and will reduce the workload on any one individual by making it more of a group effort. To get started, consult the environmental history chapter (chapter 1) as well as the bibliography and timeline at the end of this book.

Pu'u Loa Petroglyphs, Volcanoes National Park, Hawai'i. David D. Vail

As you read through these sources, pay particular attention to the ways the authors treat the environment. Do they revere it or ignore it? Do they consider it a resource to be exploited by clear cutting, mining, channeling, or cultivating? Traditional history may mention such actions but does not go into them. Take notes because these mentions, however brief, will become the basis for further exploration.

After you increase your understanding of your place and space over time, ideally from before contact to the present, you can begin to identify themes in environmental history that relate to your museum's or historic site's mission. The book, *Major Problems in American Environmental History*, or other surveys of environmental history, provide a good place to start. Check the footnotes as you read to identify additional relevant readings.

Follow similar note-taking strategies that you used as you collected data about your place or space over time. Think about how the authors identify their focus. What sorts of evidence do they use to build their case? Do you find their argument persuasive?

The real fun begins as you begin to see how your museum or historic-site resources can make the historians arguments more relevant to visitors. That's what we aim for.

At the same time you identify secondary historical resources to consult, you should be identifying additional publications that provide other disciplinary perspectives on the same subject matter. Look for county soil and water conservation district reports prepared by county agricultural extension agents or U.S. Department of Agriculture employees in county offices. Farm bureaus in some states undertake comparable studies. These usually include information drawn from county histories, the same county histories that you should include on your reading list. The soil scientists, geologists, and agricultural technical experts will not take the time to debate the validity of 1870 or 1880 or 1910 interpretations. That is not their job, though it is the job of staff in history museums and historic sites. Instead, they use these published county histories to establish the context for their discussion of soil types, watersheds, vegetation cover, and other details about flora and fauna.[5] You have the advantage, having read the historical scholarship, to screen the information. The soil and watershed experts may draw their historical information from too small a pool of resources to satisfy public history criteria, but you should not be tempted to do the same with the scientific evidence. This is where breadth of knowledge comes in handy. Challenge yourself to be well-read in the science and the history. This will prepare you well to construct as comprehensive an environmental history overview of your place and space as possible.

After you gain an introduction to the environmental topics that authors include in their histories and their reports, then you can begin to synthesize your findings into a narrative about the environment at your museum or historic site. You should arrange it by topic (the themes most relevant to your situation), and chronologically within each topic.

Include in your summary the points of agreement and of disagreement among the authors you read. This is a natural outcome of detailed reading. Some call it the "meta-discourse" about the past. Authors do not agree in their interpretation of evidence. Their class, political perspective, personal values, and familiarity with the subject may all affect their interpretation. The issues of their time also affect their interpretations. The more we read about a topic, the more obvious different interpretations become. Patterns develop, and these make it easier to categorize interpretations. These patterns might well reflect public opinion. It is important to determine the sources of the different interpretations and organize evidence to offer the best defense of the interpretation(s) that your museum or historic site may express.

A useful exercise (after you have collected your notes from secondary sources) involves putting the authors into the context of their times. This will help you identify factors that affected authors and will help you explain the reasons why they came to the conclusions that they did. This is important because you have to determine the veracity of their interpretations. To do this you have to know who the authors were, what they believed, and what outside forces affected their lives and may have influenced their interpretations. Compiling this information will help you understand what factors affect your own goals.

Regarding content, you will likely read about timber, water, fertile land, coal, iron ore, or other natural resources in county histories. This reflects the mindset of the time. Settlers perceived an environment replete with natural resources waiting to be exploited, whereas others perceived settlement as a land grab. Because victors wrote the history, the perspective of the settlers took precedence, and their agendas drove both economic development and the main themes of historical overviews. They established sawmills and grist mills and diverted flowing water to mill races to power their mills. The settlers populated the countryside, thanks to proactive land policy that facilitated settlement. They grew marketable commodities and reinvested their hard-earned income into improvements to their farms.

The stories of settlers tend to celebrate innovation, ingenuity, and resourcefulness and often fail to address exploitation of natural resources and evidence of how this hurt others—displaced, enslaved, and underpaid people—as well as the negative effects on the environment that resulted. The environmental history that you write will support your interpretation, so it is essential to incorporate the good, the bad, and the ugly in your overview.

Primary Sources

After reading secondary sources to gain the broadest vantage point on your place and space, start hypothesizing or asking questions that you need to know more about to interpret your site. These should relate to the big themes you documented as relevant to your place and space.

What natural resource did residents depend on for survival?

Who controlled the resource? How did that affect who profited from the resource?

Who labored in the mines (or mills)?

What caused pollution? What ended pollution?

What policy affected your place and space? What effect did land policy have? Or soil and water conservation management? Or Environmental Protection Agency regulations?

What commodities drove the local economy? What did it take to produce them? How did this affect the environment?

What names did local residents give creeks, streams, or rivers, and why?

What natural disasters affected residents? When did natural disasters occur?

What public lands exist in the area?

What current environmental issues galvanize the community?

Can you document examples of recycling historically?

You cannot answer all of these questions at once, but you can prioritize them and chip away at them with your team. You can categorize your research agenda. Select the most important topic—a coal mine that operated locally, or a bridge project, or a devastating flood or storm that forever changed a community—and focus energies on it first.

Natural catastrophes such as tornadoes, earthquakes, and floods disrupted routines, and many sites include collections accumulated at the time of these events. This evidence documents community resilience revisited during anniversaries of the catastrophe. An exercise in historical thinking by avoiding presentism can focus research on a local event based on almanacs and historic evidence rather than defaulting to Weather Channel reporting. That said, after documenting major events, the next step involves taking that past forward. This requires transferring historic evidence to contrast with or accentuate current conversations about environmental themes. It is key to know the historic facts before moving toward relevance.

If you have a well-documented event that relates to the environment, organize primary evidence about it to determine what perspectives might be missing. What more do you need to know? Why has no one studied it? Does evidence exist to document it? Where can you find it? What do you need to document all perspectives about a controversy? Pursue all lines of inquiry, and make note of all of them, even if you cannot find primary evidence about it. You may not be the only person looking. Collection development can help you fill in the gaps.

Agriculture will factor into stories about the environment everywhere. Growing commodities, processing them into foodstuffs, trading and transporting foodstuffs, and then marketing of those foodstuffs transformed environments at every step along the route from farm to consumer. Rural counties included large numbers of farmers, and their agricultural practices transformed local environments. Urban counties included market gardeners and plots of land owned not by wholesale grocers but farmers by local residents. Transportation systems connected the food producers with the consumers. These farmers sought bone meal, which facilitated bison hunting. Explore those connections as you do your primary research.[6]

Diaries, letters, account books, land records, personal correspondence, photographs, real and personal property tax rolls, maps, and manuscript census data—all these traditional archival sources will likely factor in to local research about the environment. So will published primary sources such as city directories that itemize producers and processors. Additional primary sources include topographical maps and plat maps that document private ownership of land at specific points in time. State historical societies, or state archives, county courthouses, and land-grant universities maintain these records. Call archivists to inquire about their holdings. Their job is to provide access to their collections.

The more you read, the more you know. This may include learning about what does not relate to your site's history. Document that, too.

Remember that engaging in higher levels of thinking involves new and deeper thought about a subject. If little attention has been paid to environmental history in your location, developing new understanding may seem easier. Even well-studied topics, however, leave room you room to add value based on your primary research. Your contribution might rest on the incorporation of relevant archival sources from your institution into the mix of primary sources about a major topic.

Based on what you have learned, review your institutional mission and interpretive plan. Do your research findings align with the mission as it exists? Does it leave room for new or refined interpretive directions? If so, move forward. If not, reassess your situation. Your institution could benefit from a review of your mission or interpretive goals. This could increase your engagement with your community and constituents. It could expand your circles of engagement. You may find that you generate more enthusiasm for local history when you ally with some new partners with shared but nonduplicative goals.

Artifacts: Identifying Collection Strengths

The research process supports intellectual control over existing collections. Knowing more about environmental history, and knowing how existing collections fit in, can help you say "yes" to artifacts that tell important stories not otherwise documented in your three-dimensional collection. It can also help you say "no" to artifacts that add little to your storytelling capacity.

The research process increases your understanding of stories you can tell or need to tell. Transfer this new understanding to the curation process. Add environment-related information to object records for artifacts already in your collection. Include environment-related justification and historical significance to your overall proposal to acquire a new object.

For example, you identified characteristics of soils and sediments in your location during your research project. This can help you determine the ways that soil properties affected human decisions in your area. Did clay draw potters or support brickmaking trades? Did fertile alluvial sediment lure farmers? Which type of plow did farmers use to turn the sod? Different plows fit needs partially dictated by soil and topography. Try to apply details from your research findings as you answer these questions during the cataloging process. Form a cataloging team that can pursue these lines of research that may not have been addressed already. Consider exploring a different subject each month to vary the topics and to add the science to your historical assets.

An exercise in cataloging collections can help you rethink how you describe your historical artifacts as evidence useful to tell the environmental-history story. The exercise starts with the environment, likely the largest artifact in your collection. First, answer these questions:

1. Does your institution consider the environment that it occupies an asset? Not an asset on a balance sheet but an intellectual asset. If so, congratulations. If not, now is the time to start.

2. Does your institution have a historic landscape plan or landscape stewardship plan? If not, start one. Environmental history does not just apply to historical resources; it relates to modern settings, which are part of the globe's overall package. Consult the bibliography for resources.

3. Does your institution have historic structure reports on file for buildings at your site? If not, add it to your list of things to do. Consult the bibliography for resources.

4. Have you accessioned your landscape into your collection? This is a major step in the process toward stewardship of your collection. If you already consider your landscape an interpretive asset, treat it like an artifact. Cataloging it makes a statement.

5. How do you catalog "landscape?" Consider it a tangible thing. Proceed as you do with other items in your collection. Measure it. Describe it. Document materials (this includes topography, soil and sediment, watersheds, vegetation, and woodlands, among other things). Document ownership and users of the site over time. State the landscape's significance in relation to your mission and in relation to environmental history.

6. Have you cataloged the structures at your museum or historic site? Documenting historic structures is essential for historic sites, and they factor into environmental history in numerous ways—made from natural resources, shelter for consumers of fossil fuels, clad in nonrenewable resources. Museums may not consider the structure that houses their collection as an intellectual asset. If that is the case, the structure still warrants attention because visitors associate the structure with the institution, and the structure may be a jumping off point for interpreting environmental history even if it is not considered a historical asset.

7. Repeat the cataloging exercise for other objects in your collection, starting with the most significant and working toward your backlogged collection. This will help you see how your porcelain and bone china, your walnut rocking chairs and mahogany sideboards, your landscape paintings and photographs of house lawns fit within this large subject of environmental history.

Thoughtful cataloging of collections will, in the short term, help you retrieve information about existing collections more quickly as you develop relevant interpretive and educational programming. You will be able to distinguish between objects essential to tell a story and those only tangentially relevant or irrelevant to your goals of interpreting the environment. In the long term, this information will inform deaccessioning decisions. Ultimately, it will become the basis for proactive collecting to fill the gaps needed to tell your environmental history.

This will take time. Make it a component of master planning to build your collection. You will not be disappointed in the results.

Collection Development

Many sites may not have everything they need to document their place and space. How to proceed? You have already started the process of proactive collecting if you have done your homework and have bolstered object cataloging. Next, link objects to relevant themes.

1. The three to five environmental history topics most relevant to your museum or historic site becomes the basis of your environmental history collection development plan. Topics such as food security and environmental sustainability, or human-livestock-soil mutual dependency, or food, fuel, and resource management become hooks around which you can categorize existing collections and plan future acquisitions.
2. Itemize existing collections by theme. Veritably everything in your collection can help you interpret the environment that sustained humans at your museum or historic site.
3. Not all objects will fit your environmental themes. Just because something does not fit does not automatically doom it to deaccessioning. It may be essential to telling other stories required at your site. Yet, this is the point in the process where difficult decisions can be made about objects suitable for deaccessioning. Proceeds from sold items should be dedicated to collection stewardship, and this can include acquiring more relevant objects.
4. Identify gaps in your collection. Prioritize the gaps. For instance, your institution may sit in a location protected by a levee. You have identified water transportation as a significant environmental story to tell. Your collection assessment confirms that you have nothing documenting the Army Corps of Engineers construction of the levee, built in 1935. Which of the following three themes do you need to address first? The government programs that funded levee construction. The memories of residents about floods before (and since) the levee. The builders of the levee, including the engineer and the hired laborers. You should collect all three, eventually, but in the next year, which *one* should you pursue?
5. Begin proactive collecting strategically. You do not want to broadcast your interest widely unless you want to be inundated with offers to purchase items. You also want to document as many perspectives on topics that can be controversial, and you do not want to scare away some of your best informants. Develop a plan and a budget, review it regularly, and proceed with proactive collecting.

Well-curated collections yield gems that support interpretive programming. They may have value even if secured in environmentally controlled storage. They contribute most to your institution's purpose when used to engage the public.

Environmental Literacy

The North American Association for Environmental Education (NAAEE) defines an environmentally literate person as

someone who, both individually and together with others, makes informed decisions concerning the environment; is willing to act on these decisions to improve the well being of other individuals, societies, and the global environment; and participates in civic life. Those who are environmentally literate possess, to varying degrees:

- the knowledge and understanding of a wide range of environmental concepts, problems, and issues;
- a set of cognitive and affective dispositions;
- a set of cognitive skills and abilities; and
- the appropriate behavioral strategies to apply such knowledge and understanding in order to make sound and effective decisions in a range of environmental contexts.[7]

Environmental literacy gains its strengths by facilitating higher levels of thinking as outlined in Bloom's taxonomy. Ultimately, evidence collected needs to be analyzed and

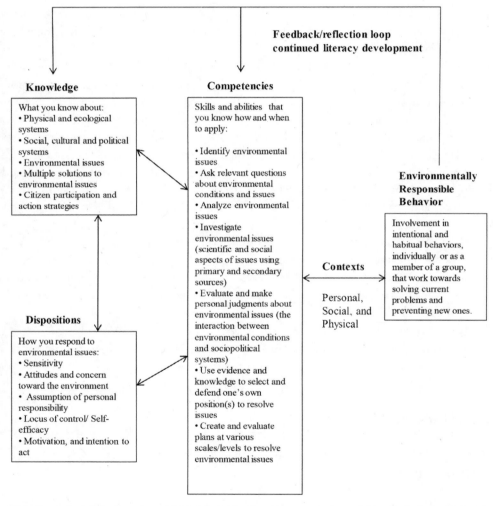

The Domain of Environmental Literacy. Used with permission of North American Association for Environmental Education; published in *Developing a Framework for Assessing Environmental Literacy* (2011), 3-2 (pg. 17 in the PDF). Available at http://www.naaee.net (accessed September 1, 2018). https://cdn.naaee.org/sites/default/files/devframewkasses-senvlitonlineed.pdf.

interpreted in ways that create new understanding. The NAAEE's Environmental Literacy framework lays out quite nicely the connections between learning about the local environment, engaging with it, and taking action to sustain it. The framework or domain incorporates social-science subjects (e.g., society, culture, politics). Scientists, including social scientists, engage with historical evidence that documents change over time as they pursue environmental literacy. Museums and historic sites can contribute to this process by reinforcing historical thinking as a component of all elements of the domain.

The NAAEE devised a curriculum to sustain environmental education in K–12 classrooms. The organization did this as national and state standards change, and the revisions may or may not remain supportive of environmental education. The matrix, Understanding the Local Environment, can provide useful resources for staff in museums and historic sites seeking a framework relevant to K–12 curriculum, specifically for fourth, eighth, and twelfth grades. Many states have adopted the NAAEE recommendations, so they can support new educational offerings that your research findings about the environment, and your artifact analysis can help support.

The NAAEE also provides guidelines to partner with community organizations. Museums and historic sites do not have to do this alone. The NAAEE Community Engagement Guidelines include five characteristics of successful community-based initiatives. See *Community Engagement: Guidelines for Excellence* for additional details. A summary of recommendations follows.[8]

First, the initiative should put the community at the heart of environmental education. Many communities already have ongoing initiatives. Museums and historic sites can find a place at the larger table. They do not have to create and manage these themselves. Partnering with others already involved in community-centered projects increases the energy dedicated to community interests, issues, and resources.

Second, the initiative should further established principles of environmental education as articulated in NAAEE educational guidelines and in NAAEE environmental literacy domain.

Third, the initiative should pursue collaborative and inclusive relationships, partnerships, and coalitions. This includes valuing and ensuring diversity, equity, and inclusion in the process. No one partner should dominate; the project should be planned and implemented collaboratively. Practice conflict resolution throughout the process to ensure complete engagement.

Fourth, the initiative should, as NAAEE explains, support capacity building for ongoing civic engagement in community life, contributing to long-term community well-being, sustainability, and resilience. It involves integrating environmental education with communication goals, and it should aim toward social change. This often requires civic action.

Fifth, participation in the initiative requires a long-term investment in community engagement and relationship building. Is your museum or historic site ready to participate? If not, but if the will exists, determine changes necessary to position yourself as a community partner in the process.

Understanding the Local Environment

Experiencing and observing the local environment is an essential part of environmental education. Understanding their surroundings helps learners build a strong foundation of skills and knowledge for reaching out further into the world and deeper into the conceptual understandings that environmental literacy demands. Direct experience in the environment also helps foster the awareness and appreciation that motivate learners to further questioning, better understanding, and appropriate concern and action.

The following chart suggests ways in which learners at different grade levels might explore and understand the local environment. It is printed in each grade level section of these guidelines to help show progression as learners mature. Other ideas are included in the guidelines.

Grades Pre K–4

Identify basic types of habitats (e.g., forests, wetlands, or lakes). Create a short list of plants and animals found in each.

Trace the source of their drinking water and where it goes after it is used.

Recognize resident animal species, migrants, and those that pass through on migratory routes.

Collect or produce images of the area at the beginning of European settlement.

Describe aspects of the environment that change on a daily, weekly, monthly, and yearly basis.

Record weather observations such as precipitation, temperature, or cloud cover.

Identify food crops that are grown or processed locally.

Grades 5–8

Classify local ecosystems (e.g., oak-hickory forest or sedge meadow). Create food webs to show—or describe their function in terms of—the interaction of specific plant and animal species.

Describe how drinking water and wastewater are treated.

Map migratory routes of birds, butterflies, and other animals that pass through the area. Identify their local habitat needs.

Monitor changes in water or air quality, or other aspects of the local environment.

Identify species that are locally threatened, endangered, or declining in population. Describe their habitat needs.

Identify sources of electricity used in the community (e.g., hydroelectric, fossil fuels, solar, nuclear).

Describe the area's climate and identify factors that contribute to it and have changed it over time.

Create a map for the local area that shows where food that is consumed locally comes from.

Grades 9–12

Identify several plants and animals common to local ecosystems. Describe concepts such as succession, competition, predator/prey relationships, and parasitism.

Evaluate sources of nonpoint source pollution of local bodies of water, including sources that are not local.

Investigate short- and long-term environmental changes in a local watershed, and aquifer, or in air quality. Or document changes in land use and their environmental effects.

Research population trends for a locally threatened species. Describe changes, activities, and other factors that seem to affect the population trends.

Calculate the potential for generating wind or solar power on a particular site.

Identify local sources of greenhouse gases. Examine the relationship between greenhouse gases in the Earth's atmosphere and climate change.

Trace human population trends and make research-based projections.

Understanding the Local Environment. *Excellence in Environmental Education: Guidelines for Learning (K–12)* (4th ed., 2010), pg. 50. https://cdn.naaee.org/sites/default/files/learner-guidelines_new.pdf (accessed September 1, 2018).

Interpretive Planning

If you help visitors learn about a place that's important to you, you're an interpreter!

NATIONAL ASSOCIATION FOR INTERPRETATION (2018)

Every day, thousands of us share the stories of our land and its people.

INTERPRETATION CANADA (2018)

The National Association for Interpretation (NAI) defines interpretation as "a mission-based communication process that forges emotional and intellectual connections between the interests of the audience and the meanings inherent in the resource." NAI attempts to expand its relevance beyond park systems and park and recreation districts by defining "resource" (i.e., important natural, cultural, and historical resources) and "museum" (e.g., "parks, nature centers, historical sites, aquariums, zoos, and anywhere that people come to learn about places") broadly.[9] This complies with the broad definition of museums as advocated by the American Alliance of Museums.

Interpretation Canada defines interpretation as "a communication process, designed to reveal meanings and relationships of our cultural and natural heritage, to the public, through firsthand involvement with objects, artifacts, landscapes and sites." (1976)[10]

Numerous how-to books exist to guide interpretive planning. *Interpreting the Environment* does not propose a new methodology. Instead, it emphasizes content as the basis for engagement. It embraces the six principles of interpretation as proposed by Tilden in *Interpreting our Heritage*, but it does not encourage any museum or historic site to blindly follow those principles. Use them as a jumping-off point for increased intellectual engagement in the content that your resources convey. Improve on them by drawing on more than sixty years' worth of thought and action in museum and interpretive practice that has occurred since Tilden's first edition, published in 1957. Embrace, particularly the potential of the first principle: "Any interpretation that does not somehow relate . . . will be sterile," to pursue environmental literacy and formal environmental education. Practice higher levels of thinking yourself. Develop strategies that capture the attention of your own undecided constituents, starting with volunteers and board members.

How to do this? A balanced interpretation documents both the positive depictions as well as the evidence of change wrought by people in the past, be they millers, farmers, public officials, local businessmen, railroad magnates, or river boat captains. They all factor into the overall use, and misuse, of the environment over time.

Remember the need to conceptualize interpretation as "a" whole, not "the" whole. Not one fact after another and not details that take visitors into too many weeds. What's the powerful point you need to make? What three artifacts can you see that help you tell it? What is your deliverable two-minute message? Now, proceed to construct that story.

Case Study

Interpretation should encourage intellectual engagement, what we call "minds-on" rather than just "hands-on" learning. Kinesthetic, or hands-on, learning has value, but thought can be kinesthetic, too. A case study focused on interpreting agriculture seems appropriate because of the ways that the business of farming changed the environment locally, regionally, and globally. Marsh provided a case study to convince Professor Baines of this in 1860. The following synthesizes some of the themes addressed already to make a point about how much potential exists with ubiquitous objects and big messages.

During fall 2017, Reid worked with Ben Thomason, an intern from Wright State University in Detroit, to document visitor interests and visitor-object interactions. He conducted his study between October 7 and November 4, 2017, completing 50 tracking study observations and collecting 102 closed-ended surveys and 51 open-ended interviews with visitors. Evidence indicated two areas of strong interest. The first related to machine functionality—how the agricultural machines operate, how productive they could be, and what improvements were made over the previous machines/tools. The second strong area of interest related to the methods and processes of agriculture, meaning that visitors wanted The Henry Ford to explain the entire process of agriculture, with both the overarching history and developments, as well as the ground-level seasonal labor that farmers of the past and present carried out.

These conclusions indicate that the public equates agricultural technology with improvements. The Henry Ford exists to complicate that impression. It emphasizes the quest for improvement and not the misperception that new machinery means better machinery. Thomason summarized the potential this way:

> I think that the functionality of the machines and the processes of agriculture are what people were most interested in and there is a lot the exhibit can teach them. . . . Building up the information on machine functionalities and agricultural processes will give a strong foundation on which to build other topics . . . like political, environmental, and public health issues as well as the connection of farming to city life and the economy. More specialized subjects will appeal to people who may be more politically, environmentally, or health minded which could keep people in the exhibit longer and make it more memorable for many visitors (excerpted from January 15, 2018 e-mail from Benjamin Thomason).

One popular seasonal visitor engagement involves soil testing. Museum presenters have soil samples from specific locations in Greenfield Village, including Firestone Farm, a living history farm, and Ford Home, the birthplace of Henry Ford, but also the location of a kitchen garden. The activity includes determining the best crop to grow on the soil given the farm's chronology and geographic location. Corn and vegetables, including peanuts, grow best in slightly acidic soil (with a pH between 5.8 and 6.8). Wheat likes a more acidic soil, as do sweet potatoes (pH of 5.5 to 6.5). Horticulturalists seek neutral or slightly more alkaline soils for flowering shrubs or ornamental plants, as do market gardeners or truck farmers who might specialize in asparagus (pH as high as 8). Guests walked away from this activity with new understanding and the knowledge of testing so they could apply it to their home gardens.

Visitors to Greenfield Village at The Henry Ford can engage with several working environments, including Firestone Farm, the birthplace of Harvey Firestone. It opened in 1985 after staff relocated the house and barn and outbuildings from Columbiana County, Ohio, and after conducting intensive research in foodways and farm practices for the third-generation German-American Firestone family. The farm models farm-to-fork concepts. The kitchen garden lies just past the kitchen window. "Chinese weeder" geese, a heritage variety, help pull weeds, and their eggs join those from the chickens as part of the daily fare cooked by presenters in the farmhouse kitchen.

The market production of wool and of wheat, plus the coal stove in the kitchen complicates the preconceived ideas that visitors might have. They could easily walk away thinking the Firestones modeled farm-to-fork agriculture and embraced "organic" operations. Instead, the kitchen becomes the location to discuss the relationship between the Firestones and fossil-fuel consumption in the mid-1880s, long before Firestone's rubber tires significantly increased fossil-fuel use. The coal used daily in the kitchen stove eased the burdens of male family members by reducing the quantity of wood required to keep the home fires burning, specifically the wood-burning fireplace in the parlor and the hearth in the basement. Farmers could transfer that labor savings into a few more head of sheep or pigs or beef cattle. But more livestock required more pasture and hay or corn acreage. This could not be increased by reducing acreage dedicated to other cash crops, but clearing a bit of woodlot could help increase pasture, and pasture could shift to wheat acreage in a coal-stove world. Investing in equipment helped farmers manage the increased acreage.[11]

The loss of biodiversity, the depletion of nonrenewable natural resources including fossil fuels, and the warming climate and extreme weather affect the daily life of everyone on the globe. Museums and historic sites can make a difference by adopting interpretive goals that create environmentally literate citizens. The process starts by documenting local environments and changes in those places and spaces over time. It continues by offering educational programs that increase environmental literacy and by partnering with community organizations to change local practices.

Notes

1. John Richard Green, *The Making of England* (1881), vii. The complete quote reads: "Archaeological researches on the sites of villas and towns, or along the line of road and dyke, often furnish us with evidence even more trustworthy than that of written chronicle; while the ground itself, where we can read the information it affords, is . . . the fullest and the most certain of documents. Physical geography has still its part to play in the written record of that human history to which it gives so much of its shape and form." Freeman Tilden, *Interpreting Our Heritage*, 3rd ed. (Chapel Hill: University of North Carolina Press, 1977), 41, 42.
2. James Deetz, *In Small Things Forgotten* (1977), 21–22. The complete quote reads: "Historical archaeology places less reliance on the natural sciences than does prehistoric archaeology. . . . This lessened dependency on the natural sciences is but a reflection of the role played by the natural world in the history of human development. The earlier in time one goes, the more people were directly and intimately tied to their environment. . . . As culture became more complex, our removal from the natural world increased."

3. William T. Alderson and Shirley Payne Low, *Interpretation of Historic Sites* (Nashville, TN: American Association for State and Local History, 1976).

4. This outline follows recommendations made in "Documenting Agriculture in Two Dimensions: Background Research," in Debra A. Reid, *Interpreting Agriculture at Museums and Historic Sites* (Lanham, MD: Rowman and Littlefield, 2017), 61–83.

5. For more about county histories, see Reid, *Interpreting Agriculture at Museums*, 62, including the footnote on county historical and biographical atlases.

6. Reid, *Interpreting Agriculture at Museums*, 67–68.

7. K. S. Hollweg, J. R. Taylor, R. W. Bybee, T. J. Marcinkowski, W. C. McBeth, and P. Zoido, *Developing a Framework for Assessing Environmental Literacy* (Washington, D.C.: North American Association for Environmental Education, 2011), 3-2. Available at: http://www. naaee.net. Accessed September 1, 2018.

8. See *Community Engagement: Guidelines for Excellence* (Washington D.C.: North American Association of Environmental Educators, 2017), 17. Available at: https://cdn.naaee.org/sites/ default/files/eepro/resource/files/community_engagement_-_guidelines_for_excellence_0. pdf. Accessed September 1, 2018.

9. "About Interpretation," at National Association for Interpretation. Available at https://www. interpnet.com/. Accessed June 22, 2018.

10. Interpretation Canada, available at: https://interpretationcanada.wildapricot.org/. Accessed June 22, 2018.

11. Reid developed this case study during an ongoing conversation held as part of the 2017 working group, Public History and Agriculture, sponsored by the National Council on Public History. Reid and David D. Vail co-chaired the group. It featured practical approaches and lessons learned. Lasting products included working group papers, a blog, and case studies that found their way into *Interpreting the Environment at Museums and Historic Sites*.

Part II

TELLING STORIES ABOUT HUMANS AND THEIR ENVIRONMENTS: TOPICS AND PRACTICE

CHAPTER 4

Creating Working Environments

Debra A. Reid and David D. Vail, with contributions by Ann Birney, Al Hester, and Joyce Thierer

W E HAVE REACHED THE POINT where we use the IE Toolkit to put the pieces of environmental interpretation together. The ultimate goal is "to present history to nature lovers and nature to history lovers while upholding our missions and growing our audiences." Hillary Pine established this goal to guide her work at Hartwick Pines State Park, near Grayling, Michigan. The 9,762 acres of parkland, including a 49-acre stand of old growth pine, two lakes, and rolling hills on glacial deposits, draw a loyal nature-loving crowd. Yet, the historic landscape was not a wilderness getaway, as the Hartwick Pines Logging Museum makes clear. Infusing history into naturalist interpretation (and vice versa) best conveys the natural and cultural history of working landscapes like Hartwick Pines.[1]

Interpreting the Environment takes a functionalist approach: you and the environment work together. The environment-centric approach will encourage bredth and depth of exploration. Museums and historic sites then build their interpretation of the environment around artifacts, objects as large as the working landscape, or as small as a living microbe.[2]

One object can help us tell many different stories. Deciding what stories to tell and what objects to use can prove challenging. Environmental history, that first tool in the IE Toolkit, helps guide your thinking along chronological, thematic, and symbolic lines. A chronological overview, as presented in *Down to Earth*, helps put your place and space into a sequence of events and determine cause and effect. A thematic approach, as taken in *Major Problems in American Environmental History*, highlights debates in the field that your collection can help inform. The construction of wilderness as symbol, featured in *Wilderness and the American Mind*, stresses human agendas. Museums support the cause by putting artifacts at the center of their intepretation of the environment.[3]

Landscapes and buildings constitute the largest artifacts, and they document human manipulation of the environment in numerous ways. We start with these largest artifacts to test the IE Toolkit. Academic study of "environmentalism," one of nine trends in material culture studies identified by Thomas Schlereth, featured the approach of cultural and historical geographers, regional ecologists, and cultural anthropologists who interpreted "all landscape features, especially housing," and sought "to depict cultural adaptations across space." Schlereth singled out the work of Frank Kniffen, John Brinckerhoff Jackson, and Pierce F. Lewis as models, and he included examples of Kniffen's and Lewis's work in his 1982 anthology, *Material Culture Studies in America*. Schlereth acknowledged that other approaches incorporated evidence of the built environment—historic battlefield sites (symbolist), historic houses and outdoor museums (cultural), living history farms, and historic houses (social history), but he also indicated that interpretation often did not convey the complexity of the past.[4]

A lot of good work has occurred since Schlereth's *Material Culture Studies in America* appeared. Yet, more remains to be done. Advocates for environmental stewardship have called for action through articles published in *The Public Historian*, the journal of the National Council on Public History. A special issue, *Public History and Environmental Sustainability*, recognized that protection and preservation started the process, and Leah Glaser urged public historians to take the next step, "to chart change and analyze the unsustainable uses of natural resources within racial, social, and economic contexts." Cathy Stanton edited a collection of essays about the roles that public historians need to play relative to climate change. Sarah Sutton provided a road map to green choices in her book, *Environmental Sustainability at Historic Sites and Museums*. Jeffrey Stine synthesized efforts to date in "Public History and the Environment," published in *The Oxford Handbook of Public History*.[5]

The approach taken in *Interpreting the Environment* does not duplicate this work. Instead, it features case studies of research, artifact-rich interpretations, and public engagement that indicates additional possibilities of environmental interpretation.

Managing the Landscape

Humans transform natural resources into their houses, the barns that house their livestock that fertilize their fields, and the tools and utensils that they use in every aspect of their daily lives. The environments we all inhabit and work in provide evidence of historic as well as current human manipulation. They provide evidence of environmental exploitation and degradation, but they can also prompt discussions about stewardship of working environments.

Fire is one tool humans use to sustain environments on which they depended. Foresters use controlled burns to contain the spread of invasive species and sustain native woodlands. Controlled burns of phragmites help sustain a healthy wetland. These scheduled burns can provide opportunities to discuss historic strategies. The process requires a clear goal and plan, careful selection of wetland or woodland areas, expert management of the setup and supervision of the burn, and ideal weather conditions.

The idea of scheduling a fire to manage an ecosystem is not new. Indians across North America used fire in specific situations and with clear goals in mind. Historian Richard

White explains that Indians living in lowland saltwater marshes in Puget Sound burned berry patches regularly to force a succession of plants to grow, including fireweed, a plant they processed and wove into blankets, and berries, an important food source. Indians burned grasslands to destroy shrubs and sustain habitats where deer and bison thrived. They also used burns to improve land used for agriculture. In general, Indians managed the environments in which they lived to ensure a consistent food supply and preserve unobstructed views to fend off rivals. They conducted burns seasonally to accomplish those goals.

Excessive burning, on the other hand, sparks controversy. Slash-and-burn agriculture destroys woodlands and edge environments needed to sustain mixed farming. Even more destructive, the process of assarting destroys forests, roots and all, but clears the way for soybean, cotton, and corn fields. Clearing fields by burning crop residue, a common historical practice, generates too much pollution, and local ordinances and sometimes national legislation have made such agricultural burns illegal. With all controlled burns, the key lies in moderation, preparation, and a manageable plan.[6]

Fire, especially, defines the environmental history of the Great Plains. Indian peoples implemented fire on the prairie, as in other places, to manage landscapes. The prairies have both natural and human ignition sources to fuel the fire. Fire has a central place in the natural and cultural history of the Great Plains. Biological and ecological science as well as historical records of settlement document its influence. All of the historical threads are there to discuss: plant, animal, and human communities all reflect fire's utility in maintaining a working landscape.[7] In the words of environmental historian Stephen Pyne, fire in the Great Plains was "a precondition to successful habitation on the plains and prairies; even nomadism was in part an adaptation to fire, both natural and anthropogenic."[8] Burning the grasslands also worked as a control technology to fight weeds and insects. As assistant Army surgeon George Sternberg observed in 1879, much of Kansas's healthy grasses could be linked directly to intentional burnings of the land.[9] A few years previously, famed landscape architect and social critic Frederick Law Olmsted journeyed across the Great Plains, observing in his account that "fire served as the 'Master of the Plains.'"[10] Historian Julie Courtwright's book *Prairie Fire: A Great Plains History* underscores just how key fire is to this region's history:

> Prairie fire is as fundamental to the Great Plains as the sun, soil, wind, grazers, and grass. It influences grass composition; allows for more nutritious growth on which cattle can graze; and, when applied regularly, prevents trees from intruding into native prairie grasses. . . . Whether absent or present, it [fire] plays a pivotal role in the environmental history of the Plains.[11]

Museums and historic sites in the Great Plains such as the Tallgrass National Prairie Preserve in Strong City, Kansas, or Theodore Roosevelt National Park in Medora, North Dakota, frequently include fire in their displays, experiential interpretations, and park-management plans. Not all agree on the utility of fire to manage spaces to maintain the prairie ecosystem. Debates address the health and well-being of rural communities because of the significant decline of air quality during the burning months on the one hand compared with the ecological and economic benefits of burning agricultural lands on the other.

Symbolism and Working Landscapes

Decorative art pieces often depict romanticized working landscapes. Artifacts such as paintings or sketches, transferware ceramics, and bank notes and official currency likewise include multifaceted scenes. Currency issued by the Department of the Treasury of the Confederate States of America (CSA), or by individual Confederate states, included engravings on the front of the bills to document the denomination. They often featured public buildings and elected officials and other imagery appealing to the wealthier investors in the war. The engraving on a ten-cent note, issued by the Bank of Tennessee on December 1, 1861, included a train with a steam engine and several rail cars.

Some notes featured fields at harvest time. It should come as no surprise that agriculture—especially cotton—featured prominently on larger denomination CSA notes because cotton was a source of wealth for many Southern planters. Cotton also was the crop that drove the slave economy. An interest-bearing note valued at 100 CSA dollars, issued in late 1862, showed two men hoeing rows of cotton plants, and a third man carrying a full basket. This large denomination note was not a small piece of paper, either. It measured 3 inches by 7.25 inches.[12]

By 1863, the CSA took notes higher than five dollars out of circulation and issued bonds instead. Wealthy Southerners considered these a reasonable investment given a high rate of return over a relatively short time. For example, H. C. Canada invested $2,000 on July 15, 1863. He could redeem his bond, with interest at the rate of 7 percent annually, after July 1868. Of course, with the Confederate defeat, such notes became worthless. Some bonds featured rice production. The wealthy Southerners who held such bonds might have overseen their own rice fields (not cotton) being harvested. A planter or overseer astride a fine horse watched two men cutting tall rice, one man binding rice into sheaves, and other men loading the sheaves into a cart drawn by two horses.[13]

These wartime depictions of large plantations in the coastal South, cultivated and landscaped by enslaved people, continued to affect impressions of Southern landscapes into the

Detail of rice harvest depicted on a $2,000 CSA bond, issued July 15, 1863. Image from the Collections of The Henry Ford.

twentieth century. Wealthy Northern industrialists invested in these properties and remade the landscapes into rural retreats. Historians who have studied these so called "sporting plantations" have documented, among other things, African Americans residents who earned their living as local guides for Northerners who transformed former rice fields into waterfowl game preserves.[14]

Not all investors focused on recreation. Henry Ford purchased at least 85,000 acres in Bryan and Chatham counties in coastal Georgia near Savannah during the 1920s and 1930s. He and Clara Ford wintered in Bryan County at their Richmond Hill property. Ford sustained the working environment, but he shifted to new commodities such as soybeans for industrial processing and truck farming, specifically growing and marketing another new commodity, iceberg lettuce.

Ford's introduction of these new crops to the region followed a pattern established by colonists and antebellum plantation owners who had cultivated rice, indigo, even soybeans, and other nonindigenous species on the properties since the 1760s. Ford's iceberg lettuce emphasized the complete disconnect between urban Northern sensibilities and rural Southern realities.

The vegetables grown at Richmond Hill reflected the different tastes of the year-round Richmond Hill residents and the migrants who traveled to the warmer climate and resided there temporarily. Collards and iceberg lettuce provide a good place to explore the differences.

The collard plant is a member of the species *Brassica oleracea acephala*, which includes kale and spring greens and other loose-leaved cultivars. Plants in the *acephala* group of *Brassica oleracea* do not form a head, whereas plants in the *capitate* group (cabbages) do. The collard leaves are rich in Vitamin K (which facilitates blood coagulation and protein and calcium synthesis) as well as Vitamins A (supportive of the immune system and vision) and C (which prevents scurvy). The plant tolerates the heat and became a staple of Southern diets.

Oral histories document local practices of residents. Amos Mattox, Jr. remembered growing collard greens in the family garden. A mouth-watering dish of collard greens and "fat back," a cut of pork that included the hard fat along the back, provided calories as well as nutrients to Southern families, including the Mattox family.

In stark contrast to collards, iceberg lettuce (a type of *Lactuca sativa*) is heat-sensitive and not well suited to humid Southern climates. It has a high-water content, less flavor, and less nutritional value than other lettuce. Regardless, it gained in popularity during the 1930s because it shipped well and appeared in urban markets before other lettuces, so it drew a following. Leslie Long, in *The Henry Ford Era at Richmond Hill, Georgia* (1998) explained that Ford grew iceberg lettuce for ten years on his property in Bryan County. Ford's staff at Richmond Hill planted lettuce in a 300-acre field, one of the former rice fields at the Cherry Hill Plantation. Those employed by the Richmond Hill Plantation, Inc., packed the lettuce in wooden crates, affixed the labels, and sold the lettuce through a Savannah company that shipped the perishable produce north to urban markets on the east coast.

Brightly colored labels, printed on durable stock and pasted or stapled on the end of packing crates, helped agricultural and horticultural producers gain brand recognition in urban markets. The Richmond Hill Iceberg Lettuce label fits the "commercial" era of

The collards grown near a school on Ford's Richmond Hill property, circa 1940. The photograph shows the lush edible foliage, the hallmark of this prized Southern crop. Image from the Collections of The Henry Ford.

packing-crate labels because the label, despite the romanticized image, featured the brand and produce name. It did not depict the perishable commodity being marketed.[15]

Henry Ford's Richmond Hill Plantation's Iceberg Lettuce label romanticized Southern agricultural landscapes. The lettuce takes second stage to reinforced stereotypes that emphasized lazy Southern days. The artwork depicts a laborer dozing under the ubiquitous spreading live oak tree shading a stereotypical Southern plantation mansion. The artwork also conveyed an enduring romanticized notion of antebellum agricultural landscapes with manicured lawns and sweeping porches (ala the Lost Cause myth of the Old South) and not the fields and packinghouses of the modern truck farm growing lettuce.[16]

The mythologized working landscape producing iceberg lettuce stood in stark contrast to the reality of daily life for rural Southern residents more inclined to eat collard greens than rarified iceberg lettuce. The packing-crate label further romanticized working landscapes built on the backs of unfree laborers and sustained through racial oppression. The imagery marketed a distinctly non-Southern crop, iceberg lettuce. Across the country from Ford's Georgia acreage, Arizona lettuce producers commissioned artwork for labels that featured brand name and geographic location. These labels were also bright and colorful. Some Arizona citrus growers also coopted imagery of pueblos and indigenous people to sell products such as Ariz-Glow and Ariz-Sun oranges and grapefruits.

A New Way of Looking at Landscapes

Agricultural Sites as Environmental Sites of Conscience
Al Hester, South Carolina State Park Service

For me, one of the most compelling questions to ask about the environment involves histories of agriculture and their connection to present issues, particularly modern concerns about health, the environment, sustainability, or other polarizing subjects. We are all aware of the transformative power of farming when it comes to landscapes and natural resources. And as historians and humanists, we are also cognizant of the role that power and inequity play in these changes. The "environmental sites of conscience" concept has the potential to make these lines of connection much more apparent to the public, especially at historic sites. This argument, best expressed by the International Coalition of Sites of Conscience, is probably a familiar one to most public historians. The Coalition defines a "site of conscience" as "any memorial, museum, historic site, memory initiative or non-governmental organization that commits to . . . interpreting history through site; engaging the public in programs that stimulate dialogue on pressing social issues; sharing opportunities for public involvement and positive action on the issues raised at the site; and promoting justice and universal cultures of human rights."[17]

Others have taken this model and applied it to sites associated with environmental catastrophes, or even places that simply help us explore our country's "past and present relationships with the environment."[18] Agriculture is often the central story at many of these places, and more often than not, struggles about race, gender, ethnicity, and class are also critical parts of their history. Not surprisingly, the interweaving of past environmental damage and human oppression are what makes them places of conscience.

Rose Hill Plantation State Historic Site, located in Union County, South Carolina, has a complex history that reflects the consequences of the slave-based plantation agriculture of the southeastern cotton region. The site is the former home of Governor William Henry Gist, a pro-slavery planter and politician who worked diligently to bring about Southern secession on the eve of the Civil War. Rose Hill, because of its association with the history of slavery, secession, the outbreak of the Civil War, racial terrorism during Reconstruction, and land degradation, could be considered both a social and environmental site of conscience. As a historic site, Rose Hill is already interpreting history through the site's cultural and natural resources. It is, however, only just beginning to address the present in its interpretation. Pressing modern issues that Rose Hill could address include the legacies of slavery, tenant farming and Jim Crow; racial terrorism; the decision to go to war and its consequences; environmental stewardship, especially of forests and soils; and environmental justice.

Environmental historian Paul Sutter has written on the historical and present meanings of land damage in the Southern piedmont, which suffered from extreme soil erosion before the 1930s. He noted how Southern cotton land experienced severe degradation over a century, caused by interwoven environmental and cultural factors, ranging from the farming of highly erodible soils to the effects of the racism central to slavery and sharecropping. Places like Providence Canyon in Georgia and Rose Hill in South Carolina can serve as reminders that historical abuse of people and land has lasting consequences that can still be felt and seen today.

This long-lasting impact of the past on the present especially stands out in the research of scientists working at the Calhoun Critical Zone Observatory (CCZO), which surrounds Rose Hill. Beginning in 1947, the Calhoun Experimental Forest measured the impact of efforts to restore the land in Union County. After soil erosion reached its peak in the 1930s, the U.S. Forest Service worked to convert damaged cotton cultivation areas to productive forest across the new Sumter National Forest, which included portions of surrounding counties and large areas of Rose Hill Plantation. Despite eighty years of Forest Service stewardship, CCZO researchers are finding that restoration of the land is incomplete and may ultimately be impossible. According to lead investigator Dan Richter, "our study is guided by a hypothesis that the impressive-looking reforestation masks fundamental alterations to the local and regional hydrology, biology and chemistry, . . . much of the Piedmont may not be recovered so much as it has been re-stabilized in a highly altered state."[19] The implications of this long-running study are potentially of global importance because the type of soils found at Rose Hill, ultisols, are also common around the world, especially in tropical areas where some of the poorest people live. In these areas, intensive conversion of forest to cropland is occurring at a rapid pace. At the heart of the CCZO project is the idea that lessons learned on the South Carolina piedmont can inform present-day environmental choices.[20]

Rose Hill's connection to the present seems clear, and I think encouraging dialogue among visitors about these topics could help make the site more relevant. But some historic site managers (not necessarily at Rose Hill) have shied away from the sites of conscience approach because its emphasis on *action* seems potentially too political. Though some sites pursue a more activist type of history, there is little consensus about what constitutes "action." How does this type of interpretation square with the work of peer agencies, such as the South Carolina Department of Agriculture, which often focuses on business promotion? Are there nonpolitical approaches that staff can use to encourage change? What about visitor expectations, especially when public memories of agriculture are often infused with nostalgia? Finally, can sites like Rose Hill engage in conscience work that helps visitors see problems on a global scale, without falling into oversimplified, formulaic narratives? Soil erosion in the Southern piedmont is not the pressing issue that it once was, so does this emphasis on past agricultural damage there direct us to think mainly about international issues to the exclusion of the local? Shouldn't we focus on the lines connecting histories of slavery and Jim Crow directly to modern racial struggles happening much closer to home? In addition to environmental recovery, can places like Union County recover economically and socially? What other agricultural sites have successfully taken on these questions, and can they serve as examples to emulate?

One option is to focus on the modern issues surrounding cotton itself, both locally and internationally. We could encourage visitors to consider whether there are more sustainable and just agricultural methods that could be brought to cotton production. Contemporary issues range from damaging fertilizer and pesticide use in the Southeast, to human trafficking and forced labor in cotton-producing countries like Uzbekistan and Cameroon. Organic cotton farming is underway in North Carolina, and visitors could reflect on how it could be done in Rose Hill's neighborhood as well. Textile history sites, such as Lowell National Historic Park, might provide a good model for this approach. Finally, despite difficult environmental and social challenges, a community still exists in the area surrounding Rose Hill. Our interpretation of agriculture at this place should also incorporate stories of resilience and should cause us to reflect on how communities adapt and survive.

A New Way of Interpreting the Built Environment

Interpreting Rachel Carson and DDT
Ann E. Birney and Joyce M. Thierer, Ride into History

Ride into History is a historical performance touring troupe. Its members do first-person narratives of historic figures or composite characters, monologues of about forty-five minutes, followed by taking questions in character and then as the scholar. As the founder and manager of Ride into History, we have strong opinions about the environment writ large and its influence on us, and us on it.

We take seriously the findings of Bonnie Sachatello-Sawyer, in *Adult Museum Programming*, that "dramatic performances tend to have a long-lasting learning effect on audiences because of their emotional impact." Learning in museums as elsewhere involves engaging emotions through the senses. Martin J. Packer, in "Interpreting Stories, Interpreting Lives," notes that narrative is recognized in such fields as philosophy and psychology as "a necessary part of any attempt to understand ourselves and the world in which we live."[21]

Historically, "the environment" and environments in general have been gendered. One of the first ways that many girls learn what it means to be gendered female is when her environment becomes more constrained than that of her brother(s). The brother can go with his buddies to the construction site down the block. She is not allowed to leave the fenced-in yard by herself. He is to be home by dark. She is to not leave home unless her mother knows where she is.

Our name, Ride into History, represents movement through time and space, a claiming of all environment of all time. We call what we do "sneaky history" because we do theater for audiences that don't go to plays unless their children or grandchildren are in them. And we do history for audiences who shudder when they remember having to memorize dates and presidents. We sneak in our gendered emphasis because, even though we perform our first-person narratives as women, we are careful to use program names that are not labeled "Women." In our experience with rural audiences in the Central Plains, the "w" word continues to send the terror of girl cooties through grown men (homophobia being, of course, the source). And if the men don't go, their wives won't go. It's not only marketing; it's also wanting to reach the people who do not seek opportunities to explore ideas about how the gender messages that have been prescribed over time have not necessarily been the gender roles that have been lived at various times. "Fighting Beside My Brother," for instance, is about a woman who disguised herself to fight in the Civil War. "Settling in Kansas Territory" is told by a woman.

Narrative transformed into dramatic performance conveys lessons about marginality and confinement in physical environments. The Wyoming Territorial Prison State Historic Site interprets a dramatically charged two-story prison, the doors of which clanked shut behind both women and men. Prisoners were not allowed to speak and were allowed only to listen. How do you interpret the auditory experience of an environment in which there is no speaking? In the immediate yard is a broom factory. Prisoners worked in the broom factory. Were they allowed to speak as they made brooms? Outside the jail were areas that at first blush might not appear to be related to incarceration. The warden's home, for instance, was also the home of children and surrounded by gardens, including flowers. A nearby river might be viewed as a moat, but it could just as likely be seen as a means of escape. An experimental farm replaced the prison, and a Wild West "front street" theme park replaced the experimental farm, entertaining families without imparting much knowledge. The prison itself is the most obvious draw, but the outside physical environment can be at least as intriguing. The outside comes inside; townspeople were invited to tour the prison when it was still operating as a prison. The prisoners became exhibits, animals in their "cages" to be gawked at by those strolling by the bars.

The perspectives of past migrants inform us about how those migrants misunderstood the environment. Migrants across and settlers on the plains misinterpreted the Flint Hills, thinking that seven-foot-tall bluestem grass promised similar crops of wheat and corn. They soon found that the roots of the grasses were at least as deep as the stems were tall, necessary for the roots to find the crevices in the rock ledges, which were far too massive to be removed and soil far too remote to be plowed. These were not the rocks of Pennsylvania as Mary Fix and other settlers understood.

Archival evidence documents human interaction with the environment, often from the eyes of female migrants and settlers. Julia Archibald Holmes described how the environment changed (interspersed with complaints about the only other woman in the forty-seven-person group sojourning the Santa Fe Trail from east of Council Grove to the Pikes Peak area). Holmes noted decreased vegetation as tallgrass yielded to short bluestem and trees to occasional bushes. Buffalo or cow chips become prized as fuel, and the travelers become quite casual about their hands moving from food to fuel back to food. Walking great distances gave her pride in her strength and enhanced her feminism.

Effective first-person narrative featuring environmental content requires deep knowledge of the environment in general and the setting in particular. In fact, the setting is crucial. One takes the audience back in time to a particular environment—a place and a time. That environment, the changes going on around the historic figure, affect the historic figure's decision making, and each story the historian-as-historic-figure tells should suggest, if not out-and-out inform, the audience, how what is going on in the larger world is affecting them. For instance, Amelia Earhart fell in love with flying during "the war"— World War I to us now. She saw wounded soldiers on a Toronto street while visiting her sister and decided to volunteer as a soldier at a military hospital. She listened to soldiers tell their stories during her work breaks and thought the pilots had the best stories. A trip to an airfield where warriors were practicing led to her determination to become a pilot. [A war "over there" affecting her life's work, proving the intimacy of environment.]

Earhart was aware of environment as gendered even as she fought against the limitations of gender proscriptions. Although she was allowed outside the fence around the yard of her childhood home, the air space over that fence were, she was told, limited to boys. She wrote that, in the earliest days of aviation, the various talents of everyone who wanted to be involved with airplanes were welcome. Skills, however, were quickly gendered. She described as an example the parachute industry that evolved to restrict women to sewing chutes and men to packing them. She wrote that she hoped one day there would be enough women seeking admittance to the doors of aviation that those doors would be open to them, but she also advised that in the meantime each woman who approaches that door take an ax with her because she will probably need it to break through into what had become an environment gendered male.

Controversial topics add another layer of urgency to our historical performances. Consider the nostalgia for DDT. One day when Ride into History scholar/performer Ann Birney was eating in the local very-small-town café she heard one of the older farmers lament that he no longer had access to DDT. The man he was talking to made understanding noises and then said that Rachel Carson had ruined "it" for them, but also said that he had a stash of such chemicals tucked away for emergencies. Birney lived on a farmstead but was a transplant to the country. She knew vaguely that Carson was identified with the environmentalist movement, but here were some pretty conservative men, her neighbors, giving Carson credit for the power to change their farm practices. About that time Birney read Mil Penner's *Section 27* in which he noted Carson's *Silent Spring* as influencing his own practices and philosophy of farming.[22] Who was this woman? What was her backstory? What factored into her influence?

Ann tried to convince a colleague who interpreted Gene Stratton Porter to add Carson to her repertoire, but that person said Stratton Porter was her reason, and her only reason, for historical performance. Birney let Carson drift off to the sidelines until she completed some other projects (including a Ph.D. dissertation). Then, having found no other Chautauquans bringing Carson to her primary audiences, she rolled up her sleeves and started researching. Besides, she wanted a historic figure with whom she could age, someone older than she was at that time.

Two surprises led to two challenges in sculpting the script. The first surprise was that Carson was only fifty-six when she died of breast cancer, about Birney's age at the time she began researching Carson. Her illness, and she was quite ill during most of the four years she spent researching and writing *Silent Spring*, meant that Birney could interpret Carson for many more years. But what to do about the setting? The date would need to be in the narrow window after the publication of *Silent Spring* but before, of course, Carson's death. Energy is crucial in a performance. One could not engage an audience for more than an hour as a weak Carson. Carson's passion would need to surface somewhere, somehow. This led to the second surprise.

"What about her family? You didn't say anything about her family. Did she have a family?" That was Birney's mother's response to a workshop performance of Carson. Ah, yes, the backstory. The ultimate source of all passion—human relationships. Personal relationships, not the drama, played out on the national stage between Carson and the chemical companies, but the affection and conflicts that almost all of us experience within private settings. In what kind of setting would Carson have said that she had provided a home and financial support for her birth family—her parents, her siblings, and the children and grandchild of one of her sisters? In what setting would the audience understand that her most significant relationships were consistently with women, especially Dorothy Freeman? Who is intimate/close, and who is at arms' length? What are the environmental (ultimately intimate) changes that inspire changes in degrees of physical or emotional intimacy?

Gender affected Carson's career path at all levels and across time. Who had the authority to interpret the environment? Men. The public could imagine a "purely" masculine environment, one in which the objectivity of science was protected from the feminine emotionality. In the 1930s and 1940s, when Carson was known as "Ray" among her friends and when her first writings were published, and during the 1950s when she worked for the Bureau of Fisheries, she was counseled to use her initials "R. L." to mask her female gender. After publishing bestsellers with her full name, and as her influence galvanized special-interest groups and policy makers, hysterical chemical company executives accused Carson of being a "hysterical woman," but Carson identified herself as a "bird lover—a cat lover—a fish lover—a priestess of nature—a devotee of a mystical cult having to do with the laws of the universe, which my critics consider themselves immune to."[23]

Conclusion

Museum collections, including the landscapes and environments, tell important stories. Interpreting natural and human-manipulated landscape help visitors become more aware of the places they pass through daily and of the human effect on those environments. Numerous examples exist.

The Byron Forest Preserve District in Illinois committed to preserving the remains of a tallgrass prairie as the basis for telling stories about environmental destruction that resulted from human construction of working environments. The two-year, award-winning project tells the story of the tallgrass prairie and human interactions with that landscape that led to its near extinction.

Georgia Humanities hosted "Coastal Nature, Coastal Culture: Environmental Histories of the Georgia Coast Symposium" to collect stories from residents to link their American South to the booming field of environmental history.

More attention to people who lived in places over time will enhance public understanding of and engagement with landscape changes over time. For example, Mark David Spence's history, *Dispossessing the Wilderness: Indian Removal and the Making of the National Parks* (1999) can help readers comprehend the connection between forced removal of indigenous populations and deconstruction of their working landscapes in favor of conservationists' goals for wilderness spaces.

Notes

1. Hillary Pine, organizer for the panel "Interpreting History and the Environment in Unexpected Places," proposed for the 2019 joint conference of the Michigan Museums Association and Association of Midwest Museums, October 2–5, 2019, Grand Rapids, Michigan. Michael Williams, "The Clearing of the Forests," in *The Making of the American Landscape*, ed. Michael P. Conzen (Boston: Unwin Hyman, 1990), 146–68, notes, 385–86; bibliography, 396–423; Michael Williams, *Americans and Their Forests: An Historical Geography* (New York: Cambridge University Press, 1989).
2. The American Alliance of Museums and the International Council of Museums have expanded their definitions to stress fulfillment of their responsibilities to the public trust. AAM—"Public trust is the principle that certain natural and cultural resources are preserved for public benefit. In essence, it means the public owns the collections, and they should be kept available so the public can study them, enjoy them, and learn from them." Available at: https://www.aam-us.org/programs/ethics-standards-and-professional-practices/public-trust-and-accountability-standards/. Accessed February 26, 2019. International Council of Museums (ICOM)—which acquires, conserves, researches, communicates, and exhibits the tangible and intangible heritage of humanity and its environment for the purposes of education, study, and enjoyment." This is part of the ICOM definition of a museum adopted by the ICOM General Assembly in 2007. ICOM broadened its definition during 2017 through 2019. See "Museum Definition." Available at: https://icom.museum/en/activities/standards-guidelines/museum-definition/. Accessed February 26, 2019.
3. Ted Steinberg, *Down to Earth: Nature's Role in American History* (New York: Oxford University Press, 2002). Carolyn Merchant, ed., *Major Problems in American Environmental History: Documents and Essays*, 2nd ed. (Boston: Houghton Mifflin Company, 2005). Roderick Frazier Nash, *Wilderness and the American Mind*, 5th ed. (New Haven, CT: Yale University Press, 2014).
4. Thomas J. Schlereth, "Material Culture Studies in America, 1876–1976," in *Material Culture Studies in America* (Nashville, TN: American Association for State and Local History, 1982), 1–75; for the summary of "environmentalist" see Table 1.2 (Part II): "Current Research Trends in American Material Culture Scholarship," 51. According to Schlereth, environmentalists focused on cultural and historical geography, regional ecology, and cultural anthropology. For examples of "environmentalism" reprinted in *Material Cultures Studies in America*, see Pierce F. Lewis, "Axioms for Reading the Landscape: Some Guides to the American Scene," 174–82, and Fred Kniffen and Henry Glassie, "Building in Wood in the Eastern United States: A Time-Place Perspective," 237–50.

5. See the bibliography for suggested readings on preserving and interpreting historic landscapes and buildings and for professional organizations that have written about object-centered or object-enhanced environmental interpretation. Leah S. Glaser, "Introduction: Public History and Environmental Sustainability," *The Public Historian*, vol. 36, no. 3 (August 2014), 13. Cathy Stanton, ed., *Public History in a Changing Climate: A Digital Publication from the Public History Commons of the National Council on Public History*, as part of "Explorations: Public History and Environmental Sustainability" (March 2014). Available at: http://ncph.org/wp-content/uploads/2014/03/PHCC-2014.pdf. Accessed June 23, 2018. Jeffrey Stine, "Public History and the Environment," in *The Oxford Handbook of Public History*, edited by Paula Hamilton and James B. Gardner (Oxford: Oxford University Press, 2017).

6. William Cronon, *Changes in the Land: Indians, Colonists, and the Ecology of New England* (New York: Hill and Wang, 1983); Richard White, *Land Use, Environment, and Social Change: The Shaping of Island County, Washington* (Seattle: University of Washington Press, 1980); and Richard White, *The Middle Ground: Indians, Empires, and Republics in the Great Lakes Region: 1650–1815* (New York: Cambridge University Press, 1991).

7. Richard J. Vogl, "Effects of Fire on Grasslands," in *Fire and Ecosystems*, ed. T. T. Kozlowski and C. E. Ahlgren (New York: Academic Press, 1974), 139–82.

8. Stephen Pyne, *America's Fires: A Historical Context for Policy and Practice* (Durham, NC: Forest History Society, 2010), 7; Pyne, *Fire in America: A Cultural History of Wildland and Rural Fire* (Princeton, NJ: Princeton University Press, 1982).

9. George Sternberg, "The Causes of the Present Sterility of Western Kansas and the Influences by Which It Is Gradually Overcome," *Junction City (Kansas) Union*, February 5, 1870, 1. See also James E. Sherow, *The Grasslands of the United States: An Environmental History* (Santa Barbara, CA: ABC-CLIO, 2007), 32–33. For agricultural fire as a precursor to farm chemical applications, see David D. Vail, *Chemical Lands: Pesticides, Aerial Spraying, and Health in North America's Grasslands since 1945* (Tuscaloosa: University of Alabama Press, 2018), 10–22.

10. Frederick Law Olmsted, *A Journey through Texas: Or, a Saddle-Trip on the Southwestern Frontier* (New York: Mason Brothers, 1859), 262.

11. Julie Courtwright, *Prairie Fire: A Great Plains History* (Lawrence: University Press of Kansas, 2011). See also Courtwright, "When We First Come Here It All Looked Like Prairie Land Almost': Prairie Fire and Plains Settlement," *Western Historical Quarterly* vol. 38, no. 2 (Summer 2007), 157–79.

12. Banknote inscription: RICHMOND NOV 2 1862 / THE CONFEDERATE STATES OF AMERICA / WILL PAY TO THE BEARER ON DEMAND / ONE HUNDRED DOLLARS / WITH INTEREST AT TWO CENTS PER DAY / KEATINGE & BALL COLUMBIA S.C. / NO. 66229. Object ID: 00.3.9146. From the Collections of The Henry Ford.

13. A $2,000 CSA bond, issued July 15, 1863, engraved by J. T. Paterson & Co., Columbia, South Carolina, featured rice. Object ID: 30.1104.1827.3. From the Collections of The Henry Ford. A five-dollar note issued by the State of Alabama in early 1864 included the same engraving but with the cart and horses cropped off. Object ID 29.1420.6. From the Collections of The Henry Ford. View the Confederate currency and bonds in the digitized collections at TheHenryFord.org.

14. Dan Vivian and Julia Rose, eds., *Leisure Plantations and the Making of the New South: The Sporting Plantations of the South Carolina Lowcountry and Red Hills Region, 1900–1940* (Lanham, MD: Lexington Books, 2015).

15. Packing-label expert, Royal John Medley, explains that "the stylistic shift to featuring brand names occurred when artists and produce growers recognized the value of the strong visual impact of thousands of stacked crates all bearing a specific growers' single dynamic brand name." See Medley's typed manuscript, "Lettuce and Landscapes: An Illustrated History of Commercial Row Crops in the Arizona Desert, 1920–1960," 5–6, in accession files, The Henry Ford.

16. The Lost Cause myth gained traction during the 1880s and 1890s, and it experienced several rebirths, including during the period of Richmond Hill lettuce production with the popularity of *Gone with the Wind*, a novel by Margaret Mitchell, published in 1936, and the Technicolor film, released in 1939.

17. International Coalition of Sites of Conscience. Available at: http://www.sitesofconscience. org/en/who-we-are/faqs/. Accessed July 13, 2017.

18. David Glassberg and Sarah Pharaon, "Witnessing Climate Change: Toward a Network of Environmental Sites of Conscience," in *Public History in a Changing Climate* (National Council on Public History, 2014), 5–6. (n.p.: National Council on Public History, 2014).

19. Sarah Farmer, "The Calhoun Critical Zone Observatory: Recovery after Extreme Soil Erosion and Land Degradation." Available at: https://www.srs.fs.usda.gov/compass/2014/04/22/ the-calhoun-critical-zone-observatory/?utm_source=rss&utm_medium=rss&utm_cam paign=the-calhoun-critical-zone-observatory. Accessed July 13, 2017.

20. "Study of Earth's "Critical Zone," January 15, 2014. Available at: http://criticalzone.org/na tional/news/story/introducing-calhoun-czo/. Accessed July 13, 2017.

21. Bonnie Sachatello-Sawyer, *Adult Museum Programs: Designing Meaningful Experiences*. (Walnut Creek, CA: AltaMira Press, 2002), 57. Martin J. Packer, "Interpreting Stories, Interpreting Lives: Narrative and Action in Moral Development Research," in Mark J. Tappan and Martin J. Packer, eds., *Narrative and Storytelling: Implications for Understanding Moral Development*. (San Francisco: Jossey-Bass, 1991), 64.

22. Mil Penner, *Section 27: A Century of a Family Farm* (Lawrence: University Press of Kansas, 2002).

23. Linda Lear, *Rachel Carson: Witness for Nature* (New York: Henry Holt and Co., 1997); David K. Hecht, "Constructing a Scientist: Expert Authority and Public Images of Rachel Carson," *Historical Studies in the Natural Sciences*, vol. 41, no. 3 (Summer 2011), 277–302; Michel M. Haigh and Ann Marie Major, "Rachel Carson's War of Words against Government and Industry: Challenging the Objectivity of American Scientific Discourse," in *Green Voices: Defending Nature and the Environment in American Civic Discourse*, Richard D. Besel and Bernard K. Duffy, eds. (Albany: State University of New York Press, 2016), 153–73, quote from critics and self-description, 159.

CHAPTER 5

Getting Water

Debra A. Reid and David D. Vail, with contributions by Charles R. Foy and Julie Mulvihill

THE HUMAN-WATER RELATIONSHIP runs deep. All living organisms on Earth need water to survive. Water helps cells function. It facilitates photosynthesis in plants that humans eat, burn, or build into their homes and furniture. It sustains saltwater and freshwater organisms, many of which humans eat. Humans depend on water for their livelihood, working on the water, hauling water to livestock, cutting ice, irrigating fields, and keeping toilets flushing. They travel on waterborne craft. They harness fast-flowing waterways using millraces and dams to channel the flow and generate energy. Many turn to water for rest and recreation. They invest in lakeside property, build summer camps, go fishing or swimming, visit nature preserves, and seek the headwaters of major rivers.

Water supports buffer zones between larger bodies of water and land. Farm families along coast and floodplains made good use of these lands, harvesting tidal marsh hay, running hogs among nut trees, and harvesting greens and berries from the natural areas. Those who did not farm undervalued the lands but developed them nonetheless. Ted Steinberg, in *Gotham Unbound*, explains how tidal marsh buffer between New York City and the Atlantic Ocean sustained families who foraged and hunted and farmed the land. The demise of the tidal marsh, combined with rising ocean levels as a result of global warming, puts the largest city in the nation at risk, as it does many other coastal cities. Henry Ford purchased 1,500 acres of lowland along the River Rouge south of Detroit to build his Ford Rouge plant. Historians have interpreted this land as unused marsh, but plat maps and census returns show otherwise. Farm families made good use of it for grain and hay crops and for vegetables and fruit for sale to wholesale grocers and urban markets.[1]

Water can generate emotional responses. Some worry while crossing bridges, or they fear drowning. Some react emotionally, believing in the powers of holy water. Some construct their cultural identity around water as the source of life and reason for their being. Natural disasters exacerbate fears and stress levels. Heavy rains, hurricanes, and tornadoes deposit too much rain too quickly and cause floods. Droughts resulting from too little rain threatens water supplies in aquifers and reservoirs. Famines result when droughts stunt crops and reduce yields. Fire also can parch dry grasslands and destroy forests, habitats, and homes.

Water also factors into debates about the sustainability of biofuel production. Irrigation to maintain crop fields affects aquafers. Extracting the ethyl alcohol from corn is water intensive, as is refining the oil from soybeans, part of the process of producing biodiesel. Research continues to reduce the environmental consequences of extracting and refining renewable energy.

History museums and historic sites engage the public in ongoing conversations about water. For example, the Smithsonian Institution and *National Geographic* organized the first Earth Optimism Summit as part of Earth Day 2017. The summit addressed four environmental concerns of global proportions, including threats to the ocean, water pollution, deforestation, and food-production concerns. The 2018 Earth Optimism Summit emphasized conservation success stories and welcomed partners to host sister events.[2]

Water contributes in many ways to interpreting the environment from nature centers to historic houses. Staff can develop context by turning to monographs or topical essays that address water and issues that arise as a result of human intervention. Mark Fiege's book, *Irrigated Eden: The Making of an Agricultural Landscape in the West*, explores the origins of irrigation as a modification to the environment that could make the desert bloom. He focuses on the Snake River valley of southern Idaho and indicates that ways that human strategies to control the environment can create challenges that result from natural forces that are beyond their control. James Sherow's *Watering the Valley: Development along the High Plains Arkansas River, 1870–1950* studies the environmental, technological, agricultural, and political intersections of water development in the Arkansas River Valley. Key in this work is the tensions between the "intricate role of water in the ecology" of the River Valley and how hydrologists, producers, and politicians "viewed water as something extractable from the valley, a commodity that could be used by them to further their ideas of growth."[3] As they modified the ecological relationships in the valley, westerners continued to experience "great difficulty in putting together a workable approach that fulfilled their cultural aspirations and corresponded to nature's rhythms."[4]

Other historians, such as John Opie in *Ogallala: Water for a Dry Land* and Char Miller in *Fluid Arguments: Five Centuries of Western Water Conflict*, examine important environmental, technological, agricultural, cultural, and political themes in the history of water in the American West and Great Plains—two regions with "often-tangled relationship[s] between the history of and public policy concerning water use . . . incurred with the construction of hydraulic systems that carry water from source to tap." The anthology edited by Carolyn Merchant, *Major Problems in Environmental History*, also includes a chapter with essays featuring different interpretations of water as an energy source during the twentieth century.[5]

Museums and historic sites can incorporate water-related topics in discussions of plumbing, gardening, cooking, eating and drinking, laundry, and bathing. They can interpret water sources including hauling water from creeks, digging wells, building cisterns, and installing public water systems. They can interpret health and safety issues through discussions of microorganisms that infect humans who drink unsanitary water or eat foods washed in

Landmark, El Rancho de los Golondrinas, Santa Fe, New Mexico, June 2007. Photograph by Debra A. Reid.

unsanitary conditions. Waterborne bacteria cause illnesses such as cholera, dysentery, and typhoid fever. These diseases not only closed port cities such as New Orleans, historically, affecting human survival, but also the transport of goods between the Mississippi River port and destinations up river.

Reducing water contamination facilitated private and public solutions to managing water. Plumbing provides a good example of the combination of public sanitation systems and individual homeowner installation of domestic water systems. The interpretation can be memorable. Mike Follin, coordinator of Interpretive Services as the Ohio History Connection, Columbus, Ohio, remembers visiting Piatt Castle, a historic site in Ohio, when he was five or six years old. It was one of the first places his parents took him, and the experience proved pivotal in his worldview. Mike recalled that "the thing I remembered most from the house was the "water closet" just think a bathroom started me down the road to where I am!"[6] Sites can develop this subject matter to engage their audience in environmental issues related to water management.

Farm families often tried to reduce labor demands of securing water by installing windmills to pump water. Electrical generators and eventually public utilities made private windmills obsolete, until the increase in interest in harnessing wind power and selling it to public utility companies.

Water relates to other big issues, beyond private or public corporate investment. Riverways, lakes, and oceans often help distinguish geopolitical borders. The Ohio River factors heavily into Matthew Salafia's *Slavery's Borderland*, which explores the meaning of freedom on both sides of the river, and in Nikki Taylor's *Driven Toward Madness*, which explores Margaret Garner and her family's quest to secure freedom. Toni Morrison used this real-life tragedy as the basis for her novel, *Beloved*.[7]

Compelling interpretation can spring from conversations that start with water and the environment. Joel Stone explores this in *Interpreting Maritime History at Museums and Historic Sites*. Charles Foy's contribution to *Interpreting the Environment* explores the ways that certain maritime occupations involved free and enslaved men of color and the ways that their geographic location on waterways affected their status as enslaved or free. Foy's database of black mariners grows through a collaborative effort with organizations with evidence of these men. In turn, the database can support interpretation of a person aspiring to freedom, willing to take personal risk to acquire freedom, and using waterways as the route to freedom.[8]

Using Data to Understand Maritime Flight in the Chesapeake during the American Revolution
Charles R. Foy

One of the more difficult challenges public historians face is demonstrating movement and change over time. With runaway slaves who sought to flee their masters via the sea, this can be a particularly daunting task. The *Black Mariner Database* (*BMD*), a dataset of more than 27,000 eighteenth-century maritime fugitives and black seamen, can demonstrate how maritime fugitives moved across the Chesapeake Bay during the American Revolution, when they did so, and why they choose particular means to escape via waterways.[9]

During the eighteenth century, bondsmen seeking freedom via the sea, individuals I refer to as "maritime fugitives," were fairly common. The *BMD* contains more than 5,000 such runaways.[10] Many fled by stealing small vessels. They were able to do so because British colonial economies were dependent on maritime labor, with small craft plentiful in the Chesapeake region. With considerable numbers of black boatmen and seamen employed throughout the British Americas, many maritime fugitives were capable of using such small craft to quickly escape from their masters. The result was that the Chesapeake Bay and the numerous rivers and creeks flowing into it was a transition zone in which enslaved individuals were able to use waterways to transform themselves into free men.

Although some Chesapeake runaways sought to obtain berths on oceangoing ships, many used maritime flight as a means to cross the bay and put distance between themselves and former masters. However, during wartime, the nature of maritime flight changed dramatically. By looking at maritime flight during 1777, when the British brought more than two hundred vessels into the Chesapeake, a clear picture of how war and the Royal Navy's presence shaped maritime flight can be seen.

From the beginning of the revolution, slave masters feared their bondsmen would flee to British forces. To limit maritime flight, officials took measures, including the removal of small craft at landings, having militias "strictly" watch rivers, and decreeing that slaves taken up in arms would be transported and sold in the West Indies.[11]

American and British officials each noted that Royal Navy vessels often offered "asylum to the distressed."[12] With the entry of Lord Howe's fleet into the Chesapeake in August 1777 slaves made it their "declared intention . . . to get on board the fleet." Scores of slaves maneuvered small boats or swam long distances to reach British vessels.[13] They did so because Royal Navy ships offered protection of the British military and opportunity to be quickly transported out of the bay, away from their former masters. By transporting runaway slaves from the Chesapeake, Royal Navy vessels such as HMS *Brune* that carried fifty-four slave runaways to New York, served as taxicabs to freedom. In this way, bondsmen such as Adam Bush were able to flee their masters and, once in New York, go on to find freedom in other regions of the British empire.

Blacks served on colonists' naval ships in the Chesapeake Bay during the revolution. Free blacks, such as Joseph Ranger, and slaves enlisted by their owners, such as Pluto, served on Virginia and Maryland State Navy vessels. However, not a single runaway in the *BMD* served in a state navy vessel in the Chesapeake. This was undoubtedly because runaways who sought refuge on colonial naval ships would have been returned to their owners. Instead, free blacks, including Abel Spriggs, deserted from colonial state navy vessels.

The dramatic change of Chesapeake maritime flight is evident both from the increase in total maritime fugitives and the number who fled onto Royal Navy vessels in 1777 as compared to the Seven Years' War. From 1754 to 1763, there were forty-nine Chesapeake maritime fugitives, 6 percent of all maritime fugitives in that time period. During this period, the Royal Navy's absence is apparent because not a single Chesapeake maritime fugitive sought haven on British naval ships. In contrast, in 1777 there were 178 identified Chesapeake maritime fugitives, comprising 66.9 percent of all maritime fugitives that year.

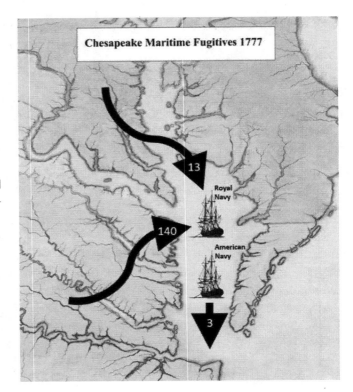

Chesapeake Maritime Fugitives 1777

Royal
Navy

American
Navy

13

140

3

Chesapeake maritime flight and naval ships, 1777. Created by Michael I. Bradley.

The presence of Lord Howe's fleet clearly was the reason for this substantial increase in maritime flight. In 1777, 153 runaways, or 86 percent of all Chesapeake maritime fugitives, found protection on Royal Navy vessels.

Through the use of the *BMD*, public historians can demonstrate that not only the Chesapeake but also other maritime regions (e.g., the waters between Jamaica and Cuba) operated as zones of transition in which waterways were highways to freedom and the critical role war and naval ships played in runaways obtaining freedom. In doing so, they will be able to provide greater detail and complexity to the choices and lives of enslaved peoples.

The second case study shifts from using waterways as a zone of transition during wartime toward an exploration of a big theme—Water/Ways—in local context. The Smithsonian Institution's Museums on Main Street (MoMS) created the traveling exhibition *Water/Ways*. It focused on the meaning and symbolism of water. MoMS staff reach rural audiences through partnerships between MoMS and state humanities councils. Each year, humanities councils in five different states host the exhibition. The humanities councils usually select six rural communities across the state as local hosts. Each community develops place-specific programming and an exhibit that supplements the MoMS exhibition. Humanities Kansas engaged local residents in even more communities across the state in an effort to generate discussion about an environmental subject at the heart of much debate in the semi-arid prairie state.

Water/Ways in Kansas
Julie Mulvihill, Executive Director, Humanities Kansas

When a state *humanities* council decides to undertake a science-based project centered on water, the reason for doing so must be clear. For Humanities Kansas it was to explore how the water resources found in Kansas have shaped the lives of Kansans over time and across generations.

Anchored by a Smithsonian Institution traveling exhibition of the same name, the *Water/Ways* initiative explored water through the lens of the human experience. Humanities Kansas worked with sixteen local museums and libraries to host the exhibition, research key themes, identify a water story unique to their community, and plan public events that would engage Kansans.

With one foot in the Prairie and the other in the Great Plains ecosystem, Kansas has a complex water story, and it informs how Kansans from east to west talk about water. Rex Buchanan, retired interim director of the Kansas Geological Survey, wrote in his foreword to the Humanities Kansas *Ebb and Flow* publication,

> In some respects, Kansas is really two states—not one—when it comes to water. Eastern Kansas gets lots of rain and thus relies on rivers and lakes for much of its water supply. In western Kansas, precipitation is scant, water is rare at the surface. But groundwater (found in the pore spaces of underground rocks like the Ogallala aquifer) is plentiful. Or at least it once was.

It is reasonable to consider that not having scientists on staff at Humanities Kansas would be a problem for *Water/Ways*. Except for one environmental library and one natural history museum, none of the museums and libraries involved were science-based either. The solution was twofold. First, Humanities Kansas would partner with the state's Water Office to learn important background information about the state's water resources. Second, the Smithsonian Institution traveling exhibition would cover the water data; the water stories would come from Kansans.

And the stories to choose from were plentiful. Water determined where Kansans broke ground for farms and which crops were planted. Water was behind the decisions determining where towns were platted—some to handle the cattle business and others to replenish the steam engines driving the trains carrying settlers west. And with businesses came more people, colleges, and libraries and, ultimately, highways and suburbs. Water also served as a ready division in many communities, separating black families from white, Spanish-speaking families of Mexican workers from others, and the poor from the affluent. Even to this day, water pits people, towns, and states against one another as lawsuits roil over water rights and claims about unfair usage. As Buchanan writes, "Water is not an abstract concept to the people of this state. It is a very real, very tangible issue."

To make *Water/Ways* a statewide initiative, Humanities Kansas depended on the expertise of the project collaborators representing the sixteen libraries and museums who signed on to tackle the project. How would they address the water issues? What unique story would each tell?

Most dug into their history. The Old Depot Museum in Ottawa located in northeast Kansas returned to the 1860s and the early days of town settlement and the decision to build in a crook of the Marais des Cygnes River, a river prone to frequent flooding. Before long, homes and businesses scrambled to move away from the heart of the city, leaving behind a town with a distinctly elongated shape.

The Eudora Area Historical Society, also in northeast Kansas, took on a similar flood story that happened generations later in 1951. The museum researched stories of residents loading clucking chickens into pick-up trucks to move to higher ground before the flood hit and afterward cruising Kansas Highway 10 in a boat. Even before this legendary flood, lawmakers knew flooding was a frequent problem in parts of Kansas; after 1951, more than twenty dams and reservoirs were built. This brought new water stories to many communities, as the government purchased personal property, towns, and cemeteries to make way for these flood mitigation efforts.

At the Prairie Museum of Art and History in Colby in western Kansas, the community honored Joe Kuska, a longtime employee at the Colby Branch Station. The Colby Branch Station, an agricultural experiment center, was opened by an act of the Kansas Legislature in 1913 to find solutions for northwest Kansas farmers concerned with erratic rainfall, drying winds, temperature extremes, and periodic drought. Kuska was hired in 1914 to research how to successfully farm in dry conditions. He spent his career working on behalf of Kansas farmers, encouraging them to apply methods that allowed for adaptability and flexibility, even as irrigation brought changes to Kansas agriculture throughout the twentieth century.

Boot Hill Museum in Dodge City, located in the state's drought-prone southwest corner, embraced its wild frontier image and tackled the story of Soule's Folly, named for the flamboyant Dr. Asa T. Soule, worldwide Hops Bitter King who peddled a medicinal combination of alcohol, bitters, and hops to cure all ailments. Approached by brothers George and John Gilbert in the 1880s, Soule was impressed by the idea of a canal that could divert the Arkansas River through potential farmland with a large-scale irrigation project. Backers boasted that the canal would ensure vegetable crops and homes with water views. The canal was built with Soule's money, but it failed from lack of water. It would not be the last time the idea of water diversion would capture the attention of Kansans.

Other communities told stories of artesian springs in the heart of the Flint Hills and curing mineral springs near Marion, whereas others shared stories of big wells and fish fossils left behind when the prehistoric sea receded.

The *Water/Ways* initiative was a success because Kansans could relate to these stories past and present. Do Kansans have a right to water? Of course. But how water is used is still up for discussion and debate. Residents, city officials, wildlife preservationists, and sportsmen, in addition to farmers and ranchers, have strong opinions about how water should be used in Kansas. This is a timely and timeless story that defines the human experience and captures the imagination of Kansans of every generation. "Water, and the myriad of challenges it presents, unites us as a people . . . [and] water will continue to unite us for the foreseeable future," Buchanan shared.

Humanities Kansas featured *Water/Ways* projects in its publication, *Ebb and Flow*, created additional *Water/Ways* resources including lists of scholars, books, and films. Humanities Kansas also created a Readers Theater project called "Shared Stories of the Kansas

Land." These resources helped share the interpretation of the environment from a humanities perspective far beyond the six host institutions and their communities.[14]

Conclusion

Many opportunities exist to incorporate water into humanities-oriented programming. Topographical maps support close investigation of communities and their resources. Global positioning systems (GPS) and geographical information systems (GIS) have revolutionized mapping, and the combination has made paper copies of topographical maps obsolete. Geographer Richard Sleezer, Emporia State University, is salvaging these historical resources, often discarded from county Farm Bureau or U.S. Department of Agriculture Soil and Water Conservation offices. He has used the county-level maps of Kansas townships to identify human intrusion on the changing landscape, including sources of groundwater and aquifer pollutants. A similar project, undertaken by archivists at the University of Nebraska at Kearney, will create a public repository of maps relevant to interpreting the environment.

Anniversaries of natural disasters such as hurricanes, fires, tornadoes, and floods cause people to pay attention to the history of local events. *Legacy*, the magazine of the National Association for Interpretation, published the special issue, "Interpreting Disaster," in 2014. Stone addresses maritime disasters in *Interpreting Maritime History at Museums and Historic Sites* (2017), and Kimberly Kenney touches on natural disasters in *Interpreting Anniversaries and Milestones at Museums and Historic Sites* (2016).[15]

Evidence documenting these localized events often document the destruction and the community resilience. These become the basis for commemorations during anniversaries of the event. An exercise in historical thinking by avoiding presentism can engage the public in an exploration of a local event based on almanacs and other historic evidence rather than the Weather Channel worldview.[16]

Notes

1. Ted Steinberg, *Gotham Unbound: The Ecological History of Greater New York* (New York: Simon & Schuster, 2014). Reid's research into Ford's transformation of the Rouge continues.
2. Earth Optimism Summit, https://earthoptimism.si.edu/. Accessed June 16, 2018.
3. James E. Sherow, *Watering the Valley: Development along the High Plains Arkansas River, 1870–1950* (Lawrence: University Press of Kansas, 1990), 4.
4. Sherow, *Watering the Valley*, 4.
5. Char Miller, *Fluid Arguments: Five Centuries of Western Water Conflict* (Tucson: University of Arizona Press, 2001), xvi. John Opie, *Ogallala: Water for a Dry Land* (Lincoln: University of Nebraska Press, 1993; 3rd ed., 2018). Carolyn Merchant, *Major Problems in Environmental History*, 2nd ed. (Boston: Cengage Learning, 2006). For a general environmental history of water and the American West, see Donald Worster, *Rivers of Empire: Water, Aridity, and the Growth of the American West* (New York: Oxford University Press, 1992).
6. E-mail communication between Mike Follin and Debra Reid, December 6, 2017.

7. Matthew Salafia, *Slavery's Borderland: Freedom and Bondage Along the Ohio River* (Philadelphia: University of Pennsylvania Press, 2013). Nikki M. Taylor, *Driven Toward Madness: The Fugitive Slave Margaret Garner and Tragedy on the Ohio* (Athens: Ohio University Press, 2017) puts the escape of Margaret Garner and her extended family into context. Toni Morrison, Beloved: A Novel (New York: Alfred A. Knopf, 1987).

8. Joel Stone, ed., *Interpreting Maritime History at Museums and Historic Sites* (Lanham, MD: Rowman & Littlefield, 2017).

9. The *BMD* contains fifty-three fields of data: age, ethnicity, place of birth, ships served on, etc. It includes references from ship musters, court records, fugitive slave advertisements, newspaper dispatches, merchant records, governmental records, and a wide variety of miscellaneous documents from more than thirty archives across the Atlantic. As was done in Merseyside Maritime Museum's "Black Salts" exhibit, the *BMD* can also demonstrate global movement of black mariners.

10. Chesapeake maritime fugitives were identified through a review of newspapers, secondary sources, as well as a random sampling of the 1777 musters of six Royal Navy vessels: HMS *Apollo, Brune, Emerald, Phoenix,* and *St. Albans,* and HM Sloop *Senegal.* Given the size of Lord Howe's fleet, it is clear that the numbers of maritime fugitives in 1777 are considerably higher than presently shown by the *BMD*.

11. *Virginia Gazette,* December 2, 1775; Hening, ed., *Statutes at Large: Being a Collection of all the Laws of Virginia,* Vol. IX (1809), 106.

12. *Virginia Gazette* (Dixon & Hunter), Williamsburg, November 18, 1775; John A. Nagy, *Invisible Ink: Spycraft of the American Revolution* (Yardley, PA: Westholme Publishing, 2011), 130.

13. *Maryland Gazette,* October 16, 1777; W. Calderhead "Slavery in Maryland in the Age of Revolution 1775–1790," *Maryland Historical Magazine* vol. 98 (Fall 2003), 303–324, 310n24; *Virginia Gazette* (Dixon and Harper), December 19, 1777.

14. Humanities Kansas included special *Water/Ways* features in its publication, *Ebb and Flow,* http://kansashumanities.org/v2/wp-content/uploads/2015/11/ebb-and-flow_web.pdf; created additional *Water/Ways* resources and made these available to other Kansas organizations, regardless of whether they were host or partner sites or not (http://kansashumanities.org/v2/wp-content/uploads/2011/12/WaterWays_catalog_MAY-2017.pdf). Humanities Kansas also created a Readers Theater project called "Shared Stories of the Kansas Land." The scripts can be found in the second step of the five listed. http://kansashumanities.org/programs/shared-stories-of-the-civil-war/. Accessed August 30, 2018.

15. "Interpreting Disaster," special issue of *Legacy* vol. 25, no. 5 (September/October 2014). https://www.interpnet.com/nai/docs/Publications/Legacy-v25n5-SeptOct.pdf. Accessed August 30, 2018. Stone, ed., *Interpreting Maritime History at Museums and Historic Sites.* Kimberly A. Kenney, *Interpreting Anniversaries and Milestones at Museums and Historic Sites* (Lanham, MD: Rowman and Littlefield, 2016).

16. Ted Steinberg, *Acts of God: The Unnatural History of Natural Disaster in America* (New York: Oxford University Press, 2000; 2nd ed, 2006).

CHAPTER 6

Generating and Harnessing Power

POWER COMES FROM MANY SOURCES and takes many forms. Geophysical forces such as thermonuclear fusion in our Sun, collisions of the Earth's tectonics, and decay in uranium isotopes on the Earth generate power naturally. Humans harness geophysical forces and other natural energy such as the wind, flowing water, and gravity to accomplish goals of grinding flour, sawing lumber, and extracting ores and fuels. All of this has profound effects on the environment. Natural features and the products of humans, artifacts, can help tell these stories.

Hydroelectric plants and nuclear reactors might be the first things that come to mind when discussing power generation. Action to protect resources in proximity to these facilities gained traction during the 1960s. President John F. Kennedy designated 170,000 acres in the area transformed by the hydroelectric projects of the Tennessee Valley Authority (TVA), as the Land Between the Lakes National Recreation Area in 1963. By the early 1970s, the United Nations Educational, Scientific and Cultural Organization (UNESCO) began the Man and the Biosphere Program to help educate the public about humans and the environment. Land Between the Lakes received Biosphere designation in 1991. These decisions drew attention to landscapes disrupted by human manipulation of the environment to create power. The lesson does not end with designation, however, because private property concerns, corporate interests, and concerns about sovereignty continue to challenge efforts to conserve or at least sustain existing landscapes. *National Geographic* reported that seventeen U.S. sites voluntarily withdrew from UNESCO's Biosphere program, including Land Between the Lakes, in 2017.[1]

Many artifacts connect to these public lands and their histories. Windmills become the starting point for conversations about global jet streams. A 1935 electric range or refrigerator or radio becomes a touchpoint for discussing the TVA and the New Deal's Rural Electrification Administration. Radium began appearing as artifacts during the early twentieth century, to create a glow on watch dials, jewelry, and other consumables. The women hired to paint with radium suffered from radiation poisoning, as did consumers who wore some of the products.[2]

Numerous objects lead us to the discussion of harnessing power. The following case studies address one topic you might not consider "power," the weather, and the other addresses numerous topics to explore relative to commercial production, distribution, and use of fuels for household consumption, culminating in the changes that electrification wrought on local systems and well as individual households.

Anticipating Natural Forces: Almanacs

The Sun's rays affect seasons and climate, and humans have no control over these natural rhythms, but historical attempts to anticipate and respond to these forces exist in museum collections. You may associate astronomy, the study of the heavens, with the job of being either a sailor or psychic. Navigators and fortune tellers both set their sights on the stars, and so did farmers. Just pick up the *Farmers' Almanac* at your local newsstand, or browse some historic almanacs in museum collections to get a sense of the relationship between astronomy and agriculture. While you can debate the modern science, the publications convey a historical way of thinking about and practical application of astronomy and astrology.

Almanacs from the 1810s to the 1910s can introduce you to the resources that farmers referenced as they went about their daily business. The publishers included weather predictions. In 1817, August 17 was the eleventh Sunday after the Trinity [after Pentecost], and the Farmers Almanacs for the Years of Our Lord 1816 and 1817 indicated that the weather would be "sultry and hot."[3]

Publishers linked celestial bodies with the months of the calendar. In August 1817, the astrological sign Pisces (associated with February 19 to March 20, based on the Sun's position relative to other constellations) appears in August. Why? Because the almanac publisher incorporated movements of other celestial bodies (the Moon, the planets) in addition to the Sun, and included the sign associated with the human form, rather than with the Sun. Aries is the first zoological sign and is associated with the head. Pisces is the last zoological sign and is associated with the feet.

The *Farmers and Dairyman's Almanac for the Year 1852* explained the signs of the zodiac in relation to the body as follows: "The above presents the anatomy of the human body as governed by the constellations, ascending in ancient astrology. In order to know where the sign is, find first the day of the month in the calendar page, and against the day in the sixth column, you have the sign or place of the Moon. Then find the sign here, and it will give you the part of the body it is supposed to govern."

Farmers took these astrological associations to heart in an era before enlightened science, and they performed tasks that seemed to turn out better because of "following the signs." For instance, some swore by (and some continue to swear by) the practice of castrating animals when the sign is in the feet because of observed benefits, such as less blood loss. Scientists, however, began questioning these best practices during the Enlightenment, labeling astrology a pseudoscience. The *Farmers and Dairyman's Almanac for the Year 1852* explained the debate clearly: "Although this table is becoming obsolete, there are many persons who have confidence in it, and persist in weaning their children and killing their pigs by the signs! Wherefore it is retained."[4]

Farmers almanacs also listed eclipses, both lunar and solar eclipses, scheduled to occur in a given year, and the location in which they could be observed. Even today, almanacs include a human-zoology chart, weather predictions, and advice about gardening in concert with lunar phases (plant belowground crops when the Moon in waning, and plant aboveground crops when the Moon is waxing), among other things.

These almanacs provided advice that farmers could use to make decisions about when to plant or harvest. The publication of the almanacs coincided with availability of barometers and thermometers, other tools used to predict the weather. Most farmers, however, had nothing but local patterns on which to base their decisions. They had no assurance (historically or today) that the weather would cooperate.

Natural Resources, Fuel Needs, and Human Intervention

Humans manipulate natural resources to extract various fuels. The process of creating the fuels or using the fuels is just one part of a much larger story of human influence on the types of fuels used at different points in the past and in the future. In the monograph *Energy: A Human History* (2018), Richard Rhodes surveys the political and public as well as the individual and personal factors that affected energy use over time, from wood to coal to oil to electricity, natural gas, nuclear power, and renewable energy.[5]

Debates about fossil fuels, renewable energy, and sustainable practices revolve around human needs for fuel. Wood has provided fuel to cook and heat since humans learned how to make fire. Farmers with land increased their income by selling firewood. Those who burned wood could convert the wood ash to potash, an essential ingredient in gunpowder and, thus, an asset to the growing United States during the early nineteenth century.

Wood, a renewable resource, grew back slowly, but clear-cutting destroyed ecosystems. Coal, a nonrenewable fossil fuel, replaced wood as the preferred fuel to propel traction engines and generate power through stationary steam engines. Coal became a preferred fuel for domestic use, especially in cities where residents had no ready wood supply. By-products of coal, including coal oil and kerosene, became indispensable in modern homes, and in industrial processing by the 1870s. All fossil fuels support interpretation of domestic as well as industrial environments.

Can you identify a popular nineteenth-century fuel based on these clues?

A clear liquid.

Low volatility.

First documented during the ninth century.

A distillate derived from petroleum; also distilled from oil extracted from shale and bituminous coal.

Trademarked in 1854.

Still used throughout the world to fire up jet engines and speed boats.

Most people historically benefited from the relatively clean and bright light that this fuel generated when burned in lamps.

The answer?[6]

During the 1860s, kerosene table lamps and chandeliers lit up domestic and work spaces from coast to coast. Companies catered to consumer tastes by producing a variety of pressed and cut patterns in clear and colored glass, in bright tin, and in painted and polished metal finishes. The lamps reflected popular decorating trends that featured marble bases and brass or bronze columns and molding.

Between the 1860s and the 1920s, changing burner design created more intense light. The popular lighting fuel became even more essential to domestic life on farms and in town as inventors created new uses. Advertisers emphasized the merits of the clean fuel in contrast to smoky and sooty wood or coal fuel. Companies began advertising kerosene cooking apparatuses as early as the 1860s. In 1888, the Perfection Stove Company began marketing a "lamp stove," that used store lamp wicks (circular wicks, standardized for different size jobs). The circular wicks became the basis for even brighter burning kerosene lamps and as the heating element in the lamp stoves. A portable heater appeared in 1894.

By 1901, the Perfection Stove Company worked out arrangements with Standard Oil, so the company that delivered the clean fuel, kerosene, also had a role in marketing the Perfection Stove. By the early twentieth century, companies advertised "smokeless" oil heaters and stoves, fueled by "coal oil" or kerosene. Patented improvements in the burner and lamp stoves in 1913 and 1919 provided advertising opportunities for Perfection Smokeless stoves that consumers could use to cook their meals (not just heat their homes).

The utility of kerosene heaters and stoves influenced life beyond the home. Food preparation remained an essential part of traveler duties. Seasoned travelers, like Charles and Anne Lindbergh, depended on a gasoline-fueled automobile to move their stagecoach travel trailer down the road, but the home-away-from-home needed other fuels and fuel-specific appliances to function. In 1948, the Lindberghs updated technologies by installing a new International Oil Burning Trailer Heater, along with a Willis cook stove. Although both ran on kerosene, the directions for the "practical and economical" Willis stove also specified the use of alcohol to preheat the burners described in advertisements as "ingenious." "The self-cleaning, wickless burners are simple to operate, economical to use, and perhaps the most efficient portable heating units on the market."[7]

Rapid adoption and wide application made kerosene an indispensable fuel. The transition away from wood- or coal-fueled cook stoves to kerosene stoves prompted changes in other technology. No longer could people heat their sad iron on a stove top without turning on the fossil fuel. A variety of kerosene-fueled irons appeared on the market during the late nineteenth and early twentieth centuries.

Farm families used kerosene to fire-up hit-and-mis engines. They ran a variety of machines, including pneumatic milking machines and corn shellers, off the power generated by the engine. Familiarity with these engines paved the way for adoption of tractors with internal combustion engines. In 1914, the Allis-Chalmers Manufacturing Company produced its first farm tractor—the Model 10-18. The suggested retail price of $1,950 put it beyond the reach of many farm families, but Allis-Chalmers tried to reduce the cost of operation by incorporating two fuel tanks, one five-gallon tank for the starter fuel—gasoline—and one twenty-gallon tank for the cheaper operating fuel—kerosene. A heat valve on the manifold routed the exhaust gases around the intake pipe. An electric spark ignited the vaporized kerosene. An International Harvester advertisement for Mogul and Titan tractors put the argument into simple economic terms: "the average price of gasoline in the United States is 16 9-10c per gallon; kerosene is 7 7-10c."[8]

Adopting the cheaper operating fuel, kerosene, made good economic sense. Corn belt farmers also called for use of ethyl alcohol, derived from corn, as an alternative fuel for tractors. This compares to 10 percent ethanol (ethyl alcohol) added to automobile gasoline today and the processing of soybeans into biodiesel as an alternative fuel source. These fuels derived from biomass used large amounts of water in processing, and this can negatively affect watersheds near processing areas. Furthermore, some processing facilities rely on coal for fuel, adding to the debate about the sustainability of corn-based ethanol as a fuel additive.[9]

Automobiles and trucks used more than one fossil fuel too. Engineers experimented with fuel mixtures and burner technology to create a bright light that helped early automobile drivers see the road. In addition to the gasoline tank under the hood, the International Harvester Company's 1912 commercial truck had holders for kerosene lamps on the side and rear that customers purchased as "extras." Customers could also purchase "gas lights" for the front of the vehicle. These burned acetylene gas, or carbide, generated by a reaction of calcium carbide and water. This variety proves that current discussions of Flex Fuels had historic precedence.

Keeping the Home Fires Stoked

Domestic technologies and decorative arts convey the variety of options available to heat homes and prepare home-cooked meals. Before rural electrification, farm families that lived close enough to municipal power plants, and who could afford it, could pay for power lines to their property. Power companies, however, realized little return on lines in the country given maintenance costs.[10]

Families not on the grid could invest in a Delco-Light Farm Electric Plant, introduced in 1916, or an electrical generating plant produced by one of several competing companies during the 1920s and 1930s. The Domestic Lighting Company (Dayton, Ohio) manufactured twenty-five Delco-Light models ranging in price from $250 to $1,675 in 1921. The popular model, a 32-volt, 600-watt generator, ran on kerosene. Advertisements claimed it could power a ½-horsepower engine. Full-page advertisements for light-plants sometimes showed the benefits of power in the barn and work sheds and in the farmhouse. This affirmed that the plant was not a frivolous purchase. The farmer (always depicted as male) used the machine to light the barn, pump water for livestock, run the fanning mill or grindstone, or power the vacuum pump milking machine. The farm wife (always depicted as female) used the plant to power the electric motor on the washing machine or cream separator or to light a reading lamp. In 1926, farm families could buy the smallest light plants and pay for wiring the farm house and the farm barn, all for $248.[11]

In rural Southern Illinois, Edith Rendleman, recalled that she and her father convinced her husband to rent a farm that had an electrical generating plant. She used it to pump water and run the washing machine.[12] The Anna and Fredrick Schupbach family, farm owner-operators of a 175-acre farm near Eden in Randolph County, Illinois, owned a 32-volt light plant. They used it to power the water pump, the washing machine, and other small motors.[13] The plant, however, had its limitations. The popular 32-volt model did not produce enough power to provide consistent light or heat an electric iron, a hot water heater, or an electric range.

Laundry, a laborious task, required physically hauling water from a creek or a well to the house and then boiling the water in a pot on the stove or hearth or in a cauldron over a pit. Then women and girls, usually the members of the family relegated to the work, had to use a scrubbing board to clean clothes. Manufacturers responded to the demand for tubs with motors and marketed both gas and electric models. The engine, situated under the tub of the washing machine, had a foot pedal that the operator used to give the engine gas. Thus, a farm wife could get some reprieve from the scrub board even without owning a generator or being wired to a utility company.

Families that had no light plants managed their work in traditional ways, lit with kerosene lamps, and performing physically taxing labor. Farm women milked and made butter when the cows were fresh. They cooked three meals a day, did laundry, and ironed clothes for large families. They repeated the tasks, day in and day out. When families first became connected to public utilities, they did not lament changing routines. Instead they remembered purchases of wringer washing machines, refrigerators, and electric stoves. Some remember increased comfort, too. Edith Rendleman recalled that "we could have a bathtub, a bathroom."[14]

Conspicuously absent from most promotional materials about electrifying the farm home—the kitchen cook stove. Various reasons account for this. Electric stoves, irons, and hot water heaters, required more voltage than small generators produced. But women had alternatives. They could cook with gas.

Two- and four-burner kerosene cook stoves, available since the late nineteenth century, allowed women to light a wick and cook a meal. By the 1930s, other fuels included inexpensive bottled gas. Eiker & Son in Sparta, Illinois, purveyors of PurOPane Bottled Gas, claimed that "The finest cooking in the world is done on a gas stove!" and that PurOPane was the "fastest heating fuel known." They would install a stove, with fuel, for seventy-four dollars.[15]

The pace of change remained inconsistent even after rural electrification. Eugenia "Jean" Stanley Reid (1922–2018), who married John Russell "Bissell" Reid on October 8, 1938, cooked on a two-burner coal oil stove in the early months of their marriage. They set up housekeeping during the spring of 1939. Then founders of the local rural electrical cooperative, Egyptian Electric, and launched their membership drive. She recalled that she and her new husband "didn't really need electricity." They had a gas stove, wood heat, a cool breeze, and coal oil lamps. Others in the town of Rockwood, Illinois, electrified after the Egyptian

An unidentified woman (likely the farm wife) stands in the backyard doorway of a farmhouse occupied by tenant farmer John Simmons and his ten children near Marseilles, Illinois (LaSalle County). A bench in the background holds two large wash tubs on a stand, as well as a copper boil kettle, all upended to drain. Women and girls spent countless hours hauling water and heating water and scrubbing and rinsing laundry in these tubs if they could not afford a washer with a gas motor before electrification. Russell Lee, photographer. January 1937. LC-USF34- 010178-E [P&P]. Library of Congress Prints and Photographs Division Washington, D.C.

Electric Cooperative ran the wires, but Aunt Jean and Uncle Bissell did not. They could not afford it, and they did not need it to live the life they chose.

Those farm women who could afford all of the commercial trappings of innovation became models during the Egyptian Electric membership drive. The Sparta [Illinois] *News-Plaindealer* featured the "Modern Kitchen on Red Bud Farm" in the June 16, 1939 issue. The *News-Plaindealer* staff photographed Mrs. William Sauer, a "prominent farm woman of near Red Bud," mixing up "home-made" bread. The caption indicated that "Mrs. Sauer has all the conveniences of a city home in her up-to-date kitchen, including electric lights, an electric refrigerator, a sink and running water." The caption does not mention the type of stove she used to bake the "home-made" bread that the staff photograph showed her mixing. Nor does it explain how she got the electricity, whether it came from the Red Bud grid or from the family generator. But Mrs. Sauer's kitchen reflected a trend among those who had electricity before the Rural Electrification Administration (REA)-supported local cooperatives began. The stove in the background appeared to be a white-enameled gas model popular during the later 1920s and early 1930s.

Rural electrification, despite all the attention, had the potential to serve only about one-quarter of the Illinois population. In 1930, 26 percent of the state's residents lived in rural areas, and only 2.8 percent lived on farms. This represented one of the lowest rural population ratios in the Midwest, largely because of the concentration of the state's population in Chicago and smaller cities. By 1950, 24 percent of Illinois residents lived in rural areas, and only 2.2 percent lived on farms.[16]

Census returns indicated that Illinois farms, on average, had some of the highest land valuations in the nation but also some of the highest mortgages. But southern Illinois counties had some of the lowest valued land in the state, and many had little interest in mortgaging their farm to improve their standard of living. But these farm families had to participate for the cooperative utility to come to fruition. Investing in farm improvements offered more suasion. Farm families that owned their homes could rationalize their involvement as a cost of doing business: the membership fee, the wiring fees, the monthly utility fee, and the investment in new light fixtures, motors, and pumps in barns and more lights, pumps, and appliances in homes.

The cooperative ideal fit an approach to farm purchasing and marketing that farmers understood, too, when they saved through collective action and realized a return on their collective investment. The Egyptian Electric Cooperative Association began on paper in August 1938. The cooperative had to recruit at least three families per mile as members to meet the minimum requirement of $10 per mile in monthly bills. By early 1939, organizers had recruited enough members per miles of line in Jackson, Perry, and Randolph counties to apply for REA funding. The cooperative received its initial REA loan on February 20, 1939; set the first electric pole on September 13, 1939; and switched the breaker to light the first section of line on March 30, 1940. Contractors ran 402 miles of lines to about 1,500 farm homes, most in Randolph County, but others in Jackson, Perry, Washington, and St. Clair counties during initial construction.

The Sparta *News-Plaindealer* headlined the pole-setting ceremonies with the headline: "Happy Days Ahead for Rural Folk" (September 22, 1939). Advertising emphasized the potential of electric lights, water pumps, washing machines, and vacuum cleaners to lighten the heavy lifting of a farm wife's routines. The women themselves recounted these tales of modernization. The Egyptian Electric Cooperative featured six farm wives conducting a memorial service for their obsolete appliances: Bonnie Well Bucket, Bennie Broom, Willie Washboard, Fanny Flatiron, Lula Lamp, and an old-fashioned ice box. The casual observer might interpret this as endorsement of the advertisers' messages and the newspaper hype, but it also indicated the ways that women managed the transformations.

The Egyptian Electric Cooperative held public meetings to "assist farmers and homemakers in securing the most efficient and economical use of equipment they plan to purchase."[17] The breadth of the work, with farm wives in the 1,000 homes scheduled for wiring during summer 1939, represented sales opportunities for local businesses. Jim Frazier Furniture in Chester, Illinois, wired houses and sold appliances. W. W. Lynn of Lynn Furniture Company in Sparta tried to help customers realize that "the modern electric range is by no means the high-priced luxury it has been pictured." Lynn paid for a news story that featured the 1939 GE model B-20 and its Thriftomatic time switch (March 24, 1939).

The Illinois Iowa Power Company paid for advertising that promoted electric ranges too. This coincided with the Egyptian Electric membership campaign to recruit rural subscribers. The Sparta *News-Plaindealer* carried stories for several weeks in May and June 1939 about the Illinois-Iowa Power Company's offer of a rate reduction if twenty new users of electric ranges signed up for service within thirty days (May 19, 1939). The power company targeted housewives to realize the goal. In one instance it offered a two-day cooking school, presented by Ruth Graham of the Electromaster Factory (Michigan) to increase interest in adoption of electric ranges. The company featured electric ranges because they used more power than other household appliances.

Businesses joined the promotion. Lynn Furniture Company urged customers to come in to see the new Frigidaire Electric Range: "Buy your stove now and help reduce electric rates in Sparta. Models priced from 120.50 and up" (May 19, 1939). An advertisement for the power company's Electric Range Exposition, an annual fall sale, featured a cartoon of a lovely couple with the woman holding a "low electric cooking bill," and the man thinking "Costs <u>only</u> <u>half</u> as much as I thought. . . Electric cooking's cheap. . . like electric light" (September 22, 1939). A week later Egyptian Electric set its first pole.

Some families invested in rural electrification with many of its trappings when rural electrification came. Others did not. Cora Eva Frazier Reid and her two youngest daughters, Tirzah and Alice, bore responsibility for domestic chores on the 100-acre family farm in Rockwood, Illinois. They got power in 1940, a result of Egyptian Electric Cooperative initiative. Jim Frazier, who owned the a furniture store in Chester, Illinois, wired the Reid house, hanging a single bulb from the ceiling in the two-room house. Aunt Alice remembered that the family replaced the wood cook stove with a gas stove but could not remember when that happened, before or after electrification. She recalled vividly, however, that her mother won an electric skillet from the REA. They used the skillet to fry chicken, sitting the skillet on a counter in the kitchen, and they continued that method long after the first skillet wore out.

Some families did not purchase refrigerators when they electrified. The ice delivery man came regularly to restock the ice block for the ice box. Icemen in Rockwood, Illinois, Alfred Durkee and Roy Merden [Merton] remained in business during rural electrification. Neither did many invest in bathrooms. The Reids did not build an indoor toilet until the early 1960s when walks to the outhouse became risky for the blind patriarch of the family.

Even being in town did not translate into equal opportunity when it came to electricity. Families retained their personal preferences about the appliances they owned and the investments that they made in their homes. Francis Surman was a teenager when electricity came to rural Randolph County, but her family, tenant farmers, did not live in a house with electricity until they moved to Chester, Illinois in 1943. But they did not purchase new equipment as a result of their move or because of the new resource at their disposal. They had no indoor bathroom. They still boiled water on the stove to heat water and heated the iron on the stove, but their washing machine had a motor. They had an apartment-sized stove that required them to pump the fuel. They also had an ice box and the ice delivery man came regularly. And they had a coal furnace. In the instance of my mother and her family, at least, their move to town brought electric lights and running water into their life.

The electric cooperatives offered other centralized services to rural families, specifically freezer facilities or locker plants (Paulter meat locker in Chester, Illinois). These cold-storage units appealed to families who could put their butchered meat into the rented freezer compartments. The freezers allowed families to change their traditional butchering practices. They could take the hogs to the butcher, who wrapped the cuts in freezer paper. Then the families could take the meat directly to their rented locker.

Marion Post Wolcott took this photograph of a Polish miner in Westover, West Virginia. Her notes described him as well-to-do and thrifty, with a fastidious Hungarian wife. The miner listened to the radio after his night shift ended, and before he washed his face. September 1938. Farm Security Administration, Office of War Information. Library of Congress Prints and Photographs Division, Washington, D.C.

Even with selective purchasing, wiring a home took money. Other New Deal agencies, specifically the Federal Housing Administration (FHA) offered "modernization loans." A bank in Sparta brought the opportunity to the attention of *News-Plaindealer* readers in 1939: "Home is what you make it. . . . Would installing new conveniences make it more liveable?" Monthly payments up to three years—Sparta State Bank (June 16, 1939).

Jean and Bissell Reid did not save enough money to electrify until 1949. After they ran the wires up the hill to their house, they bought a Frigidaire refrigerator, the first item they purchased on credit. Jean earned the money to pay for it while working at the International Shoe Factory in Chester, Illinois. She equated the refrigerator "with a whole new world." She could make all the ice cubes she could use and buy hamburger ahead and extra loaves of bread at five cents a loaf.

What farm women perceived as the most important change that electricity brought to the farm may vary depending on the person. But the coming of electricity to Illinois farms meant a complete transformation that only money could buy. Farm Security Administration (FSA) photographer John Vachon photographed a tenant farm family in Crawford County, Illinois, in May 1940. The images emphasized incorporation of the radio into farm homes and the addition of evening leisure for families who electrified. The radio spread news and market reports during morning and noontime broadcasts. FSA photographer Marion Post Wolcott documented a Polish miner who listened to the radio before he even washed his

Solar panels viewed from airplane approaching Las Vegas for the National Council on Public History Conference. April 2018. Photograph by Debra A. Reid.

face after coming home from his night shift in the mines. The coal he mined earned him a paycheck, and it fueled the power plant that lit up rural America.

The 1950 Census of Agriculture reported that in 1900, "practically no farms used electricity," but by 1950, "more than three-fourths of all the farms had electric service from central-station sources" (80). Half of that number received service between 1945 and 1950. The mass production of electricity radically changed extraction of fossil fuels, energy production and distribution, and the consumption of appliances to use the new services.[17]

Conclusion

Today, kerosene remains a popular fuel to power modern appliances in homes off the grid and in Old-Order Amish homes with kerosene-fueled appliances as small as portable heaters and as large as absorption refrigerators. Today, wind has become an alternative energy source, though not without its controversies. Windmills, once a necessity on farms to lessen the burden of pumping water, have gained new symbolism for harnessing the power of the wind and adding it to the public electrical grid.[19] Today, solar panels tend to symbolize personal investment in energy regeneration, but some airports, and some municipalities, such as Las Vegas, maintain acres of solar panels to reduce their dependence on fossil fuels. Almost every artifact in museum and historic site collections from tools and equipment to appliances and decorative arts can help tell a story about energy and the environment.

Notes

1. Casey Smith and Michael Greshko, "UN Announces 23 New Nature Reserves while U.S. Removes 17," *National Geographic*, June 14, 2017, available at https://news.nationalgeographic.com/2017/06/unesco-new-biosphere-reserves-us-withdraws-reserves/ Accessed February 27, 2019. The seventeen sites that withdrew voluntarily include: the Aleutian Islands National Wildlife Refuge, U.S. Fish & Wildlife Service; Beaver Creek Experimental Watershed, US Forest Service; California Coast Ranges, University of California Natural Reserve System; Carolinian South-Atlantic, Non-Game and Heritage Trust (South Carolina); Central Plains Experimental Range, USDA Agricultural Research Service; Coram Experimental Forest, U.S. Forest Service; Desert Experimental Range, U.S. Forest Service; Fraser Experimental Forest, U.S. Forest Service; H. J. Andrews Experimental Forest, U.S. Forest Service and Oregon State University; Hubbard Brook, U.S. Forest Service; Konza Prairie Research Natural Area, Kansas State University; Land Between the Lakes, U.S. Forest Service; Niwot Ridge Mountain Research Station, University of Colorado; Noatak National Preserve, National Park Service; Stanislas-Tuolumne Experimental Forest, U.S. Forest Service; Three Sisters Wilderness, U.S. Forest Service; Virgin Islands, National Park Service.
2. Kate Moore, *Radium Girls: The Dark Story of America's Shining Women* (n.p.: Sourcebooks, 2017).
3. "Farmers Almanacs for the Years of Our Lord 1816 and 1817," Object No. 00.4.679, from the collection of The Henry Ford. The complete title, printed across the top of a piece of linen fabric: The FARMERS ALMANACS for the Years of our LORD / 1816 Being Bissextile or

Leap Year: & 40th to AMERICAN Independence, & 1817 Being the 1st after Bissextile or Leap Year. & 41st of AMERICA Independence. / CALCULATED FOR THE MERIDIANS OF MARYLAND. PENNSYLVANIA. VIRGINIA. KENTUCKY. AND TENNESSEE. Two flying eagles bearing American flags bookend the title. The twelve months of 1816 appear on the left-hand half (minus September, which was cut out of the lower left corner of the Almanac). The twelve months of 1817 appear on the right-hand half of the printed linen. Each month is illustrated with a sign of the zodiac. A decorative border of looped and intertwined vines in red and black runs around all four edges of the linen almanac.

4. *The Farmers and Dairyman's Almanac for the Year 1852* (Albany, NY: A.C. Grant & Co., 1852). Object No. 71.1.842, collection of The Henry Ford. The principal of the New York State Normal School, George R. Perkins (1812–1876), completed the "astronomical calculations." In addition to his calculations, the almanac included astrological signs for each month, the phases of the Moon, the sunrise and sunset times for the entire year, and historical events for each day of the year.

5. Richard Rhodes survey, *Energy: A Human History* (New York: Simon and Schuster, 2018).

6. Kerosene.

7. *Motor Boating* vol. 73, no. 1 (January 1944), 191.

8. Allis-Chalmer Manufacturing Company, Trade Catalog Collection, The Henry Ford, Pearton, Michigan.

9. *Farm Implements* 30, no. 2 (February 29, 1916), 32–33.

10. Jane Adams, *The Transformation of Rural Life: Southern Illinois, 1890–1990* (Chapel Hill: University of North Carolina Press, 1994), 25. See also Katherine Jellison, *Entitled to Power: Farm Women and Technology, 1913–1963* (Chapel Hill: University of North Carolina Press, 1993). Ronald R. Kline, *Consumers in the Country: Technology and Social Change in Rural America* (Baltimore: Johns Hopkins University Press, 2000). Ronald C. Tobey, *Technology as Freedom: The New Deal and the Electrical Modernization of the American Home* (Berkeley: University of California Press, 1996).

11. Delco-Light Farm Electric Plant, 1916–1947. http://www.doctordelco.com/Dr._Delco/Delco-Light/Delco-Light.html Accessed January 2, 2015. Delco-Light Plants. http://delcolight.com/index.html. Accessed January 2, 2015.

12. Adams, 151, 187. Rendleman lived in Union County.

13. Sparta [Illinois] *News Plaindealer*, April 14, 1939.

14. Adams, *The Transformation of Rural Life*, 153.

15. Sparta *News-Plaindealer*, May 19, 1939.

16. E. W. Lehmann and F. C. Kingsley. *Electric Power on the Farm* (Urbana: University of Illinois Agricultural Experiment Station, 1929). Ralph R. Parks, *Farm Electrification and your Wiring Problems* (Urbana, IL: College of Agriculture, Extension Service in Agriculture and Home Economics, [1939]). Harold Severson, *Architects of Progress: A Dynamic Story of the Electric Cooperatives as Service Organizations in Illinois* (n.p.: Association of Illinois Electric Cooperatives, n.d.).

17. Sparta *News Plain-dealer*, March 29, 1939.

18. "Agriculture 1950: Changes in Agriculture, 1900 to 1950," *1950 Census of Agriculture*, US Bureau of the Census. http://www2.census.gov/prod2/decennial/documents/41667073v5p6ch4.pdf. Accessed January 15, 2015.

19. Meghan L. O'Sullivan, *Windfall: How the New Energy Abundance Upends Global Politics and Strengthens America's Power* (New York: Simon and Schuster, 2017)

CHAPTER 7

Growing Food

Debra A. Reid and David D. Vail, with contributions by Aaron Hollis

THIS CHAPTER EMPHASIZES THE CONNECTION between people who need to eat and the places that provide them food. Growing food changes the environment. Every aspect of food production and distribution provides avenues to interpret the environment.

Debra Reid's *Interpreting Agriculture in Museums and Historic Sites* provides an introduction to the subject of agriculture, as well as more details about growing food for humans and for animal feed. Carol Kennis's chapter in *Interpreting Agriculture*, "You Can't Eat Gold," focuses on how farmers fed miners in semi-arid Colorado. It indicates the numerous layers of information essential to interpreting "a" whole story about the environment. The physical properties of the place conspired against food cultivation, including soils, sediments, and their fertility; climate and rainfall, topography, and available water supplies. Humans had to destroy American Indians and their ecosystems to secure the place. They applied their U.S. government land policy to secure private title to farmland. They had to modify the environment in numerous ways, including constructing irrigation systems and transportation routes. They grew crops suitable to their palette, rather than modifying practices to suite the indigenous flora and fauna. They imported agricultural implements to replace inadequate labor supplies.

Growing food occurs locally. Marketing and processing foods occurs locally but also regionally and globally. Families in citrus-growing regions of the United States relished the taste of fresh oranges, but they made their money from the crates of ripe fruit that they packed for shipment to consumers in the Midwest and East. International events also affected what families raised in their own yards. During World War I, the national government even mobilized school children to support the war effort by cultivating their own gardens to help provide food for residents in their own communities. Agricultural laborers mobilized local to affect change nationwide, as the United Farm Workers did through the

Postcard, "Picking Oranges in California," circa 1912. Image from the Collections of The Henry Ford.

Delano Grape Boycott of 1965–1970. In these instances, communication and transportation systems linked producers to consumers far distant from the fields.[1]

Production and distribution of food also has environmental consequences. Michael Pollan's *The Omnivore's Dilemma* makes the point about the irony, if not hypocrisy, of ordering an organic chicken from Virginia that is then flown to California for roasting. Michelle Moon and Cathy Stanton adopt a humanist approach to the topic in their book, *Public History and the Food Movement: Adding the Missing Ingredient*. They urge public historians to be more mindful of the environmental consequences of industrial farming, and they argue for more activism in food interpretation, hoping to prompt a sea change in how people farm.[2]

Museums and historic sites have numerous opportunities to explore relationships between growing food and the environment. Many artifacts support exhibitions on agricultural practices, farm production, and domestic processing of foodstuffs. The environmental factors in all levels of this production from the natural materials used in the house, to the fuel sources to heat the water, to the materials that made the ceramic or glass containers used in processing, and the feed consumed by the livestock slaughtered or the manure from livestock recycled as fertilizer. Furthermore, living history farms and open-air museums provide complete working environments that the public can explore. Michelle Moon's *Interpreting Food at Museums and Historic Sites* can provide additional guidance to developing food interpretation.[3]

In general, farmers grew many different foods to feed themselves and the livestock that they tended. Dee Brown summarized the variety in his description of Navajos culture in *Bury My Heart at Wounded Knee* (1971): "At points where the canyon widend to several hundred yards, the Navajos grazed sheep and goats on pasturage, or raised corn, wheat,

Promotional poster advertising the U.S. School Garden Army, World War I. Image from the Collections of The Henry Ford.

fruit, and melons on cultivated soil. They were especially proud of their peach orchards. . . . Water flowed pentifully through the canyon for most of the year, and there were enough cottonwood and box-elder trees to supply wood for fuel."[4] Such detail can launch further exploration of how farmers struck a balance between the need to feed themselves, within the confines of a place, and the need to trade the excess with others who needed it.

Fertilizer and Soil Nutrition

The theme of growing food can lure the general public into conversations about the environment and about modern agricultural practices, including the debate between organic and synthetic chemical applications. Steven Stoll, in *Larding the Lean Earth*, conveyed the interdependency of farmers, livestock, and soil fertility historically. Farmers in places with seasonal changes confined their livestock in barns or feedlots, and they turned the manure collected there into the nutrients that their soils needed to maintain plant growth. The practice constituted a seasonal ritual.[5]

During early spring, farmers cleaned out their barns and spread the manure on their crop fields before they plowed. This was a routine task, and carts and pitchforks the common tools to accomplish the job. During the early twentieth century, many bought manure spreaders to lessen the labor required to haul and spread.

Manure Spreader No. 3, manufactured by the International Harvester Company of Chicago in 1905. Image from the Collections of The Henry Ford.

Why would farmers spend money on a tool that looks more like a work of art than a utilitarian implement to do the job? Because the company created a spreader that doubled as a moving advertisement during a time when dairy farmers could justify buying equipment to spread a rapidly growing pile of manure.

During this Golden Age, roughly between 1900 and 1920, many farmers actually made money. They earned more for the commodities that they grew than it cost to produce them. Farmers used that capital to purchase more land and build new farm buildings, including dairy barns. They improved their herds by buying purebred livestock and reduced the strain on their backs with new agricultural equipment that helped them do their jobs more quickly.

The manure spreader reduced the labor required to move increasing amounts of manure from barns and stables and apply it to their arable land. The machine distributed the organic manure and its three essential elements (i.e., nitrogen, phosphorus, and potassium) more evenly than pitching manure from a cart onto the fields. The spreader answered the prayers of farm families with livestock housed in barns and stables and fields in need of nutrients.

A lot of changes have affected the seasonal routine of manure spreading. The known consequences of excessive runoff of fertilizers (including animal manure) into waterways concerns state departments of agriculture. In Wisconsin, the intensive dairy industry generates a lot of manure held in slurry pits or lagoons. On March 1, 2017, the Wisconsin Department of Agriculture, as part of its Manure Management Advisory System, issued a "Runoff Risk Advisory Forecast." The forecast helps farmers plan when to spread by consolidating weather forecasts, soil moisture ratings, snow cover, and GIS data to determine slope. These tools, combined, can help farmers determine what fields can hold the most manure to reduce the risk of run off.

The manure spreader has added value for furthering science, technology, engineering, and math (STEM) and science, technology, engineering, the arts, and math (STEAM) subjects, as well as Environmental Literacy. Engineers at International Harvester designed the mechanism. The company acquired ore that had to be refined and cast into a variety of parts, including chain links, cogs, gears, wheels, and rims. The company acquired trees that had to be milled into dimension lumber. Industrial laborers put the parts together and a crew painted the wooden box yellow and red, added pinstripes, and stenciled the manufacturer's name and model number prominently on its exterior. The work of art would not have held its new look for long; it certainly gave up its new spreader smell with the first pitchfork full.

Farm chemical technologies in the field offer strong historical examples for interpreting the environment, agriculture, and science. Throughout the United States, growing food meant protecting crops. Industrial technologies and farming techniques emerged in the early 1900s as a consequence of large-scale farming. That farms increasingly looked and acted like factories is key, but also important, as Deborah Fitzgerald has argued, is that these rural places remained complicated: "the sheer diversity of landscapes and climates in America, as well as the diversity of crops and livestock and humans, discredits the idea of a monolithic American agricultural aggregate."[6] Production was the goal, but it proceeded differently based on region, community, and crop and animal.

The history of agricultural chemicals is just as complicated. Diverse farming landscapes meant diverse approaches to using insecticides and herbicides. As David Vail points out in *Chemical Lands: Pesticides, Aerial Spraying, and Health in North America's Grasslands*, agricultural chemical artifacts can tell many different kinds of stories. Early attempts, for example, to combine plowing and protection came together in the "hopperdozzer," a kind of chemical plow that farmers invented in the Great Plains. Landowners designed these plows "to catch pests, especially grasshoppers, in poisoned meshes as they tilled their fields . . . which included mixing chemicals and tar together onto a tightly knitted mesh stretched over a plow blade or series of pans."[7]

With growing dependence on herbicides and insecticides after World War II, farmers looked to chemical companies and agricultural aviation pilots for help. Industrial agriculture, whether in the Midwest as J. L. Anderson traces in *Industrializing the Corn Belt: Agriculture, Technology, and Environment, 1945–1972*, in the South as Pete Daniel explores in *Toxic Drift: Pesticides and Health in the Post–World War II South*, or in the Southwest with Adam Tompkins's study *Ghostworkers and Greens: The Cooperative Campaigns of Farmworkers and Environmentalists for Pesticide Reform*, the complicated relationships among rural communities, agricultural labor, farm chemical technologies, and the health of the land and people can be told in powerful ways through documents and artifacts of these chemical technologies.[8]

Growing food also reflects cultural values. The case study by Aaron Hollis explores the ways that farmers in one area of Pennsylvania wrestled with the need to balance faith and community cohesion, with local food production, and regional commodity marketing. Aaron prepared this as part of the "Public History of Agriculture" working group, a part of the 2018 conference of the National Council on Public History. His case study explored changes in local food systems over time, the production and processing of feed for humans, feed for animals, and feed for both, and how local food systems and global commodity chains existed in one place. His contribution also indicates how presentism affects interpretation.

Whiskey and West Overton Village
Aaron Hollis

West Overton Village is in a unique position. It has existed as a historic site since 1928, but several factors have caused the relationship between the site and the public to sour. We have been working since the current director came on in 2012 to steer the organization in a better direction, striving to rebuild our relationship with our community and regain trust, while still trying to reinvent ourselves as a more modern, progressive site. Further, we are trying to convince our largely conservative community that whiskey is inherently agriculture. Mostly a challenge, whiskey has provided us with particular advantages in trying to generate interest in agriculture. With that said, because our efforts to interpret agriculture are a work in progress, the following overview includes projects that are underway and those we plan to implement in the future.

Our approach to public history and agriculture has three strata. The first stratum changes the appearance of the site to make it look and feel more like a living farm again. First, we partnered with a neighboring antique farm equipment organization to create a natural pollinator strip along a busy road. In the future, we hope to build on that partnership.

HOW TO

SPRAY & DUST

Air Applicator

INFORMATION SERIES

Vol.3

Aerial Applicator Institute, *How to Spray and Dust* (1951). Agricultural aviation pilots conducted their own toxicology experiments and designed training manuals for applying agricultural chemicals from the air. Image courtesy of the University of Nebraska-Kearney Archives and Special Collections, Calvin T. Ryan Library, Kearney, Nebraska.

Second, we recently collaborated with a local apiary group to organize the West Overton Beekeeping Association and will have bees on site within a year. Also, we are now working on partnering with a local 4-H organization to bring farm animals back to the site. Though there were at one time a variety of animals on the farm, we have chosen to begin with hogs. Hogs were important for food on the farm, but they were also critical to the complementary distilling business. To prevent waste, distillers fed used mash to hogs, which fattened them up over the distilling season. By year's end, the distillers would sell the hogs for further profit or keep them for their own family's food supply. Finally, after finding a diagram of the family's nineteenth-century garden in our archives, we are working with our volunteer garden society to at least partially recreate the family's garden.

Our second stratum of action is to create an agricultural co-op on sections of our forty acres of land. This is a new plan; we are currently in the planning stage and are searching for partners and funding. Our short-term goal for this co-op is to generate revenue and draw visitors. Long term, we hope the co-op will spark interest in visitors by enabling them to talk to modern farmers and purchase local produce in a cohesive public history network.

Third, we plan to offer new programming and events to build on our other projects. So far, we hope to include historic trades weekends, hands-on-history programs, and nineteenth-century cooking classes. As we develop these programs, it is a requirement that they do more than demonstrate. I want our audience to take part in the program and, if possible, leave with something in their hands.

Because these are all such new initiatives for us, we face many challenges and still have much to consider as we move forward. We are working on building relationships with our audience and community, so we do not yet know how they will respond to our new projects. Also, it is much easier said than done to start an agricultural co-op and, doing so, has proven to be a great challenge itself.

Above all, our most unique and most difficult connection to agriculture is whiskey. Because of the boom in craft distilling, we have a new audience that is interested in agriculture only because of its connection to whiskey. For those visitors interested in alcohol, we have the opportunity to share with them its roots in the region's culture, and they have so far proven interested and responsive. On the other hand, we are in danger of losing touch with our local, more conservative audience. Because of our recent push to open a distillery, some community members have attacked us and spoken out against us publicly for "embracing drunkenness." Though there are folks that will never accept our changes and connections between alcohol and agriculture, we are hoping our other agricultural projects will be a gateway for us to have that conversation with our community.

Ultimately, because we are not building on decades-old programming, we have the opportunity to create modern, progressive programming and to get it right the first time. We can increase visitation and simultaneously engage our visitors in deeper conversations, encouraging them to connect with ongoing issues about health, sustainability, and even alcohol. If we find a responsible way to do so, a goal of mine for our agriculture and alcohol programming would be to connect that conversation to our region's modern opioid epidemic. Because alcohol is often considered a gateway drug, that conversation would be a difficult one for us to embrace but is a conversation our community needs to have. We can explore issues of gender and ethnicity at our site and challenge the patriarchal stereotypes of agriculture by researching and incorporating the role of women, children, and the village's two hundred inhabitants into the second and third strata of our project.

Conclusion

Cultivating crops for home consumption and for market tends to dominate food and environment interpretation in museums and historic sites. Great potential exists for historical institutions to embrace their natural environments, and even their cultivated ones, to talk about foraging for food. This can include berry picking, mushroom hunting, and collecting greens in spring and nuts in the fall. Numerous indigenous plants supplemented human diets, and history institutions can often launch interpretation of the environment by taking this approach.

Cultivating crops for human and livestock feed provides countless opportunities that can be overwhelming. When in doubt, return to the main ideas identified through research and itemize resources to tell specific food-environment stories. Each day of the week could feature a different artifact and theme. Articulating the goals and objectives for each and summarizing talking points about them can launch dynamic interpretation.

Notes

1. Matt Garcia, *A World of Its Own: Race, Labor, and Citrus in the Making of Greater Los Angeles, 1900-1970* (Chapel Hill: University of North Carolina Press, 2001). See also Thomas Okie, *The Georgia Peach: Culture, Agriculture, and Environment in the American South* (New York: Cambridge University Press, 2016); Shane Hamilton, *Trucking Country: The Road to America's Wal-Mart Economy* (Princeton, NJ: Princeton University Press, 2008).
2. Michael Pollan, *The Omnivore's Dilemma: A Natural History of Four Meals* (New York: The Penguin Press, 2006); Michelle Moon and Cathy Stanton, *Public History and the Food Movement: Adding the Missing Ingredient* (New York: Routledge, 2018).
3. Michelle Moon, *Interpreting Food at Museums and Historic Sites* (Lanham, Maryland: Rowman & Littlefield, 2016)
4. Dee Brown, *Bury My Heart at Wounded Knee: An Indian History of the American West* (New York: Bantam Books, 1970), 24.
5. Steven Stoll, *Larding the Lean Earth: Soil and Society in Nineteenth-Century America* (New York: Hill and Wang, 2002).
6. Deborah Fitzgerald, *Every Farm a Factory: The Industrial Ideal in American Agriculture* (New Haven, CT: Yale University Press, 2003), 5.
7. David D. Vail, *Chemical Lands: Pesticides, Aerial Spraying, and Health in North America's Grasslands since 1945* (Tuscaloosa: University of Alabama Press, 2018), 16–17.
8. For a more comprehensive survey of these works, see chapter 1 and the bibliographic essay.

CHAPTER 8

Traveling and Trading

Debra A. Reid, with contributions by
Ann E. Birney and Joyce M. Thierer

Some years ago. . . . I thought I would sail about a little and see the watery part of the
world. It is a way I have of driving off the spleen. . . . I quietly take to the ship.

HERMAN MELVILLE, *MOBY DICK* (1851), [1]

NATURAL FORCES CREATED THE LANDSCAPES that all humans navigate as they live their lives. As glaciers expanded, they churned up soil and rocks. As they receded, they deposited this rubble into features that geographers call moraines, unstratified soil, sediment, and rocks. Glaciers also left parts behind, and these fragments, as they melted, left kettles or sediment-filled depressions. The wind played a role in landscape formation, as well, depositing particulates at the edges of glaciers, which soil scientists describe as loess. Each of these affected trails that humans navigated since prehistoric times, and each influenced the agricultural practices that farmers adopted as suitable to topography, soil types, and climate.

This chapter explores those pathways and thoroughfares. Cow paths followed a landscapes' contours historically. Humans eventually deviated from the path and moved earth and blasted mountains to create more direct paths. Elevated railway systems in places like Cincinnati conveyed the public up and down steep hillsides, while the railway system affirmed national investment in a private enterprise. Tunnels and bridges facilitated movement. A photographic essay features canals and railways and other engineering feats that helped move natural resources to production centers and manufactured goods back to consumers.

Museums and historic sites hold evidence of private and public efforts to manipulate the landscape and facilitate travel and trade in the public trust. Some preserve complete canals and railways and runways and cargo planes. Some operate canal boats and preserve bridges that carried canals over creeks. Most have artifacts that either facilitated movement—wag-

Mount Adams Incline Railway, Cincinnati, Ohio, 1907. Image from the Collections of The Henry Ford.

ons or other freight hauling equipment—or have evidence of the objects distributed to consumers via sailing vessels, railway lines, Conestoga wagons, and eighteen-wheelers. No matter the scale, artifacts bridge the distance between the subject of travel and trade and the environmental context.

Private Investment or Public Infrastructure

English common law protected the public's right of passage through private lands. Rights of way continue to apply, but public access and private ownership often generate tension. So too do debates about public investment in private transportation. Government support of private railway companies provides one example. The national government granted land to the companies that the companies then sold through public land sales. The companies retained the proceeds and used the funding to develop rail lines. Entrepreneurs positioned themselves strategically at places where steam engines needed to restock coal and take on water. The private-public venture facilitated antebellum Manifest Destiny and displacement and annihilation of indigenous peoples.

During the 1820s, political debates pitted Whigs, nee National Republicans, against Democrats. Whigs argued for national investment in public transportation systems and infrastructure. The US Army Corps of Engineers, stationed at West Point, engineered the public infrastructure, which remains foundational for many transportation systems across the eastern United States.[1]

Romanticized views of the Military Academy at West Point often featured the Hudson River, which facilitated travel and trade from the largest city in the nation, New York, up to Albany, and then west on the Erie Canal.

The Military Academy at West Point provided much inspiration. William Guy Wall (1792–1864?) painted West Point from various vantage points. The Irish-born painter spent the summer of 1820 traversing 212 miles of the Hudson River's 315-mile course. John Hill (1770–1850), a master printer, created aquatints of twenty of Wall's body of work, and New York printer, Henry Megarey, published them between 1821 and 1825. Wall's paintings, transformed into aquatints by Hill, depicted the buildings and landscapes of West Point and its environs. Details showed men climbing rocks, a sidewheel steamship navigating the Hudson River, and sailing ships and even rowboats at the river's edge. The scenes became

Platter, circa 1840. Depicts steam ships and sailing vessels on the Hudson River at West Point. Made by Enoch Wood & Sons, Burslem, England. Inscribed Larsen 73 on bottom. Image from the Collections of The Henry Ford.

popular as inexpensive prints of the views and tablewares with transfer prints of the scenes appeared on the market.[2]

Other painters copied Wall's work. Thomas Chambers made a living by painting scenes of West Point and the Hudson River. Shorelines, rock outcrops, and hill orientations allowed viewers to pinpoint the location of the artist. Many painters, including Chambers, set up their canvases on the northwestern tip of Constitution Island, looking south and west toward West Point.

Why did so many paint West Point? The site became popular because of its strategic location and military significance. The United States built bulwarks on the Constitution Island in 1778 during the Revolutionary War, and in 1802 the U.S. government opened West Point Military Academy. The military academy hired artists because accurate depictions of landscapes played a critical in military strategy and in postbattle reports. Many faculty with artistic aptitude taught at West Point including artist Seth Eastman. His body of work includes a view he painted of the Hudson River from West Point. Eastman may have taken inspiration from earlier paintings by William Guy Wall and engraved by John Hill.[3]

West Point's beautiful location inspired traveling artists as well, and their landscapes took on added significance during the era of national expansion. Printers created lithographs from the paintings and consumers framed and hung them in their houses. Some also made their way onto transfer prints used to decorate ceramics. These helped publicize and popularize civil engineering undertaken during the tenure of West Point Commandant Sylvanus Thayer (1817–1838?) as he fulfilled his charge to build a national transportation infrastructure. The landscapes became public reminders of the public investment needed to facilitate travel and trade.

Picturing Trade Infrastructure

Paintings and photographic prints capture routine events of moving cargo overland. They also featured the engineering feats required to facilitate inland water transportation without benefit of navigable waterways.

Canal building included aqueduct and bridge construction to carry canal water over seasonal creeks or rivers. These maintained the grade of the canal and helped ensure consistent seasonal travel.

Canals existed to carry goods to markets. Many canals continued into metropolitan areas to deposit their cargo and to collect new cargo.

Locks held water and boats and moved them up or down to the next stage of the canal. A series of photographs at a lock on the Morris Canal in New Jersey shows how a series of water-driven inclined planes to move barges full of anthracite coal across northern New Jersey from mines to factories.

Interpretation of travel and trade can also incorporate programs designed to explore centers of trade that have declined if not evaporated from the landscape. The case study by Ann E. Birney and Joyce Thierer features Main Street, the business center of most communities, in the small Kansas town of Allen.

Canal bridge, Chesapeake and Ohio Canal, over a river at Williamsport, Maryland. Image from the Collections of The Henry Ford.

The Lower Locks, Chesapeake and Ohio Canal), Washington, D.C. Image from the Collections of The Henry Ford.

Boat ascending inclined plane of Morris and Essex Canal, Boonton, New Jersey, circa 1900. Detroit Publishing Company, P.DPC.011523; THF204090. Image from the Collections of The Henry Ford.

Morris and Essex Canal near Hopatcong, New Jersey, circa 1900, Detroit Publishing Company. P.DPC.011551 THF204078. Image from the Collections of The Henry Ford.

Main Street: Night at the Museum
Ann E. Birney and Joyce Thierer, Ride into History

Ride into History conducts week-long camps, usually with young people, in addition to the week-end intensive workshops that are primarily for adults. The camps were created to supplement week-long Chautauquas in which a national theme is brought to a local setting and scholars come from across the country to portray national figures. Our Youth Chautauqua Camps bring rising fifth through ninth graders together to research and portray local figures, people who lived and worked in their community while also within the context of the national scene.

One question we ask local historians as they prepare for our arrival is, "How did the national event(s) affect the local scene, and who might be good examples of people whose lives were changed by those national events?" The question could also be, "How did the environment affect the local scene?" How did the decisions made in Washington, D.C., Chicago, or Tokyo change lives in Fall City, Nebraska?

On the last of five days, the young people each cross the Chautauqua stage and present a short first-person narrative. After the last Young Chautauquan has greeted the audience in character, talked about what was happening in his or her life, and then excused himself or herself, they all line up on stage and invite questions, first as historic figures and then as scholars.

A take-off on this program is Night at the Museum, where the search for history's stories begins not with a single theme and local people but with intriguing museum artifacts. Museum staff introduce a group of not more than twenty young people to some intriguing artifacts for which provenance is known. The young scholars research the artifact, getting to know its physical being, its donor history, and how it is similar to and different from other artifacts. They will likely interview someone who made or donated the object. Then they decide which of the actors in the artifact's history they would like to become to tell that object's story and what setting (place, date) they would choose. For instance, a young man selected a shell casing from World War I that had been artistically altered. He talked to the grandson of the soldier about the meaning of this object in his family. The result was that he portrayed the grandson's father as a boy who could talk to us about the shell there on the back porch, but we were not to touch it and what was realistic was that he kept hoping that his older brother would come out because he knew more about it.

This happens in the format of tours about every thirty minutes that are framed by a story about a vintage docent who is looking forward to taking all night to tell us everything she knows about every object in the museum but instead is constantly being interrupted by costumed interpreters (a mortician calls our attention to a child-sized portable cooling table and passes out his card; the sound of a basketball hitting the cement floor leads to the discovery around the corner of a girl whose team earned the trophy in the case; tapping sounds lead to an archeologist who explains some of his finds; a cradle begins rocking and the mother of the child is soon telling us about bringing the cradle and the children out here on a covered wagon). Stagnant objects come to life *and* their environment does, too. The lucky people who signed up for the tours now see the museum building as harboring ceaseless surprises, surprises that continue after the museum is closed for the night.

We also designed this manner of pop-up exhibits for a very tiny town. Our North Lyon County Historical Performance Troupe is challenged with interpreting the history of seven small communities with a lot of farmland in between each. We took on the town of Allen a few years back because they had contributed most of the troupe that summer, and Hunter was excited because the summer before he had interpreted an Admire mechanic, and as he talked with his own family members, he discovered that his great grandfather had been a mechanic in his hometown of Allen. We found a beautiful memory map and began with it, a printed town history, and the stories of the coffee drinkers.

Most of the buildings had burned down, and there was concern that people would forget that Allen once had a bank, a newspaper, a hotel, a hardware store, and a grocery—none of which exist now. So the important thing was to repopulate the town, to bring the environs back to life. What were the stories that would bring back those buildings, and what historic figures should tell them? We ended up with a flatbed trailer towed by a pickup truck on which audience members rode who were best off not walking the four blocks of Main Street (two blocks from the bank past the lumber yard down to Frizzell's Shop and two blocks back).

As in Night at the Museum, an empty street would suddenly come to life as, for instance, Doc Edwards stepped out of his office (no longer in existence, but that is what a willing suspension of disbelief can accomplish) to explain that he was off to take care of one of their neighbors. A couple of girls played a jazz tune on their trumpets, but when they saw the Methodist minister, who also had the mortuary and the coffin and furniture concession, they disappeared, and sure enough he demanded to know where those girls went who were playing that nasty music. We learned as we rode or walked up the street that the frame hotel had just burned, and Delsey Spade had lost not only her business but also her home and that of her family.

Just as the museum had come to life, the environs of Allen, Kansas, population 177 more or less, had changed with those stories. The empty lots are not so empty.

Conclusion

The energy expended to literally move mountains transformed the flow of natural resources to processing plants and from plants to consumers. The canals, railway lines, roadways, and airways transformed mobility for people and goods. The case studies in this chapter barely touch the tip of the iceberg of environmental topics related to travel and trade. Literally every artifact in a museum or historic site could launch the topic.

Notes

1. Examples include http://www.loc.gov/pictures/item/2011661799/resource/ and another 1820s view: https://www.loc.gov/resource/ppmsca.50674/; and another: https://www.loc.gov/resource/ds.10808/; and 1830s view: http://www.loc.gov/pictures/resource/pga.00210/.

2. No. 16 of the Hudson River Port Folio. C size. New York: Published by Henry I. Megarey between 1821 and 1825. Prints and Photographs Division, Library of Congress, Washington, D.C.

3. The Hill aquatint of the Wall painting comparable to Eastman's work is in the collection of the New York Public Library, available at: https://digitalcollections.nypl.org/items/510d47d9-7e48-a3d9-e040-e00a18064a99 and in the Library of Congress collection at: http://www.loc.gov/pictures/item/2011661799/. Accessed February 26, 2019.

CHAPTER 9

Building Things

Debra A. Reid,

with contributions by Nora Pat Small

UMANS BUILD THINGS WITH ORGANIC MATERIALS—carbon-based compounds, such as wood, plant materials, and animal horn, hide, and bone to name a few. They also build things with inorganic materials—stone, ore, and sand to name a few. Vernacular architecture and the built environment provide evidence of the work of local builders who used local materials and standard dimensions and construction techniques to shelter their families and neighbors. Builders incorporated natural heating and cooling systems in structures. They devised lighting systems to defy the natural course of daylight and dark and readily adopted synthetic materials with a goal of overcoming natural decay. Floor coverings, such as linoleum and synthetic carpet, vinyl siding, and asbestos and asphalt shingles, add the finishing touches to home interiors and exteriors. Powerful lobbying groups, trade unions, and mortgage systems developed around this elemental need for shelter. Opportunities to interpret the transformation of natural resources into built things abound.

Folklorist Henry Glassie explained that "history must depend on artifactual analysis." To understand the history of the region of initial English settlement in North America, the Chesapeake Bay colonies of Maryland, Virginia, and North Carolina, he conducted research in the field. He sought out houses because "of all classes of artifacts, architecture would be the most efficient guide to past culture because of its universality, tenacity, complexity, and fixedness."[1]

Anthropologists stress the utility of material culture to comprehend the ecology of building practices. The artifact resulted from the collision of the natural and the cultural. Technology is "the means by which the natural literally becomes the cultural, by which the substances won from nature become useful to man."[2]

Houses take form from materials readily available. In places with limited wood supplies, humans molded mud into adobe and clay into brick. They used stone and brick for foundations and walls and clay tile or marsh grasses for roofing material. In areas with plentiful wood, they used pliable poles to frame lodges, and they covered them with bark, tree boughs, or mats made from grasses or other organic materials. Others processed logs into temporary structures or permanent houses, or they built houses and barns with heavy timber frames, covered in riven or sawn clapboards. Wooden shakes covered roofs and lathe held plaster in place. Thus, houses and other structures provide evidence of use of environmental resources.

Studying the structures in their original locations confirms the relationships that existed between builders, residents, and their environments historically. After the introduction of air conditioning and synthetic mass-produced building materials, however, these direct connections between buildings and landscapes and relations between people and their environment become less obvious. John Brinckerhoff Jackson addressed both in his studies of vernacular landscapes. In contrast to the house types of a culture group in the Chesapeake Bay, Jackson remarked on the most extraordinary variety of types of dwellings in New Mexico, representing many culture groups and eras of construction and use. Villages of small houses, built by people with little money and big families, grew up near water sources in open rangeland where the livestock owned by all in the village grazed. They built acequia to irrigate their small fields of corn, beans, and chilis. The adobe homes with dirt floors, corrugated tin roofs, outdoor toilets, and no running water or electricity cost little to build. The traditional houses dominated in New Mexico until after World War II when trailers began to appear within villages or in new trailer parks. These low-costs structures came off an assembly line and not from local mud, but they became homes for people living in rural New Mexico.[3]

Lighthouse, Manistee, Michigan, 2012. Placard on the lighthouse (unmanned) reads: "To energize the fog / signal key your / microphone five / times on Channel 83A. Photograph by Debra A. Reid.

Structures afforded protection to humans, providing cover in inclement weather and places of rest from the elements. Some structures, such as lighthouses, mitigated environmental hazards. As Nora Pat Small explains, the U.S. government invested in the construction of a system of lights to support national economic growth.

Local preservationists rally to protect these markers on the spot where ocean or lake meets land. These sites provide ample opportunity to discuss technological innovation, economics of trade, and communication between captains of ocean- or lake-going vessels and lighthouse keepers. The natural environment is a main actor in these interpretations and not a backdrop to the story of building things.

US Government Mitigation of Coastal Hazards through Lighthouse Stations
Nora Pat Small, Eastern Illinois University

The government of the newly formed United States recognized immediately that a well-lighted coast was instrumental in ensuring the safety of mariners and of investments in ships and goods. Congress passed the first Lighthouses Act in 1789, which was one of its first official actions. In short order, the government assumed responsibility for lighting the coasts, thus building, literally, a federal presence throughout the Eastern Seaboard. The lighthouses underwritten by the new federal government attested to the widely acknowledged power of commerce to strengthen the nation; they may have reminded some that the central government played an instrumental role in providing the means by which commercial interests thrived.

In the first generation following the ratification of the new Constitution, Americans embarked on building campaigns that changed the face of public and private landscapes everywhere. Banks, churches, state legislatures, newly chartered corporations, and speculators engaged architects, engineers, and surveyors for major building commissions that reshaped old cities and embodied the ambitions of new ones; for surveys that led to the construction of roads and canals; and to the development of hitherto "unimproved" land. The United States was transformed from a small-scale, locally centered, preindustrial enterprise, to an extralocal, industrialized market economy that could not exist without the new and sprawling transportation systems (including its system of coastal lights), the mills of unprecedented size, the vast acres newly opened to agriculture, and the frenetic harbors. Farmers, merchants, and artisans hired masons, carpenters, mechanics, and millwrights to improve their holdings and to enlarge or build anew their workshops, homes, mill seats, farm buildings. The necessity of lighthouses to a great commercial nation was undeniable, and in a landscape dominated by wooden buildings and structures, stone and brick lighthouses stood out, whether viewed from land or water.

Lighthouse towers had to fulfill certain practical needs: they had to be able to be seen day and night a certain distance from the shore, they had to be constructed in such a manner as to enable a lighthouse keeper to reach and maintain the lantern, and they had to be able to withstand the more or less destructive natural elements encountered along the shoreline. Standards in lighthouse design were already well established by the time the federal government took over their construction. Towers were cylindrical, square, or octagonal, tall or short, masonry or wood. Specifications of material, size, and shape derived from local circumstance, including the availability of natural and human resources.

When Stephen Pleasonton, fifth auditor of the Treasury, was assigned the task of overseeing navigational aids in 1820, he inherited a system that had come to rely on a patchwork of customs collectors, local contractors, and entrenched practices. Pleasonton's thirty-two-year career as general superintendent of lighthouses encompassed an era of tremendous change in building technologies, engineering expertise, the size of the lighthouse system, and the consequent need for more centralized oversight of navigational aids.

Despite the attempts to standardize designs and processes, the Lighthouse Service found itself embattled in the 1830s. Architects, engineers, and Congress grew increasingly frustrated with the Lighthouse Service as it remained mired in old ways of doing business even in the face of calls for a more modern approach to coastal lighting. The benefits that had accrued to the building program as a result of standardized plans and processes, the efficiencies gained through reliance on long-standing traditions in maritime building, stood in the way of innovation and ultimately drove Congress to replace the Lighthouse Service with the Lighthouse Board in 1852. With that act, lighthouses officially became the purview of engineers rather than architects and building contractors, part and parcel of a modern industrial world and industrialized building methods. The increasing disenchantment with the Lighthouse Establishment that culminated in the restructuring of the entire system in 1852 paralleled the growth of U.S.-trained engineers. Lighthouses and other aids to navigation presented interesting technological problems to this expanding group of U.S. engineers, especially as the Lighthouse Establishment was called on to light less stable shoreline or inaccessible, wave-swept rocks.

Lighting the coasts, harbors, and waterways of the United States between 1789 and 1852 served the needs of government, commerce, and mariners. On a practical level, goods and people were brought safely to port, but the construction of coastal lights by the U.S. government also demonstrated the nation's trustworthiness as a trading partner, ready to accept the responsibilities of membership in the global network of commerce. The concerted effort by the federal government to undertake this major building campaign provided evidence of the new nation's stability and strength to citizens and foreigners alike. The prominent positions of towers along coasts and in harbors, the primary highways and population centers of the early republic, ensured high visibility not from the water alone but also to that vast portion of the U.S. populace tied in one way or another to seafaring.

The environmental conditions that confronted lighthouse designers and builders did not change markedly over the course of the nineteenth century, nor did the necessity of ensuring safe passage for freight and people, but politics, the building trades, and technology did. The Lighthouse Service's and Lighthouse Board's responses to the environmental challenges of coastal lighting were, of necessity, made in and shaped by those contexts. Never a simple functionalist calculus, their responses to the natural environment changed with the times.

Questions to consider when studying Lighthouse Stations in the context of environmental history include:

When was the lighthouse built? If there are auxiliary structures, when were they built? Were any of the structures ever altered? When? Why?

Was there another way that that segment of the coast could have been lighted? Why was this lighthouse design employed?

What materials were used to build the lighthouse and auxiliary buildings? Were they locally sourced?

How do the lighthouse and light station relate, physically or geographically, to the surrounding neighborhood or community? How did one access the lighthouse? Is the lighthouse remote? Do the lighthouse and light station share building materials with the surrounding community?

Sources to Consult

Much has been written about lighthouses, ranging from artful coffee-table treatments to historical monographs. That said, anyone wanting to delve into the history of a particular lighthouse or lighthouses in general will find they must consult the National Archives and Records Administration, Record Group 26, Records of the United States Coast Guard. For an analysis of foundational legislation, see *The Lighthouse Act of 1789*, prepared under direction of Walter J. Stewart, secretary of the Senate (1991), and for a late-nineteenth-century history of the internal workings of the office that constructed lighthouses, see *History, Organization and Functions of the Office of the Supervising Architect of the Treasury Department*, compiled by Rufus H. Thayer (1886). Francis Ross Holland's classic, *America's Lighthouses: Their Illustrated History since 1716* (1972) is a good general source, but Sara E. Wermeil's *Lighthouses* (2006) is even more thorough and provides easy access to Library of Congress lighthouse photos in the accompanying disc. There are numerous works that deal with histories of individual lighthouses, but there are also publications that examine groups of lighthouses that can help put individual lighthouses into a broader context, for example, Patrick Hornberger and Linda Turbyville, *Forgotten Beacons: The Lost Lighthouses of Chesapeake Bay* (1997) and J. Candace Clifford and Mary Louise Clifford, *Nineteenth Century Lights: Historic Images of American Lighthouses* (2000).

Most lighthouses support exploration of additional environmental themes beyond those addressed by Nora Pat Small. The two lighthouses interpreted by the Twin Lights Historical Society existed originally to increase shipping safety near Sandy Hook, New Jersey, and support national defense at a critical point, the main entrance to New York harbor. The historical society stresses other innovations that occurred over the lighthouses histories to increase relevance for today's visitors. As the website explains:

> A startling number of scientific and cultural firsts have taken place on this site a tribute to its powerful presence on the American landscape, both literally and figuratively. Indeed, the next time you answer your cell phone, checkout at a grocery store, land safely at an airport, create a family tree, or recite the Pledge of Allegiance, you are connecting with the people and events that have made the Twin Lights such a profoundly special place.[4]

Twin Lights power station (1909, left) and south tower (right), overlooking Sandy Hook, New Jersey, March 2015. Photograph by Debra A. Reid.

Congress authorized the construction of the Twin Lights in 1828, in a strategic location on the high point of the Navesink Highlands, overlooking Sandy Hook, New Jersey. The Fresnel lenses installed in the beacons in 1841 were the first installed in the United States. These, according to the Historical Society, "sparked a scientific revolution . . . that led to everything from checkout scanners and camera lenses to solar collectors and fiber-optics cables."[5]

Twin Lights helped stage other firsts in the history of technology and in social and cultural history, but the topic of energy relates most directly to this book. The site included a power station that generated the electricity for the Fresnel lights in the towers. The exhibit sign reads: "Electric Power Station: Twin Lights was the first primary seacoast light in the United States to use electricity. This building contained equipment for generating electrical power for the light that produced 25,000,000 candlepower, by far the most powerful in the United States. This building, completed in 1909, replaced an earlier wooden structure built in 1898."

Two Hornsby-Akroyd engines (patented and described as a "safety-oil engine," that is, an engine that burned kerosene fuel) turned the dynamos that generated electricity. The sole licensee and manufacturer was R. Hornsby & Sons, Ltd., Grantham, England. In 1917 the engines needed repair, and complaints about noise and excessive light prompted the Lighthouse Board to replace the Hornsby and Akroyd engine and electric light with an incandescent oil vapor lamp. The board had the engine dismantled in 1921. The lighthouse used oil vapor until 1924 when a commercial supply of electricity became available.

The natural resources that helped build Twin Lights included quarried stone, sand for window glass and for high-grade optics in the Fresnel lens, wood for building materials, clay for the brick for support structures, metal for the engines, and kerosene for the fuel (and probably gasoline to fire the engine). These resources began as tools to facilitate maritime travel and trade; they have become a tourist destination.

Conclusion

As an exercise in interpreting the environment, list the organic and inorganic materials visible in your historic structures. You can also identify the synthetic materials, which launches us into an exploration of the environmental consequences of extracting ores and other nonrenewable resources such as oil and processing them into house parts. Asphalt shingles, vinyl siding, particle board with formaldehyde, linoleum, and interiors furnished with acrylic carpet and foam padding, Naugahyde, polyester curtains, and Tyvek create hermetically sealed homes that offgas as synthetics slowly degrade. Each of these have their own histories of extraction, transportation, industrial processing, and marketing and distribution chains before arriving at the construction site. Each museum has examples to start conversations about the cost of building things.

Notes

1. Henry Glassie, *Folk Housing in Middle Virginia: A Structural Analysis of Historic Artifacts* (Knoxville: University of Tennessee Press, 1975), 14.
2. Glassie, *Folk Housing in Middle Virginia*, 122. Glassie synthesized the work of Claude Lévi-Strauss, Robert Redfield, David Pye, and Robert F. G. Spier to make these points.
3. John Brinckerhoff Jackson, *The House in the Vernacular Landscape, in The Making of the American Landscape*, 355–69.
4. Twin Lights Historical Society website: http://www.twinlightslighthouse.com/history.html. Accessed October 1, 2018.
5. Twin Lights Historical Society.

CHAPTER 10

Preserving and Conserving Natural Landscapes

Debra A. Reid, with contributions by
Chris Sommerich, Catherine Schmitt,
Tim Garrity, Maureen Fournier, and
Caitlin McDonough MacKenzie

PRESERVING AND CONSERVING NATURAL landscapes seems a fitting place to end because it is the first thing that may come to mind when many think about interpreting the environment. Readers, now conversant with numerous other ways to engage with environmental themes, can put natural landscape preservation into larger context. This can help them wrestle with the conundrum that Paul Wapner raises in *Living through the End of Nature: The Future of American Environmentalism*. He argues that "we have so tamed, colonized, and contaminated the natural world that safeguarding it from humans is no longer an option. Humanity's imprint is now everywhere and all efforts to preserve "nature'" require extensive human intervention." What is the next step for environmentalism. The North American Association for Environmental Education (NAAEE) advocates for programming that creates environmentally literate citizens. Museums and historic sites can do their share by helping guests learn more about conservation.[1]

Several studies itemize the factors that motivated scientists, conservationists, and concerned landowners to preserve the environment. Some spaces and places survived relatively unscathed because of their remoteness or imposing nature. Others survived because owners gifted property to local, county, municipal, or state conservation agencies rather than see more acreage succumb to suburban and exburban sprawl. Whatever their origin tale, these preserved and conserved landscapes take many forms, from national parks and heritage

'Typical campsite, Camp Iroquois, Glen Eyrie, Lake George, New York, 1911. Image from the Collections of The Henry Ford.

corridors to metro-parks, nature centers, and forest preserve districts. Their stories convey the benefit of partnering with special-interest groups and government agencies to secure funding, protective legislation, and broad-based commitment essential to sustain the preservation of historic and natural environments.

Conservation, Forest Management, and Interpretation

Managers at The Henry Ford's Greenfield Village have partnered with the U.S. Forest Service for years to support interpretation of a U.S. forest ranger. The program began to interpret the relationship of the U.S. Forest Service, a division of the U.S. Department of Agriculture, and working environments, particularly forests on public lands.

Management of U.S. forests began during the 1870s. Employees of the Forest Service managed timber stands, watched for fires, provided some local law enforcement, and helped standardize board feet and cutting protocols.

The Forest Service followed societal norms that linked masculinity to the outdoors and femininity to domestic duties. Civil servants considered the job of a forest ranger as physically demanding and personally risky. They considered it "man's work" and not suitable for women, whose delicate constitutions made them incapable of performing such tasks. Such

Abigail, with Orville the horse, helping make a tour group's day in Greenfield Village, August 1, 2018. Photograph by Debra A. Reid.

gendered hiring practices persisted with few exceptions. Not until 1957 did the Forest Service hire its first female forester. Slowly, the Forest Service increased the number of women in professional positions as women's liberation and the feminist movement matured. The first female chief of the Forest Service, Abigail R. "Gail" Kimbell, served from 2007 to 2009. And for the first time, Greenfield Village added a lady ranger in 2018 to increase the lessons taught through this popular program.

The Forest Service hired male staff to work in administrative offices. As more and more men took on the position of ranger, the Forest Service began hiring women to fill these administrative positions. These first jobs were mainly clerical positions, serving as secretaries and typists. Women later worked in technical drawing, data collecting, and data analysis.

As the Forest Service grew, the demand for rangers increased. The first women to experience the life that a forest ranger lived was married to one. Spouses volunteered in various capacities if their husbands already worked for the Forest Service.

Women were first hired to be fire lookouts to help the rangers in maintaining the national forests. Hallie Daggett, the first female fire lookout, got the job because no qualified males applied. Beginning in the summer of 1913, she worked at Eddy's Gulch Lookout Station atop Klamath Peak. She served as a lookout for fourteen years.[2]

Women were hired as fire watchers only when wartime duty affected society's opinion about jobs women could hold. During times of peace and economic depression, public sentiment swung the opposite direction, and the pressure to keep men employed reduced opportunities for women. Women performed the same job as a ranger but did not receive the title.

Women had few tools at their disposal. Iva Gruenewald described her lookout on Tumwater Mountain near Leavenworth, Washington, in the Wenatchee National Forest: "There was no cabin, or lookout tower but a tent down in a sheltered place among a few trees. My 'office' was a very rocky higher peak, no shelter from wind, or sun, just a map, a phone and an alidade to locate fires in all four directions."[3]

The North Pacific Region of the U.S. Forest Service (Region 6) reported on popular interest in female fire fighters. For instance, *The Woman's Home Companion and the American Magazine* described "the wild, isolated, odd, interesting, unusual, brave, courageous, noble, primal, patriotic, western, romantic life that these ladies lead."[4]

Gladys Murray, a woman lookout at the Columbia Lookout on the Colville National Forest during World War I, located and reported fifty fires. Her creature comforts come second to finding fires. She hauled drinking water only between dusk and nightfall, when fires were most difficult to spot.[5]

Fire lookouts were originally not meant to fight fires; however, some women did in emergency situations (i.e., during wartime):

> The Fremont has a woman who is not only a lookout but also a fireman. Mrs. Bertha Covert is her name, and she is stationed on Dog Mountain. She has demonstrated her ability in fighting forest fires on three different occasions, and when not otherwise engaged is not averse to using the pick and shovel with good effect on roads and trails.[6]

During World War I, some women were employed as patrolwomen. Their jobs were similar to those of male rangers:

> Miss Helen McCormick, of Eugene, has been employed to patrol in the Upper McKenzie River country. . . . Her district will embrace the territory between Blue River village and the Blue River mines [about 10 miles]. She will cover this district on horseback; carrying an emergence camping outfit, to be prepared for the nights which must necessarily be spent along the trail.[7]

A historian with the U.S. Forest Service, Gerald W. Williams, described these as "the only accounts found, thus far, of women employed in field-going positions in the national forests in something other than a lookout position in these early years."[8]

Relatively little analysis of the history of women in the Forest Service exists. Historians and rangers continue to look at diaries, letters, and journals to further expand our knowledge on the subject. Some secondary sources that can help put gender and Forest Service employment into context includes Marcia Myers Bonta, *American Women Afield: Writings by Pioneering Women Naturalists* (1991); Elers Koch, *Forty Years a Forester, 1903–1943* (1998), Susan R. Schrepfer, *Nature's Altars: Mountains, Gender, and American Environmentalism* (2005); and Roderick Frazier Nash, *Wilderness and the American Mind*, 5th edition (2014).

First Female Rangers with the National Park Service

Women found jobs in other professional "outdoor" occupations equally elusive. The National Park Service (NPS), within the U.S. Department of the Interior, hired its first female naturalist, Herma Baggley, in 1929 to work at Yellowstone National Park. The first female director of the NPS, Fran P. Mainella, served from 2001 to 2006.

Tourists on road-trip vacations to western mountain ranges or national parks may have encountered these first female employees. The contrast provides food for thought.

In 1918, the NPS first hired a female seasonal ranger. Claire Marie Hodges worked in Yosemite. She was hired because of the shortage of males seeking ranger positions during wartime. Hodges performed the same jobs as male rangers. She wore the same Stetson hat and NPS badge, but she did not carry a gun (according to a biography on an NPS website).

Women on vacation with friends and family could drive through Yosemite Valley, California, and drive through "Wawona," a giant Sequoia. Donna Braden, senior curator, has studied leisure and travel extensively. Her catalog description of the postcard explains how conservationists convinced President Abraham Lincoln to declare Yosemite Valley and the Mariposa Grove of giant sequoias a public trust of California in 1864. They hoped to reduce the threat of vandalism and commercial exploitation. As Braden explains, "this marked the first time the U.S. government moved to protect land for public enjoyment. . . . it laid the foundation for the establishment of the national and state park systems."[9] The

Postcard. "Wawona. Mariposa Big Tree Grove," 1915–1920. Printed by the Western Publishing & Novelty Co., Los Angeles, California. Heavy snow toppled the tree in 1969. Image from the Collections of The Henry Ford.

first transcontinental railroad increased traffic in the park after 1869. Automobiles did the same, especially after they were officially admitted into the park in 1913.

Fire threatened the giant trees. A fire scar, incurred by the tree at some point in its 4,800-year-long existence, helped justify cutting a tunnel through the tree in 1881, the easier for horse-drawn stage coaches that hauled tourists through the park to pass through. The more automobiles bearing tourists, the greater the fire risk, but also the more the public might support expanding the reach of the NPS.

The NPS hired a seasonal female park ranger/naturalist for the first time in 1921. Marguerite Lindsley worked in Yellowstone National Park. She knew Yellowstone well. Her father worked for the Army and then the NPS with responsibilities for Yellowstone, and she had grown up there. Lindsley became the first permanent female park ranger in 1925. After she married an NPS ranger in 1928, she continued as a seasonal ranger, and she and her husband remained residents of Yellowstone.[10]

Tourists likely never encountered the few women who worked with the U.S. Forest Service during the 1910s and 1920s, given the remote nature of their deployment as fire lookouts and patrolwomen. On the other hand, tourists may have encountered the women ranger-naturalists working (for the NPS) during the height of summer tourist season in popular destinations such as Yosemite and Yellowstone.

Women and men concerned about conservation may have encountered their stories in the special-interest publications that featured women and men and their jobs in national wilderness management and interpretation.

My Antonia at 100: The Ongoing Story
Chris Sommerich, Humanities Nebraska

Humanities Nebraska funded "My Antonia at 100: The Ongoing Story." There is a series of five community conversation programs taking place across the state, and one of particular interest took place at Audubon's Rowe Sanctuary on the Platte River in central Nebraska during the spring Sandhill Crane migration, continuing with a bus trip to the Willa Cather Memorial Prairie and other Cather-related sites in Red Cloud (where Cather grew up).[11]

Dr. Andrew Jewell, editor of the Willa Cather Archive at the University of Nebraska–Lincoln, spearheaded the project, which was billed as an ecotourism event focused on Willa Cather's *My Ántonia*, published in 1918 and the complex ecosystem of central Nebraska. The event, "My Ántonia at 100: The Changing Ecology of the Great Plains," originated with the Willa Cather Archive in partnership with the Willa Cather Foundation, Audubon Nebraska, and the Iain Nicolson Audubon Center at Rowe Sanctuary. It began with a sunrise viewing of Sandhill Cranes roosting on the Platte River in Rowe Sanctuary's viewing blinds. In addition to tens of thousands of Sandhill Cranes amassed on the river, the program participants were fortunate to observe a pair of rare whooping cranes (with a population of only a couple of hundred, they are listed as an endangered species). Participants then traveled by bus to Red Cloud, Nebraska, for tours of Cather-related sites in town, including Cather's childhood home and the Willa Cather Memorial Prairie.

The bus ride from Rowe Sanctuary to Red Cloud took the participants through the landscape that Willa Cather wrote about in *My Ántonia*. Jewell took the opportunity to read excerpts from the novel, such as this well-known passage:

> I do not remember crossing the Missouri River, or anything about the long day's journey through Nebraska. Probably by that time I had crossed so many rivers that I was dull to them. The only thing very noticeable about Nebraska was that it was still, all day long, Nebraska.

And this, as the bus continued rolling through the prairie:

> As I looked about me I felt that the grass was the country, as the water is the sea. The red of the grass made all the great prairie the colour of wine-stains, or of certain seaweeds when they are first washed up. And there was so much motion in it; the whole country seemed, somehow, to be running.

When the bus passed through the small town of Bladen, Nebraska, on our way to Red Cloud, this passage spoke to the harsh, long winters out on the Great Plains:

> In the morning, when I was fighting my way to school against the wind, I couldn't see anything but the road in front of me; but in the late afternoon, when I was coming home, the town looked bleak and desolate to me. The pale, cold light of the winter sunset did not beautify—it was like the light of truth itself. When the smoky clouds hung low in the west and the red sun went down behind them, leaving a pink flush on the snowy roofs and the blue drifts, then the wind sprang up afresh, with a kind of bitter song, as if it said: "This is reality, whether you like it or not. All those frivolities of summer, the light and shadow, the living mask of green that trembled over everything, they were lies, and this is what was underneath. This is the truth." It was as if we were being punished for loving the loveliness of summer.

After touring Cather's childhood home, the National Willa Cather Center, and other sites in Red Cloud, the program finished with a peaceful walk on the Willa Cather Memorial Prairie just south of town. Formerly owned by the Nature Conservancy, the site is managed as habitat for grassland birds and wildlife and, as such, is a precious and all-too-rare tract of native prairie that looks the way most of Nebraska looked before being ploughed up for cropland.

The Champlain Society and the Origins of Acadia National Park
Catherine Schmitt, Tim Garrity, Maureen Fournier, Caitlin McDonough MacKenzie

The Mount Desert Island Historical Society envisions an island-wide community working together to foster meaningful engagement with the histories of Mount Desert Island. As stewards of Mount Desert Island's history, we believe in developing innovative approaches to historical research and discovery. We engage third graders in a rollicking recreation of an 1892 one-room schoolhouse, where a strict schoolmarm and stern superintendent are beset with mischievous ne'er-do-wells. Our commitment to supporting the work of future historians manifests itself through partnerships with Acadia National Park, College of the Atlantic, University of Maine, and neighboring historical societies and town libraries. We take particular pride in *Chebacco*, our annual magazine. In nineteen issues published since 1998, *Chebacco* provides well-grounded and accessible public history articles that foster a deeper insight and appreciation of the natural and human history of Mount Desert Island. We provide on-site and virtual access to our archives and collections database. We sponsor scholarship opportunities for undergraduate visiting history scholars and graduate-level Eliot Fellows. For more information, please visit www.mdihistory.org.

Welcome and Introduction

The scenery of Mount Desert is so beautiful and remarkable that no pains should be spared to save it from injury—to the end that many generations may receive all possible benefit and enjoyment from the sight of it.[12]

CHARLES ELIOT

In 1880, Charles Eliot invited a group of his fellow Harvard students to spend the summer on Maine's Mount Desert Island, with the understanding that they would spent part of their time in scientific studies. Calling themselves the Champlain Society, the young men spent that summer and the following summers surveying the island's flora, fauna, geology, and climate. Their work represents the first intensive and broad documentation of the region's natural history. The Champlain Society kept detailed records in a series of logbooks, which today are held by the Mount Desert Island Historical Society.

In journals, poetry, songs, and photographs, they chronicled their days and nights living in white canvas tents at the edge of the sea. The logbooks offer a glimpse into the practice of science of the era and also reflect the experience of early vacationers on the coast of Maine.

The logbooks also reveal that Eliot and his companions quickly realized the unique qualities of the island, its vulnerability, and the value of protecting it. This concern carried into their adult lives and became inspiration in the twentieth century for conservation of lands that became Acadia National Park.

Logbook entry, March 30, 1880. This evening the gentlemen named below met at 34 Grays and had a talk about the camping expedition which has been proposed by Charles Eliot. The party is to have the use of Mr. C.W. Eliot's yacht and camping outfit, and the plan is that each member of the party shall do some work in some branch of natural history or science. Charles Eliot has invited 12 persons to be members of the club, and 7 of these were present this evening, as follows. G.B. Dunbar, E.L. Rand, S.A. Eliot, C.W. Townsend, H.M. Spelman, J.C. Monroe, H.M. Hubbard

Camp Life

The Champlain Society set up camp on the shores of Mount Desert Island in eastern Maine in the summers of 1880 and 1881. From 1882 to 1886, the camp was located at the head of Northeast Harbor, near the Asticou Inn.

Each member of the Champlain Society chose a scientific "specialty" or department for their summer work: botany, geology, icthyology, lepidoptery, marine invertebrates, meteorology, or ornithology. Harvard professor William Morris Davis visited the campers and assisted with geology. Collecting plants and animals was a popular pastime among the higher classes, and specialized disciplines within science were emerging from the broader field of "natural history." At camp in the evening, they processed their specimens: stuffing birds, pressing and identifying plants and butterflies, and making notes in the logbooks.

Explorations

To expand their scientific observations and add to their lists of plants, birds, fish, and insects, members of the Champlain Society hiked mountain summits and walked through wooded valleys and sailed along the coast in the Eliot family yacht, *Sunshine*. They created some of the first recreational walking paths on Mount Desert Island, many of which persist as trails today.

August 25 1883. Soon after breakfast great energy seized Bates, Jones, and Rand. They walked along the dusty road to Hadlock's Upper Pond, thence through the woods to the

The Champlain Society at work on scientific specialties in the parlor tent, 1881. Courtesy of Mount Desert Island Historical Society.

In the summer of 1881, the Champlain Society set up their tents on the shore of Somes Sound on Mount Desert Island in Maine. Courtesy of Mount Desert Island Historical Society.

foot of the Sargent Mt. gorge. At the logging camp the party separated. Rand roamed through the woods in search of new plants.

In later years, when camped at Northeast Harbor, they rented rowboats and small sail-boats from local residents, using them to access the village at Southwest Harbor or visit nearby islands. They also made longer sailing excursions along the Downeast Coast.

Observations

Though they were young and easily distracted by the social scene, Champlain Society members did real and valuable scientific work. Back at Harvard during the school year, they met to discuss past and future summer activities, socialize, and present summaries of their work. They also presented their scientific findings before the Harvard and Boston Natural History Societies. Edward Rand, head of the Botanical Department, engaged others in the plant collecting work, and in 1894 he published, with John C. Redfield, the *Flora of Mt. Desert Island Maine.*

During the course of their summer studies, the young scientists became concerned about the island's future. They saw trees being cut, flowers being picked, and private development of lands previously open to all. They had experienced the refreshment and beauty of Mount Desert Island, and they had gotten to know the place, its plants and animals, shorelines and lakes, mountain summits, fog, rain, and sun. They knew that such an experience should be available to anyone in search of nature both subtle and sublime. They formed a committee, led by Eliot and Edward Rand and began to organize with other seasonal and year-round residents of Mount Desert to discuss protection of the island. Edward L. Rand wrote,

> Is it possible to protect the natural beauty of the island in any way? . . . A company of interested parties could buy at a small cost the parts of the Island less desirable for building purposes. To these they could add from time to time such of the more desirable lots as they could obtain control of either by purchase or by arrangement with the proprietor. This tract of land should then be placed in the charge of a forester and his assistants; the lakes and streams should be stocked with valuable fish; the increase of animals and birds encouraged; the growth of trees, shrubs, plants, ferns and mosses cared for. This park should be free to all. . . . I hope, however that we may have the pleasure before long of listening to a paper on this subject by one of its earnest advocates, 'Captain' Charles Eliot.[13]

Impact and Conclusions

After graduating from Harvard and an apprenticeship with Frederick Law Olmsted, Eliot became a landscape architect. His work for the city of Boston resulted in the first public beach in the United States, several large jewels in the Emerald Necklace, and the beginnings of what we now know as city and regional planning. In 1891, he cofounded the Trustees of Public Reservations, the world's first land trust, to secure and steward natural areas around the city. He also continued to advocate for similar protection of Mount Desert Island. In an article in *Garden and Forest*, he wrote,

> The United States have but this one short stretch of Atlantic sea-coast where a pleasant summer climate and real picturesqueness of scenery are to be found together. Can nothing be done to preserve for the use and enjoyment of the great unorganized body of the common people some fine parts, at least, of this sea-side wilderness of Maine?

Eliot died of spinal meningitis in 1897. In compiling his deceased son's biography, Charles William Eliot reread the Champlain Society logbooks and his son's diaries and published articles. In 1901, Eliot took up his son's mission and worked with George Dorr and others to create the Hancock County Trustees of Reservations, modeled after the organization his son created in Massachusetts, acquiring the lands that became Sieur de Monts National Monument in 1916 and then Acadia National Park.

Conclusion

Interpreting the Environment addresses the early history of conserving and preserving wilderness areas and the need to mobilize public support for the national parks that resulted. Freeman Tilden's *Interpreting our Heritage* satisfied the 1950s' need and has inspired two generations of interpreters since then. The general public has embraced environmental causes since then, too, often pushing the government to act in supportive ways. Efforts to rescind restrictions on some lands already designated as off limits to drilling or mining or protected from pipelines, for instance, remind us of the need to remain vigilant about mobilizing public support. Most of us may not work at areas conserved through an act of the U.S. Congress, or designated as a state park or a metropark, but all of us can support the cause by making our buildings green to reduce energy use and reduce plastic use to reduce dependence on fossil fuels. All of us can also incorporate complicated histories of conservation and landscape preservation as part of our efforts to interpret the environment.

Notes

1. Paul Kevin Wapner, *Living through the End of Nature: The Future of American Environmentalism* (Cambridge, MA: MIT Press, 2010).
2. James G. Lewis, "New Faces, Changing Values," in *The Forest Service and the Greatest Good: A Centennial History* (Forest History Society, 2005), 172–73. See also Rosemary Holsinger, "A Novel Experiment: Hallie Comes to Eddy's Gulch," *Women in Forestry* vol. 5, no. 2 (Summer 1983), available at https://www.webpages.uidaho.edu/winr/Daggett.htm. Accessed June 10, 2019.
3. The Forest Fire Lookout Association (FFLA) documents fire finders including women such as Iva M. Gruenewald (nee West, 1899–1984). She staffed the lookout camp at Tumwater near Leavenworth, Washington, in the Wenatche National Forest during 1920, 1921, and 1922, according to the FFLA Facebook post dated April 11, 2019. She described her camp in a 1983 memoir, cited in Ray Kresek, "History of the Osborne Firefinder" (2007) available at http://new.nysforestrangers.com/archives/osborne%20firefinder%20by%20kresek.pdf. Accessed October 1, 2018.
4. See the U.S. Forest Service Region 6 periodical, *Six Twenty-Six* vol. 6 (April 1921), pg. 31.
5. For information on Gladys Murray, see Lewis, "New Faces, Changing Values," 172.
6. *Six Twenty-Six* vol. 3 (September 1918), pg. 12, reported that Bertha Covert assumed duties as lookout. She continued in 1919. See "Dog Mountain," Fremont National Forest 40S-17E-9, Forest Lookouts, available at https://oregonlookouts.weebly.com/dog-mountain.html. Accessed June 10, 2019.
7. Gerald W. Williams, "Women in the Forest Service," Rocky Mountain Region, U.S. Forest Service, available at https://www.fs.usda.gov/detail/r2/learning/history-culture/?cid=stelprdb5360500. Accessed June 10, 2019.
8. Williams, "Women in the Forest Service."
9. Catalog Record, Object#2016.57.2, catalogued by Donna Braden, The Henry Ford, Dearborn, Michigan.
10. Elizabeth A. Watry, *Women in Wonderland: Lives, Legends, and Legacies of Yellowstone National Park* (Helena, MT: Riverbend Publishing, 2012).
11. Available at: http://myantonia100.org/march-23-and-april-7-2018/; overall project web page: http://myantonia100.org/. Accessed September 23, 2018.
12. Quote about C. Eliot from *Sieur de Monts* dedication ceremony July 1916.
13. E. L. Rand, *Report of the Botanical Department 1880, First Annual Report* (Cambridge, MA: Harvard University, Gray Herbarium Archives, 1881).

Conclusion

Some might argue that ants cannot move mountains, but those who study ants know that they can move between ten and fifty times their body weight. Working together, they can make mountains, and they can move them. Some might compare global warming or environmental degradation to a mountain. Working together, we take positive action. As much as Tilden mobilized readers to spread a message about national parks, *Interpreting the Environment in Museums and Historic Sites* seeks to mobilize readers to spread a message about the environment. The artifacts in museums and historic sites are the pieces, and working together, we can move them. Putting these pieces together will enable us to tell stories about human interactions with the environment across time. This includes stories about the humans who move mountains, removing tops of mountains to access fossil fuels and other natural resources, for instance. The stories of the environment that museums and historical societies can tell need to engage with the good as well as the alarming and mediate with a goal toward saving the planet and charting a more sustainable future.

This is part of a global movement that seeks environmental justice as well as survival. The United Nations adopted seventeen Sustainable Development goals in 2015.[1] Nine focus on environmental issues and the environment affects the other eight. These goals align with environmental education best practices. They stress the need to act fast to reduce global warming or face the consequences and to be more thoughtful about water use, synthetic chemical use, waste disposal, and fossil fuel consumption, among other things. Museums and historic sites play an essential role in educating the millions who need convincing.

Going green in your museum or historic site is a form of direct action to attain this goal. This internal change will have external ramifications. Most visitors (though not all) will appreciate seeing recycling bins, low-flush toilets, solar panels, electric car hookups, and other evidence of an institutional effort. These and other steps institutions can take to go green pave the way for more environmental topics in the exhibitions and programming that museums and historic sites can deliver.

Revisiting the themes introduced in the preface provide closure. Use this as a helpful reminder of needed action as you plan your next public engagement or strategize for your institution's future.

United Nations Sustainable Development Goals (SDG), 2016–2030. Used with permission of the United Nations.

Humans ... Land ... Nature ... Conservation ... Exploitation

Interpreting the Environment recognizes the public investment in conservation of natural areas. Tensions fester over access to and control of these places. Balancing public access with private use poses real challenges, but a land-ethic statement justifies sustainable management.

The call to action involves devising a land-ethic statement or an environmental justice statement for your institution. It should take into account inhabitants over time, human but also biological and geological. It should consider the factors that contributed either to their survival or their demise. It should articulate actions to take to convey that environmental history within and beyond the institution. Ally with other social and cultural institutions in your community or region, as environmental educators urge us to do, to share this history. Individual efforts to create institution- and site-specific land-ethic statements and pledges to pursue environmental justice will make a difference. Developing interpretation around negative and positive topics as follows will help you put your institution's land-ethic statement and environmental justice pledge to work.

Pollution . . . Environmental Degradation . . . Fossil-Fuel Dependency . . . Climate Change

Some might categorize these as imaginary enemies. *Interpreting the Environment at Museums and Historic Sites* approaches them as real threats and worthy of engagement.

The call to action involves developing interpretation based on evidence of historic practices related to these negative topics. The table and chairs in the dining room provide a way to discuss deforestation historically and travel and trade networks that processed and distributed them. This might link to steam travel either by water or rail with coal as a fuel. Furthermore, the stove or fire in the hearth becomes the link to a timeless story of the need for fuel, and the products that addressed that need as they relate directly to your context. All of this helps tell a story of the human-nature continuum, the sources of the Anthropocene and climate change as it exists today. You can map these stories out for your site, identifying a variety for each vista in the landscape or room in a house. This way, anyone can refresh their memory about environmental histories to tell.

Conservation . . . Green Certification . . . Reduce, Reuse, Recycle . . . Sustainability

Some consider these as futile efforts to reverse entropy. *Interpreting the Environment at Museums and Historic Sites* approaches them as natural acts that stewards of cultural patrimony should perform and pursue.

The call to action involves developing interpretation related to these positive topics. Consider how many artifacts represent a reduce and reuse ethic. Washing dishes rather than disposing of paper plates represents a trade-off, environmentally. Washing dishes requires water and produces wastewater (but that could be recycled to water plants). Disposing of paper plates involves removing waste to a landfill or a burn barrel. Choices existed historically, but actions today can create lessons about environmental stewardship.

Going green addresses this, too. The time seems right to pursue recycling as community investments seem at an all-time high. This may require careful planning because curbside pick-up does not exists across rural parts of the nation, but a commitment to reduce waste will carry a price tag and will warrant a budget line. What cost are we willing to pay to do our part to slow environmental degradation?

You might notice increased use of compostable food containers as substitutes for plastic and Styrofoam cups and containers. Companies such as Eco-Products, Inc. or Down2Earth Materials market these items, often made of post-consumer material or renewable materials such as wood or plant by-products. Some carry a recycling symbol, designating category "7" resin, but most have a composting symbol that indicates proper disposal to industrial composting sites only. A few may be certified compostable in home compost piles. These compostable containers are often made of or coated with a bioplastic, Ingeo, produced by NatureWorks, a subsidiary of Cargill. Any institution using these containers has an opportunity to link these back to reusable materials in their collections and then link the lesson to today's generation-old industry of biodegradable or compostable products and certification through the U.S. Composting Council and Biodegradable Products Institute.

The moral of the story is that we all need to be alert for changes of a global scale to address the crisis of environmental degradation and associated climate change. It is a rapidly changing field. This can help us keep our histories vibrant as they inform us about past practices that affected the environment and that take on different meaning as the solutions to the problem continue to evolve.

Note

1. United Nations Sustainable Development Goals, https://sustainabledevelopment.un.org/. Accessed February 26, 2019.

Selected Readings in Environmental History and Interpretation: A Bibliographic Essay

History museums and historic sites need to consider public interest in current issues and then determine how the stories they emphasize can inform public understanding of current issues. A few examples suffice to illustrate potential.

These selected reading suggestions raise additional topics to consider when identifying environmental themes to feature. This is not an exhaustive list. It augments endnotes in each chapter.

Accessing Historical Resources

Digital editions of historic literature (both monographs and serial publications) abound. The Biodiversity Heritage Library, an international consortium of natural history and botanical libraries, make biodiversity literature held in their collections available, digitally and free [https://www.biodiversitylibrary.org/ (accessed June 16, 2018)]. The Core Historical Literature of Agriculture (CHLA), Cornell University, includes the Literature of the Agricultural Sciences [http://chla.library.cornell.edu/ (accessed June 16, 2018)]. The HathiTrust [https://www.hathitrust.org/ (accessed June 16, 2018)] seeks to digitize everything no longer protected by copyright, including Earth science and plant science publications. See also the nonprofit library, Archive.net [https://archive.org/ (accessed June 16, 2018)]. For grey literature, topographical maps, and government agency publication at the state and national level (i.e., aerial spraying handbooks), see the Air Applicator Information Series, produced by the Air Applicator Institute, available at https://openspaces.unk.edu/air-info/ (accessed June 16, 2018). Individual publications, such as *The Whole Earth Catalog* [http://

www.wholeearth.com/history-whole-earth-catalog.php (accessed June 16, 2018)], maintain websites worth consulting to investigate historic mindsets about themes relevant to interpreting the environment.

Environmental History

Those starting to learn about the environment in historic context should start with broad overviews or surveys. See, for example, Ted Steinberg, *Down to Earth: Nature's Role in American History* (New York: Oxford University Press, 2002), Chris J. Magoc, *Chronology of Americans and the Environment* (Santa Barbara, California: ABC-CLIO, 2011), and Jeff Crane, *The Environment in American History: Nature and the Formation of the United States* (London: Routledge, 2014).

Concepts of "wilderness" and "nature" affected constructions of national identity. Roderick Frazier Nash surveyed these connections in 1967 in *Wilderness and the American Mind* 5th ed. (New Haven, CT: Yale University Press, 2014). Max Oelschlaeger studied "wilderness" in broader context in *The Idea of Wilderness: From Prehistory to the Age of Ecology* (New Haven, CT: Yale University Press, 1991). Conevery Bolton Valencius explored the ways that the "frontier" affected settlers' perceptions of personal health and well-being in *The Health of the Country: How American Settlers Understood Themselves and Their Land* (New York: Perseus Books Group, 2002). Wilderness and nature also became associated with gender identity and gendered perceptions. Susan R. Schrepfer compared male and female mountaineering narratives in *Nature's Altars: Mountains, Gender, and American Environmentalism* (Lawrence: University Press of Kansas, 2005). Their perceptions affected wilderness preservation.

In the context of the Anthropocene epoch, humans, not nature, effect change in the "environment." Environmental historians, however, do not agree on causes or consequences. A popular collection, *Major Problems in American Environmental History: Documents and Essays* (2nd ed., Boston: Houghton Mifflin Company, 2005 and 3rd ed., Boston: Wadsworth Cengage Learning, 2012) incorporates primary documents along with excerpts from influential articles and monographs. Each provides different perspectives on big issues in environmental history that remain relevant to current debates. The editor, Carolyn Merchant, selected essays that introduce upper-division undergraduate students to historical thinking about the environment over time, but it is also perfect for anyone trying to incorporate environmental topics into public programming. As the preface explains, "As concern mounts over the quality of environments and human life in the future, the study of past environments—how they were used and how they changed—provides guidance for the formation of government policy" (xiii). Furthermore, "such histories and case studies offer valuable perspectives to a world whose very survival depends on shifting from exploitative to environmentally sustainable development, and from inequality to environmental justice" (xiv). The selections start with "What is Environmental History?" and then move chronologically from the effects of American Indian and European contact to urbanization and environmental change.

Encyclopedias provide quick overviews and suggested readings for further study. See Rachel White Scheuering, *Shapers of the Great Debate on Conservation: A Biographical Dictionary* (Westport, CT: Greenwood Press, 2004); Carolyn Merchant, ed., *The Columbia Guide to American Environmental History* (2002; 2nd ed., 2007), which explores a range of topics from wilderness to global warming; and Carolyn Merchant, co-editor, with Shepard Krech, III and John McNeill, *The Encyclopedia of World Environmental History*, 3 vols. (2004), which broadens the geographic area to encompass the globe. See also the *Encyclopedia of Life*, supported by the digital resources of the Biodiversity Heritage Library, and available at http://eol.org/ (accessed June 16, 2018).

Other overviews of big topics include David Montgomery, *The Hidden Half of Nature: The Microbial Roots of Life and Health* (2016); Carolyn Merchant, *Autonomous Nature: Problems of Prediction and Control from Ancient Times to the Scientific Revolution* (2016); Merchant, *Science and Nature: Past, Present, and Future* (2018); and Merchant, *Key Concepts in Critical Theory: Ecology* (1994; 2nd ed., 2008).

Environmental historians can use their essays as a call to action. See, for example, William Cronon, *Uncommon Ground: Rethinking the Human Place in Nature* (New York: W. W. Norton & Company, 1995) and Donald Worster, *The Wealth of Nature: Environmental History and the Ecological Imagination* (New York: Oxford University Press, 1993).

Professional Organizations (in alpha order), Date Founded, and Publications

Agricultural History Society (AHA), 1919, *Agricultural History*

Agriculture and Living History, Farm and Agricultural Museums (ALHFAM), 1970, annual conference proceedings since 1974, monthly newsletter, and quarterly *Bulletin*

American Alliance of Museums (AAM), 1906, *Museum*

American Association for State and Local History (AASLH), 1940, *History News*

American Historical Association (AHA), 1884, *American Historical Review*

American Society for Environmental History (ASEH), 1977, *Environmental History* (co-published with the Forest History Society)

Association of American Geographers (AAG), 1904, *Annals of the Association of American Geographers*

Association for the Study of Literature and Environment (ASLE), 1992, *Interdisciplinary Studies in Literature and Environment*

Environmental Protection Agency's Office of Environmental Education, *Ethics & the Environment*, since 1996, a journal published by an interdisciplinary forum

Forest History Society, 1946, a not-for profit library and archive, *Forest History Today*; *Environmental History* (co-published with the American Society for Environmental History)

History of Science Society, 1924, *Isis*; *Osiris*

North American Association for Environmental Education, 1971, *Early Childhood Environmental Education Programs: Guidelines for Excellence* (2010); *Nonformal Environmental Education Programs: Guidelines for Excellence* (2nd ed., 2009); *Excellence in Environmental Education: Guidelines for Learning (K–12)* (4th ed., 2010); and *Community Engagement: Guidelines for Excellence* (2016), all available at https://naaee.org/eepro/publication/guidelines-excellence-series-set (accessed September 1, 2018).

National Association for Interpretation, 1988, *Legacy Magazine; Journal of Interpretation Research*

National Council on Public History, 1979, *The Public Historian*

Organization of American Historians (OAH), 1907, *Journal of American History*

Society for the History of Technology (SHOT), 1958, *Technology & Culture*

Vernacular Architecture Forum (VAF), 1980, *Buildings & Landscapes*

Private Interest, Professional Organizations, and the Environment

For the first one hundred years, the U.S. Congress considered its public lands its greatest asset. The U.S. Army bore responsibility of Yellowstone between 1886 and 1918, an indication of the connection among formidable landscapes, military presence, and public investment. Interest in interpreting these otherwise nonproductive lands like Yellowstone increased after formation of the National Park Service (NPS) in 1916. Denise D. Meringolo surveys the ways that conservationists and preservationists galvanized public support (from the national government and from local special-interest groups) and the ways that historians professionalized to distinguish the "hard" work of history from the "soft" work of preservation. Historians founded the American Historical Association in 1884, and the U.S. Congress "sanctioned the [AHA's] role as the arbiter of historical significance." See Denise D. Meringolo, *Museums, Monuments, and National Parks: Toward a New Genealogy of Public History* (Amherst: University of Massachusetts Press, 2012), 31–32; quote 32.

As collecting and preservation efforts garnered more private and public support, the AHA established the Conference of State and Local Historical Societies in 1904. The American Association of Museums (now the American Alliance of Museums) formed in 1906 to support staff in institutions that collected, preserved, and interpreted flora and fauna (i.e., arboreta, herbaria, zoos, and natural history collections) as well as science, history, and the arts. In 1907, historians working in state and local historical societies launched their own organization, the Mississippi Valley Historical Association (MVHA; now the Organization of American Historians, OAH). See John R. Wunder's overview, "The Founding Years of the OAH." *OAH Newsletter* vol. 34, no. 4 (Nov. 2006), 1, 6, 8. The Agricultural History Society (AHS) began in 1919, and officials with the NPS, as well as divisions within the U.S. Department of Agriculture, joined AHS and provided leadership. The need for more service to local historians prompted formation of the American Association for State and Local History out of the American Historical Association in 1940 (summarized briefly at http://about.aaslh.org/the-story-of-us/. Accessed June 14, 2018).

Increased interest in interpretation to growing numbers of visitors prompted formation of the Association of Interpretive Naturalists in 1954 and the Western Interpreters Association in 1969. These operated separately until 1988 when they joined forces as the National Association for Interpretation (See "About NAI," at https://www.interpnet.com/. Accessed June 15, 2018).

The first edition of the classic "how-to" book, Freeman Tilden's *Interpreting Our Heritage*, appeared in 1957 (Chapel Hill: University of North Carolina Press; 2nd ed., 1967; 3rd ed., 1977; 4th ed., expanded and updated and issued as the fiftieth anniversary ed., 2007). Tilden did not emphasize a distinction between natural history and cultural history interpretation. He balanced them adeptly, and his six principles applied equally to presentation of materials "scientific, historical, or architectural" as his third principle explained. He balanced examples of what he described as "our natural and man-made heritage" as seen in national parks, state and municipal parks, historic houses and museums (3rd ed., 1977, 3).

On the heels of publication of Tilden's second edition, a new organization formed that committed to interpreting the environment. The Association for Living History, Farm and Agricultural Museums (ALHFAM) began in 1970 at an Agricultural History Society seminar. The ALHFAM drew NPS "technicians" such as Verne Chatelain, first chief historian of the NPS, who called the interpreters he needed to convey the cultural history to the general public. Denise D. Meringolo describes the process by which Chatelain developed history interpretation in national parks in *Museums, Monuments, and National Parks: Toward a New Genealogy of Public History* (Amherst: University of Massachusetts Press, 2012), xxviii–xxix. Three senior managers in national institutions and dedicated AHS members, John T. Schlebecker of the Smithsonian Institution, Wayne D. Rasmussen of the U.S. Department of Agriculture, and Ernst T. Christensen of the NPS, signed Articles of Incorporation for ALHFAM in April 1972. They pledged to:

- encourage research, publication, and training in historic agricultural practices
- facilitate the exchange of agricultural information and items
- develop a genetic pool of endangered agricultural plants and animals
- sponsor scholarly symposium and publications dealing with agricultural history
- accredit living historical farms and agricultural museums
- foster in present and future generations an appreciation and understanding of the ideas and ideals that have contributed to the greatness of U.S. agriculture.

For an overview of the influence of public history on professional organizations dedicated to studying agriculture over time, and considering it in all its context, not just its "greatness," see Debra A. Reid, "Agricultural Artifacts: Early Curators, Their Philosophies and Their Collections," *Proceedings of the 2010 Conference of the Association for Living History, Farm and Agricultural Museums* (North Bloomfield, Ohio: ALHFAM, 2011), 30–52.

An unnatural division grew, though, between sites that interpreted the natural environment (natural history) and those that interpret the built environment (local, social, and cultural history). Given an extreme example, the influential *Interpretation of Historic Sites* by

William T. Alderson and Shirley Payne Low (1976; 2nd ed., rev. 1985) defined sites narrowly by focusing on buildings and not incorporating the landscape or environment.

This abandonment of the environment on the part of history museums and historic sites may have resulted from the increased attention to other aspects of the built environment by the NPS. In 1933, the Historic American Buildings Survey (HABS) began under the NPS with support of the Library of Congress and the American Institute of Architects to document architecturally significant structures. For information on HABS and guidelines, see https://www.nps.gov/hdp/habs/index.htm (accessed June 15, 2018). The Historic American Engineering Record (HAER) began in 1969, a result of an agreement among the NPS, the American Society of Civil Engineers, and the Library of Congress. The HAER has documented bridges, an important landscape feature central to numerous environmental topics. For guidelines and a report on covered bridges, see https://www.nps.gov/hdp/haer/index.htm (accessed June 15, 2018). In 2000, the NPS created the Historic American Landscapes Survey (HALS) to document historic landscapes in the United States and its territories. Methods follow those perfected by HABS and HAER (creation of measured drawings, written histories, and large-format black-and-white as well as color photographs. The American Society of Landscape Architects (ASLA) consults with HALS staff to implement the program. Guidelines are available at https://www.nps.gov/hdp/hals/index.htm (accessed June 15, 2018). The Library of Congress includes drawings, photographs, and reports produced by HABS, HAER, and HALS at http://www.loc.gov/pictures/collection/hh/ (accessed June 15, 2018).

The NPS manages HABS, HAER, and HALS projects that document historic buildings, engineering features, and landscapes. The Department of the Interior (DOI) gained more authority to issue standards for historic preservation projects and guidelines for preserving, rehabilitating, restoring, and reconstructing historic buildings in 1966 with the passage of the National Historic Preservation Act. *Guidelines for Rehabilitating Old Buildings* appeared in 1976. For a history of the standards and guidelines, see "A History of The Secretary of the Interior's Standards for the Treatment of Historic Properties & Guidelines for Preserving, Rehabilitating, Restoring and Reconstructing Historic Buildings," at https://www.nps.gov/tps/standards/history-of-standards.htm (accessed June 15, 2018). The DOI expanded its language in 1990 and published its first guidelines to emphasize "property," not just "buildings" in 1992. The DOI released *The Secretary of the Interior's Standards for the Treatment of Historic Properties and the Guidelines for the Treatment of Cultural Landscapes* in 1995, available at https://www.nps.gov/tps/standards/four-treatments/landscape-guidelines/index.htm (accessed June 15, 2018). The DOI has also released *The Secretary of the Interior's Standards for the Treatment of Historic Properties & Illustrated Guidelines on Sustainability for Rehabilitating Historic Buildings* in 2011, available at https://www.nps.gov/tps/standards/rehabilitation/sustainability-guidelines.pdf (accessed June 15, 2018).

Since formation of ALHFAM, more attention has been paid to the historic landscape and the heritage breeds and seeds that constitute ecosystems in living historical farms. Thomas J. Schlereth urged museums to approach landscapes as they did other three-dimensional artifacts in "Landscapes as Artifacts," in *Artifacts and the American Past* (Nashville, TN: American Association for State and Local History, 1980). Debra A. Reid surveyed open-air museum approaches to landscape documentation, management, and interpretation in 1986 and published findings as "Hills and Dales of Historic Sites and Open-Air Museums," *Proceedings of the 1986 Conference of the Association for Living Historical Farms and Agricultural Museums* (Washington, D.C.: Smithsonian Institution, 1987), 92–114. The AASLH has published technical leaflets, articles, and books on interpreting historic landscapes. For an overview of interpreting historic house landscapes, see Catherine Howett, "Grounds for Interpretation: The Landscape Context of Historic House Museums," in *Interpreting Historic House Museums*, edited by Jessica Foy Donnelly (Walnut Creek: AltaMira Press, 2002), 111–27. The classic "how-to" overview of researching and implementing historic landscapes and gardens for museums and historic sites is Rudy J. Favretti and Joy P. Favretti, *Landscapes and Gardens for Historic Buildings* (1978; 1987; 2nd ed., 1995). Articles in the AASLH journal, *History News*, have featured the environment and landscapes. Cultural influences on gardens has also received coverage. See, for example, Richard Westmacott, *African-American Gardens and Yards in the Rural South* (Knoxville: University of Tennessee, 1992).

Publications encouraging museums to adopt sustainable practices include Sarah Sutton, *Environmental Sustainability at Historic Sites and Museums*. Special edition of *The Public Historian*: Public History and Environmental Sustainability (vol. 36, no. 3, August 2014); Cathy Stanton, et al. *Public History in a Changing Climate: A Digital Publication* (2014), available at: http://ncph.org/wp-content/uploads/2014/03/PHCC-2014.pdf; Jeffrey Stine, "Public History and the Environment," in *The Oxford Handbook of Public History*, edited by Paula Hamilton and James B. Gardner (New York: Oxford University Press, 2017).

Andrew Glenn Kirk provided an institutional history in *The Gentle Science: A History of the Conservation Library* (Denver: Denver Public Library, 1995), founded by Arthur Carhart in 1960 in Denver, Colorado, and then analyzed its influence in *Collecting Nature; The American Environmental Movement and the Conservation Library* (Lawrence: University Press of Kansas, 2001).

Museums might look at taxidermied collections differently after reading Karen R. Jones, *Epiphany in the Wilderness: Hunting, Nature, and Performance in the Nineteenth-Century American West* (Boulder: University Press of Colorado, 2015). Jones explores men and women who participated in "the hunt" as either hunter or trail guide or crack-shot performer, and the uses of the trophies they secured on the hunt. These include literature, paintings, photographs, taxidermied mounts, and also preserved landscapes. Monica Rico addresses class and race and perceptions of the American western wilderness across national boundaries in *Nature's Noblemen: Transatlantic Masculinities and the Nineteenth-Century American West* (New Haven, CT: Yale University Press, 2013). Rico studies British nobles on American ranches, but also international receptions of Buffalo Bill's Wild West Show and Theodore Roosevelt's white man's country.

Resources to Manage Landscape and the Environment in Museums and Historic Sites

Long before landscapes became objects to curate and interpret, the national government considered them resources to document. Responsibility for surveying public lands and documenting natural resources has rested within various departments of the U.S.

government over more than two hundred years. The General Land Office managed public land sales starting in 1788. It became part of the U.S. DOI when Congress authorized the new department in 1849. Congress appropriated funds to survey geological resources of western lands in 1869 and created the U.S. Geological Survey in 1879. Congress also created the first national park, Yellowstone, in 1872, and created the NPS in 1916 to manage properties of national significance. The maps and reports and guidelines created by the U.S. DOI over time provide useful resources to support the documentation, stewardship, and interpretation of the historic environment.

Documents created by several DOI bureaus warrant consideration when planning environmental interpretation. These include the NPS; U.S. Fish and Wildlife Service (FWS); Bureau of Indian Affairs (BIA); Bureau of Land Management (BLM); Bureau of Safety and Environmental Enforcement; Office of Surface Mining, Reclamation & Enforcement; Bureau of Reclamation (BOR); and the U.S. Geological Survey (USGS).

The "American Indian Nations" finding aid, available via the National Archives and Records Administration (NARA) at https://www.archives.gov/research/native-americans/treaties (accessed June 15, 2018) itemizes several sources to consult for historic treaties. Furthermore, the NARA provides access to BIA records including allotment records, applications and case files, and rolls at https://www.archives.gov/research/native-americans/bia (accessed June 15, 2018).

Records of the General Land Office (GLO), within the BLM, includes land patents, survey plats and field notes, land status records, and tract book records. If a historic site includes land purchased directly from the GLO, the original land patent that conveyed ownership from the national government to the purchaser will be digitized and available at https://glorecords.blm.gov/default.aspx (accessed June 15, 2018). For an analysis of the GLO, see *The Nation Possessed: The Conflicting Claims on America's Public Lands and the Commemoration of the 200th Anniversary of the Founding of the General Land Office*, a report prepared by a symposium convened by the Center for the American West, and available digitally at: https://www.centerwest.org/projects/land-use/thenationpossessed (accessed June 14, 2018).

Other agencies, particularly the U.S. Army Corps of Engineers (USACE), within the U.S. War Department, manipulated the environment historically to survey rights-of-way, channel rivers, and build levees. For an overview of its many projects, see *The History of the U.S. Army Corps of Engineers* (Alexandria, VA: Office of History, Headquarters, U.S. Army Corps of Engineers, 1998), available at https://cdm16021.contentdm.oclc.org/digital/collection/p16021coll4/id/184/rec/19 (accessed June 15, 2018). For local and regional USACE office histories, and other published reports, see the USACE Digital Library, available at http://hecsa.libguides.com/usacedigitallibrary (accessed June 15, 2018).

Institutional histories of agencies vested with responsibility for and influence on the environment warrant attention. Most are accessible via the institution's website as digital files because they are public documents. Scholars have also studied these agencies, and histories produced by outsiders can provide additional perspective on these influential agencies. See, for example, several essays in "A Centennial History: The National Park Service," special issue of *The Public Historian* (Vol. 38, no. 4, November 2016) or Dylan Zaslowsky and the

Wilderness Society, *These American Lands: Parks, Wilderness, and the Public Lands* (New York: Holt, 1986). For more on the BLM and the U.S. Forest Service (within the U.S. Department of Agriculture), see Paul J. Culhane, *Public Lands Politics: Interest Group Influence on the Forest Service and the Bureau of Land Management* (New York: Resources for the Future, 1981); and James R. Skillen, *The Nation's Largest Landlord: The Bureau of Land Management in the American West* (Lawrence: University Press of Kansas, 2009).

Many studies of public lands, particularly federal lands, have resulted from land disputes that erupt when private ownership clashes with public access and government regulation. For studies of government agencies and land issues, see Paul W. Hirt, *A Conspiracy of Optimism: Management of the National Forests since World War II* (Lincoln: University of Nebraska Press, 1994) and William D. Rowley, *U.S. Forest Service Grazing and Rangelands: A History* (College Station: Texas A&M University Press, 1985).

Ecological Design: Studies That Can Inform Artifactual and Architectural Analysis

Peder Anker, *From Bauhaus to Ecohouse: A History of Ecological Design* (Baton Rouge: Louisiana State University Press, 2010); Vera Norwood, *Made from This Earth: American Women and Nature* (Chapel Hill: University of North Carolina Press, 1993) explores women writers and illustrators, botanists and biologists, ornithologists and conservationists, and landscape and garden designers; Carol Bigwood, *Earth Muse: Feminism, Nature, and Art* (Philadelphia: Temple University Press, 1993); Norman T. Newton, *Design on the Land: The Development of Landscape Architecture* (Cambridge: MA: Harvard University Press, 1971); Barbara Novak, *Nature and Culture: American Landscape Painting, 1825–1875* (New York: Oxford University Press, 1980); Stuart Wrede and William Howard Adams, *Denatured Visions: Landscape and Culture in the Twentieth Century* (New York: Museum of Modern Art, 1991); Peter Warhall, ed., *Thirtieth Anniversary Celebration: Whole Earth Catalog* (San Rafael, CA: Point Foundation, 1999).

Foundational Studies in Environmental History

Publications around which Ideas about the Environment Changed

Digitized original classics abound, available through the Biodiversity Heritage Library, among other sources. Presses also reissue classics, such as George Perkins Marsh, *Man and Nature: Or, Physical Geography as Modified by Human Action* (1864), edited with an introduction by David Lowenthal (Seattle: University of Washington Press, 2003). Rachel Carson, *Silent Spring: The Classic that Launched the Environmental Movement. 50th Anniversary Edition* (Boston: Houghton Mifflin Harcourt, 2002). Aldo Leopold, A *Sand County Almanac* (1949).

Selected Works on Preservation and Conservation

Char Miller, *Gifford Pinchot and the Making of Modern Environmentalism* (Washington, D.C.: Island Press, 2004); Donald Worster, *A Passion for Nature: The Life of John Muir* (New York: Oxford University Press, 2008); Kevin Amitage, *The Nature Study Movement: The* Forgotten *Popularizer of America's Conservation Ethic;* Sarah T. Phillips, *This Land, This Nation: Conservation, Rural America, and the New Deal;* Karl Jacoby, *Crimes Against Nature: Squatters, Poachers, Thieves, and the Hidden History of American Conservation;* Samuel P. Hays, *Conservation and the Gospel of Efficiency: The Progressive Conservation Movement, 1800–1920* (Cambridge, MA: Harvard University Press, 1959); Carolyn Merchant, "The Women of the Progressive Conservation Crusade, 1900–1915," in Kendall E. Bailes, ed., *Environmental History: Critical Issues in Comparative Perspective* (Lanham, MD: University Press of America, 1985).

Selected Works on National Parks

Mark David Spence, *Dispossessing the Wilderness: Indian Removal and the Making of the National Parks* (New York: Oxford University Press, 1999); Alfred Runte, *National Parks: The American Experience* (Lincoln: University of Nebraska Press, 1979); Denise D. Meringolo, *Museums, Monuments, and National Parks: Toward a New Genealogy of Public History* (Amherst: University of Massachusetts Press, 2012); Hal Rothman, *America's National Monuments: The Politics of Preservation* (Lawrence: University Press of Kansas, 1994); Richard Sellars, *Preserving Nature in the National Parks: A History* (New Haven, CT: Yale University Press, 1997); Paul Sutter's *Driven Wild: How the Fight against Automobiles Launched the Modern Wilderness Movement* (Seattle: University of Washington Press, 2002); Hal Rothman, *Devil's Bargains: Tourism in the Twentieth-Century American West* (Lawrence: University Press of Kansas, 1998).

For a study of how nature writing affects perceptions of the first national park, see John Clayton, *Wonderlandscape: Yellowstone National Park and the Evolution of an American Cultural Icon* (New York: Pegasus Books, 2017). Clayton organizes the book around themes such as half-tame, rugged, patriotic, teachable, spiritual, threatened, and triumphant. See also, Chris J. Magoc, *Yellowstone: The Creation and Selling of an American Landscape, 1870–1903* (Albuquerque: University of New Mexico Press, 1999).

Selected Works on Environmentalism

Samuel P. Hays, *Beauty, Health, and Permanence: Environmental Politics in the United States, 1955–1985* (New York: Cambridge University Press, 1987); Victor B. Scheffer, *The Shaping of Environmentalism in America* (Seattle: University of Washington Press, 1991); Kirkpatrick Sale, *The Green Revolution: The American Environmental Movement, 1962–1992* (New York: Hill and Wang, 1993); Hal K. Rothman, *The Greening of a Nation: Environmentalism in the United States since 1945* (New York: Harcourt Brace, 1998); Karl Boyd Brooks, *Before Earth Day: The Origins of American Environmental Law, 1945–1970* (Lawrence: University Press of Kansas, 2009); Paul S. Sutter, "The World with Us: The State of American Environmental

History," *Journal of American History* 100 (June 2013): 94–119; John Wargo, *Green Intelligence: Creating Environments That Protect Human Health* (New Haven, CT: Yale University Press, 2009).

Local, State, and Regional Environmental Histories

Micro-history or macro-history? Both approaches can influence selection of topics to explore in history museum and historic-site interpretation.

Selected examples of micro-history, or local history, that feature the environment include Richard White, *Land Use, Environment and Social Change: The Shaping of Island County Washington* (Seattle: University of Washington Press, 1980); William Cronon, *Nature's Metropolis: Chicago and the Great West* (New York: W. W. Norton & Co., 1991); Ted Steinberg, *Gotham Unbound: The Ecological History of Greater New York* (2014); Patricia Nelson Limerick with Jason L. Hanson, *A Ditch in Time: The City [Denver], the West, and Water* (Golden, CO: Fulcrum Publishing, 2012); Michael J. Makley, *Saving Lake Tahoe: An Environmental History of a National Treasure* (Reno: University of Nevada Press,2013); and Douglas H. Strong, *Tahoe: From Timber Barons to Ecologists* (1984; reprint, Lincoln: University of Nebraska Press, 1999).

Selected examples of state history include David A. Chang, *The Color of the Land: Race, Nation, and the Politics of Landownership in Oklahoma, 1832–1929* (Chapel Hill: The University of North Carolina Press, 2010); Carolyn Merchant, *Green Versus Gold: Sources in California's Environmental History* (1998) and Samuel Trask Dana and Myron Krueger, *California Lands: Ownership, Use, and Management* (Washington, D.C.: American Forestry Association, 1958).

Selected examples of regional environmental histories include Leisl Carr Childers, *The Size of the Risk: Histories of Multiple Use in the Great Basin* (Norman: University of Oklahoma Press, 2015); Jack Temple Kirby, *Mockingbird Song: Ecological Landscapes in the South* (Chapel Hill: University of North Carolina Press, 2006); Frederick Turner, *Beyond Geography: The Western Spirit against the Wilderness* (New York: Viking, 1980); and William Cronon, *Changes in the Land: Indians, Colonists, and the Ecology of New England* (1983; rev. ed. New York: Hill & Wang, 2003).

Several regional study centers exist at universities, including the University of Colorado–Boulder's Center of the American West. That center has published books directed toward public engagement in environmental issues such as *What Every Westerner Should Know about Energy* (2003), *Cleaning Up Abandoned Hardrock Mines in the West* (2006), and *What Every Westerner Should Know about Energy Efficiency and Conservation* (2007).

Culture also affects relationships with the environment. Essays in *To Love the Wind and the Rain: African Americans and Environmental History*, edited by Dianne D. Glave and Mark Stoll (Pittsburgh: University of Pittsburgh Press, 2005), explore how humans engaged with the environment over centuries and how racism affected that interaction. See also, Dianne D. Glave, *Rooted in the Earth: Reclaiming the African American Environmental Heritage* (Chicago: Chicago Review Press, 2010).

Public Land and Conflicts over Public Land Use

For an analysis of public land and debates about access and use, see Paul W. Gates, *History of Public Land Law Development* (Washington, D.C.: William W. Gaunt & Sons, 1987), Char Miller, *Public Lands, Public Debates: A Century of Controversy* (Corvallis: Oregon State University Press, 2012), and Karen R. Merrill, *Public Lands and Political Meaning: Ranchers, the Government, and the Property Between Them* (Berkeley: University of California Press, 2002).

Disputes erupt when private use competes with public access to land held by local, state, or national governments. Several studies explore the tensions that led to the 1980s' Sagebrush Rebellion, when ranchers challenged national regulation of their public grazing lands, lands once the province of indigenous nations and now rented by ranchers who found their livestock range compromised by public recreational use. Tensions continue to simmer as increasing numbers of urban and suburban residents seek recreational access. See, for example, William L. Graf, *Wilderness Preservation and the Sagebrush Rebellions* (Savage, MD: Rowman & Littlefield, 1990); R. McGreggor Cawley, *Federal Land, Western Anger: The Sagebrush Rebellion and Environmental Politics* (Lawrence: University Press of Kansas, 1993); William Perry Pendley, *Sagebrush Rebel: Reagan's Battle with Environmental Extremists and Why it Matters Today* (Washington, D.C.: Regnery, 2013); and Michael J. Makley's *Open Spaces, Open Rebellions: The War Over America's Public Lands* (Amherst: University of Massachusetts Press, 2017).

Hunting, Fishing, and Foraging

Matt Cartmill, *A View to Death in the Morning: Hunting and Nature through History* (Cambridge, MA: Harvard University Press, 1993).

Michael Williams, *Americans and Their Forests: A Historical Geography* (Cambridge: Cambridge University Press, 1989).

Camping and Nature Recreation

Terence Young, *Heading Out: A History of American Camping* (New York: Cornell University Press, 2017).

The National Council on Public History (NCPH) published a special issue on the one-hundredth anniversary of the National Park Service. See "A Centennial History," *The Public Historian* 38, no. 4 (November 2016).

Agriculture and the Environment

Biologist Norman Borlaug experimented with strains of wheat that could tolerate drought, and these varieties helped usher in the "Green Revolution" on a global scale. Borlaug is the "wizard" in Charles C. Mann's comparative history, *The Wizard and the Prophet: Two Remarkable Scientists and Their Dueling Visions to Shape Tomorrow's World* (New York: Alfred A. Knopf, 2018). The "prophet" is William Vogt, whose book, *Road to Survival* (New York: William Sloane Assoc., Inc., 1948), helped launch modern environmentalism, distinctive because of the belief that humans should live within ecosystems and not manipulate them. Other studies of the Green Revolution include Lester Russell Brown, *Seeds of Change: The Green Revolution and Development in the 1970s* (New York: Praeger, 1970).

Commodities in Environmental Context

Kendra Smith-Howard, *Pure and Modern Milk: An Environmental History since 1900* (Oxford: Oxford University Press, 2014); Phillip Pauly, *Fruits and Plains: The Horticultural Transformation of America* (Cambridge, MA: Harvard University Press, 2008); Alan L. Olmstead and Paul W. Rhode, *Creating Abundance: Biological Innovation and American Agricultural Development* (New York: Cambridge University Press, 2008).

Farm Laborers, Health, and Environmental Reform

Adam Tompkins, *Ghostworkers and Greens: The Cooperative Campaign of Farmworkers and Environmentalists for Pesticide Reform* (Ithaca, NY: Cornell University Press, 2016).

Suburbanization, Urbanization, and the Environment

Adam Rome, *The Bulldozer in the Countryside: Suburban Sprawl and the Rise of American Environmentalism* (New York: Cambridge University Press, 2001); Anne Whiston Sprin, *The Granite Garden: Urban Nature and Human Design* (New York: Basic Books, 1984); and Ted Steinberg, *American Green: The Obsessive Quest for the Perfect Lawn* (2006).

Sarah A. Fox, *Downwind: A People's History of the Nuclear West* (Lincoln: University of BEbraska Press [Bison Books], 2014)

Special-Interest Group History

Local historical societies can often incorporate national issues into their programming by documenting localized actions relevant to nationwide public-interest groups. Histories of those organizations can inform the content. See Michael P. Cohen, *The History of the Sierra Club, 1892–1970* (San Francisco: Sierra Club Books, 1988); Carolyn Merchant, *Spare the Birds: George Bird Grinnell and the First Audubon Society* (2016). *Science for the People: Documents from America's Movement of Radical Scientists*, edited by Sigrid Schmalzer, Daniel S. Chard, and Alyssa Botelho (Amherst: University of Massachusetts Press, 2018), including selections focused on "Agriculture, Ecology, and Food," and on "Energy and Environment." Karl Boyd Brooks, *Before Earth Day: The Origins of American Environmental Law, 1945–1960* (Lawrence: University Press of Kansas, 2009); Adam Rome, *The Genius of Earth Day: How a 1970 Teach-In Unexpectedly Made the First Green Generation* (New York: Hill and Wang, 2013). For digital resources that help schools and local historical organizations participate in Arbor Day see the Morton Arboretum (http://www.mortonarb.org/) and the Arbor Day Foundation [https://www.arborday.org/celebrate/history.cfm (both accessed August 15, 2018)].

Support for and Opposition to Conservation and Environmental Movements

Public policy and public engagement with the environment predated Don't Litter campaigns, Earth Day, and the Environmental Protection Agency. For an overview, see Victor B. Scheffer, *The Shaping of Environmentalism in America* (Seattle: University of Washington Press, 1991); Hal K. Rothman, *The Greening of a Nation: Environmentalism in the United States since 1945* (New York: Harcourt Brace, 1998); David Helvarg, *The War against the Greens: The Wise Use Movement, the New Right and the Browning of America* (Boulder, CO: Johnson Books, 2004); Hal K. Rothman, *Saving the Planet: The American Response to the Environment in the Twentieth Century* (Chicago: Ivan R. Dee, 2000); and Kirkpatrick Sale, *The Green Revolution: The American Environmental Movement, 1962–1992* (New York: Hill and Wang, 1993).

Selected monographs about the contested nature of conservation and the environmental movement include Karl Jacoby, *Crimes against Nature: Squatters, Poachers, Thieves, and the Hidden History of American Conservation* (Oakland: University of California Press, 2003); Jacqueline Vaughn Switzer, *Green Backlash: The History and Politics of Environmental Opposition in the U.S.* (Boulder, CO: Lynne Rienner, 1997); and biographies such as Char Miller, *Gifford Pinchot and the Making of Modern Environmentalism* (Washington D.C.: Island Press, 2001).

Numerous monographs focus on Rachel Carson's *Silent Spring* and its role in galvanizing the Environmental Movement. See Thomas Dunlap, *DDT, Silent Spring, and the Rise of Environmentalism* (Seattle: University of Washington, 2008); Robert Gottlieb, *Forcing the Spring: The Transformation of the American Environmental Movement* (Washington, D.C.: Island Press, 1993); Frank Graham, Jr., *Since* Silent Spring (Boston: Houghton Mifflin Company, 1970). Several put *Silent Spring* into international context, including David Kinkela, *DDT and the American Century: Global Health, Environmental Politics, and the Pesticide that Changed the World* (Chapel Hill: University of North Carolina Press, 2011).

For biographies of Carson, see Linda Lear, *Rachel Carson: Witness for Nature* (New York: Henry Holt and Company, 1997) and William Souder, *On a Farther Shore: The Life and Legacy of Rachel Carson* (New York: Crown Publishers, 2014).

Several scholars have explored the relationships between public policy and environmental protection and corporate regulation. See Stephen Bocking, *Nature's Experts: Science, Politics, and the Environment* (New Brunswick: Rutgers University Press, 2004); Christopher Bosso, *Pesticides and Politics: The Life Cycle of a Public Issue* (Pittsburgh: University of Pittsburgh Press, 1987); James Whorton, *Before* Silent Spring: *Pesticides and Public Health in Pre-DDT America* (Princeton, NJ: Princeton University Press, 1974); Samuel P. Hays, *Beauty, Health, and Permanence: Environmental Politics in the United States, 1955–1985* (New York: Cambridge University Press, 1987).

Nature writers wielded considerable influence in shaping public perceptions of nature and the environment. See Daniel J. Philippon, *Conserving Words: How American Nature Writers Shaped the Environmental Movement* (Athens: University of Georgia Press, 2004). Other forms of writing convey personal notions of place and space. See, for example, Kent C. Ryden, *Mapping the Invisible Landscape: Folklore, Writing, and the Sense of Place* (Iowa

City: University of Iowa Press, 1993), David Mazel, *American Literary Environmentalism* (Athens: University of Georgia Press, 2000), and Wilson O. Clough, *The Necessary Earth: Nature and Solitude in American Literature* (Austin: University of Texas Press, 1964). Authors also convey human disillusionment with nature. See J. Richard Schneider, *Dark Nature: Anti-Pastoral Essays in American Literature and Culture* (Lanham, MD: Lexington Books, 2016).

Biographies of several influential conservationists and environmentalists exist, including Lawrence Buell, *The Environmental Imagination: Thoreau, Nature Writing, and the Formation of American Culture* (Cambridge, MA: Harvard University Press, 1995); David Lowenthal, *George Perkins Marsh: Prophet of Conservation* (Seattle: University of Washington Press, 2003); Michael P. Cohen, *The Pathless Way: John Muir and American Wilderness* (Madison: University of Wisconsin Press, 1984); Paul Russell Cutright, *Theodore Roosevelt: The Making of a Conservationist* (Urbana: University of Illinois Press, 1985); James Perrin Warren, *John Burroughs and the Place of Nature* (Athens: University of Georgia Press, 2006); Curt Meine, *Aldo Leopold: His Life and Work* (Madison: University of Wisconsin Press, 1988).

Chemical Applications

Interpretive programs about synthetic applications to agricultural lands can capture the public's attention, particularly as consumers advocate for organics and local food systems. Consumers' economic leverage prompted multinational corporations like Walmart and McDonalds to be more mindful of organic produce. For context, see Michelle Mart, *Pesticides: A Love Story: America's Enduring Embrace of Dangerous Chemicals* (Lawrence: University Press of Kansas, 2015) that provides context.

Several books study the history of synthetic applications in general. Frederick Rowe Davis' *Banned: A History of Pesticides and the Science of Toxicology* (New Haven, CT: Yale University Press, 2014) provides an overview of research in and demand for synthetic chemicals to control pests before World War II and the factors that contributed to indiscriminate use of pesticides including DDT, but also addressing use of chlorinated hydrocarbons and organophosphates. These were labeled as more toxic than DDT before the 1972 ban of DDT, but despite their effect on nervous systems, both gained in popularity after the ban.

Others consider pesticides in regional context. See David D. Vail's *Chemical Lands: Pesticides, Aerial Spraying, and Health in North America's Grasslands since 1945* (Tuscaloosa: University of Alabama Press, 2018). Pete Daniel's *Toxic Drift: Pesticides and Health in the Post-World-War-II South* (Baton Rouge: Louisiana State University Press, 2005) distinguished between the precision of private pilots in contrast to government-agency pilots who had little incentive to be precise in their applications.

Adoption of synthetic fertilizers and herbicides have received less attention from historians than pesticides. For an overview of applications, associated technological, and agricultural changes in the Corn Belt state of Iowa, see J. L. Anderson, *Industrializing the Corn Belt: Agriculture, Technology, and Environment, 1945–1972* (DeKalb: Northern Illinois University Press, 2009). Clinton L. Evans, *The War on Weeds in the Prairie West: An Environmental History* (Calgary: University of Calgary Press, 2002).

Elements of the Environment

For a general overview of tornadoes, floods, and other environmental disasters, see Ted Steinberg, *Acts of God: The Unnatural History of Natural Disaster in America* (New York: Oxford University Press, 2000; 2nd ed., 2006). For an interpreter's presentation of the Cosmos, see Neil deGrasse Tyson, *Astrophysics for People in a Hurry* (New York: W.W. Norton & Co., 2017), including a thought-provoking chapter on exoplanet Earth.

For controlled burns, see Stephen J. Pyne, *Fire in America: A Cultural History of Wildland and Rural Fire* (Princeton, NJ: Princeton University Press, 1982); and *America's Fires: A Historical Context for Policy and Practice* (Durham, NC: Forest History Society, 2010); and Timothy Egan, *The Big Burn: Teddy Roosevelt and the Fires that Saved America* (Boston: Houghton Mifflin Harcourt, 2009).

For overviews of significant ecosystems, see James E. Sherow, *Grasslands of the United States: An Environmental History* (Santa Barbara, CA: ABC-CLIO, 2007) and William Least Heat-Moon, *PrairyErth: A Deep Map* (New York: Houghton, 1992).

For recent books on petroleum and energy, see Brian Frehner, *Finding Oil: The Nature of Petroleum Geology, 1859–1920* (Lincoln: University of Nebraska Press, 2011); Richard Rhodes, *Energy: A Human History* (New York: Simon and Schuster, 2018).

Insects/Pests

Dawn Biehler, *Pests in the Cities: Flies, Bedbugs, Cockroaches, and Rats* (Seattle: University of Washington Press, 2013). James E. McWilliams, *American Pests: The Losing War on Insects from Colonial Times to DDT* (New York: Columbia University Press, 2008). Edmund Russell, *War and Nature: Fighting Humans and Insects with Chemicals from World War I to Silent Spring* (New York: Cambridge University Press, 2001).

Soil

David R. Montgomery and Anne Biklé, *The Hidden Half of Nature: The Microbial Roots of Life and Health* (New York: W. W. Norton and Co., 2015). Steven Stoll, *Larding the Lean Earth: Soil and Society in Nineteenth-Century America* (New York: Hill and Wang, 2002); Benjamin R. Cohen, *Notes from the Ground: Science, Soil, and Society in the American Countryside* (New Haven, CT: Yale University Press, 2009); David R. Montgomery, *Dirt: The Erosion of Civilizations* (Berkeley: University of California Press, 2007) and *Growing a Revolution: Bringing Our Soil Back to Life* (New York: W. W. Norton and Co., 2017).

Water / Drought

Ken Burn's documentary, *The Dust Bowl* (2012), prompted historians to debate its merits. See Pamela Riney-Kehrberg, Geoff Cunfer, R. Douglas Hurt, and Julie Courtwright, "Historians' Reaction to the Documentary, The Dust Bowl," (2014), available at https://lib .dr.iastate.edu/cgi/viewcontent.cgi?article=1067&context=history_pubs. Accessed June 10, 2019.

Donald Worster, *Rivers of Empire: Water, Aridity, and the Growth of the American West* (New York: Oxford University Press, 1985); John Opie, *Ogallala: Water for a Dry Land* (Lincoln: University of Nebraska Press, 1993). Kevin Z. Sweeney, *Prelude to the Dust Bowl: Drought in the Nineteenth-Century Southern Plains* (Norman: University of Oklahoma Press, 2016).

Timeline of Environmental Ideas, Policies, and Legislation

Portions of this chronology draw on timelines and chronologies in these sources: Debra A. Reid prepared "Timeline: National Policy and Agrarian Legislation," for inclusion in *Interpreting Agriculture at Museums and Historic Sites* (Lanham, MD: Rowman & Littlefield, 2017). Because of page restrictions, the "Timeline" appears in digital format only and is available at http://alhfam.org/InterpAg (accessed June 22, 2018). Additional timelines and chronologies appear in Kathleen A. Brosnan, eds., *Encyclopedia of American Environmental History, Volume I* (2011) and Carolyn Merchant, *The Columbia Guide to American Environmental History* (2002).

1.6 million–10,000 B.C.E. **The Pleistocene Ice Age** coincided with significant ecological and climatic changes that transformed North American topography.

11,000 B.C.E. **Disappearance of Mammoths** from North American Continent.

c10,000 B.C.E. **Holocene Epoch** denotes the end of the last Ice Age and the start of human domestication of flora and fauna.

10,000 B.C.E. or 1945 **Anthropocene Epoch** proposed, with a beginning date coincident to the domestication of flora and fauna by humans between 12,000 and 15,000 years ago (an event that began the Holocene Epoch) or that began with the detonation of the first nuclear weapon in 1945.

500–1200 C.E. Anasazi Communities in American Southwest.

700–1400 Cahokian woodland communities expand along the Mississippi River.

1400–1690s Spanish and European colonization of North and South America.

1705   Robert Beverley, *History and Present State of Virginia*: Beverley wrote on the natural resources and various communities of Virginia. In his writings, Beverley described the South as a garden where laziness had ill effect on the colonists with harmony in nature as the result.

1760s–1820s   Soil experiments in Virginia: Agriculturalists such as George Washington, Thomas Jefferson, and James Madison conducted field studies in soil health and improvement. They experimented with a variety of chemical applications, technical implements, and ecological methods to bring fertility to soils and prevent insects and weeds.

1750s–1760s   Land Riots: Disputes over land claims led to class conflict in colonies from New York to New Hampshire and Maine. Settlers and tenant farmers who had improved land challenged the claims of their proprietary landlords, and violent uprisings often resulted.

1785   Land Ordinance: The Continental Congress established the grid system of township and range lines as the basis for surveying public land. Townships consisted of thirty-six square miles; each section contained 640 acres. Investors had to purchase complete sections, at a minimum payment of one dollar per acre, but could then divide the section for resale.

1787   Northwest Ordinance: The Continental Congress created the Northwest Territory and vested the national government with oversight over lands in the public domain and authority over the process of admitting states into the Union. Owners held the land in fee simple (i.e., in perpetuity without limitation). The ordinance prohibited slavery in the Northwest Territory and gave the national government final authority over Indian relations in the west.

1801   Preemption Act: This was the first of several acts passed by the U.S. Congress that gave squatters the opportunity to purchase the land on which they had settled but not purchased because of contested land claims, inadequate financial resources, or limited access to land offices, among other reasons.

1803   Louisiana Purchase: Napoleon Bonaparte of France sold the Louisiana Territory to President Thomas Jefferson, doubling the size of the United States. The boundaries included everything west of the Mississippi, along the Arkansas, Platte, and Missouri Rivers, ending at the Continental Divide. Modern states include: Louisiana (portions), Arkansas, Missouri, northern Texas, Oklahoma, Kansas, Eastern Colorado, Nebraska, South Dakota, Iowa, half of North Dakota, half of Minnesota, most of Montana, and Wyoming.

1804–1806   Lewis and Clark Expedition: One of many westward expeditions in the early nineteenth century to explore portions of newly acquired territories, President Thomas Jefferson encouraged Congress to support an expedition along the Missouri River and on to the Oregon Territory.

1830   Indian Removal Act: U.S. policy that justified removal of Indians from the southeastern United States to Indian Territory on the grounds of protecting the Indians from extinction. Some Indians voluntarily relocated; others resisted and were forced out of the area in 1838 during the infamous Trail of Tears; and others avoided relocation by hiding out. Indians faced the total destruction of their culture as President Andrew Jackson made good his promise to further the interests of white yeoman farm families.

1836   Ralph Waldo Emerson's publication, *Nature*: Emerson published *Nature* in 1836, which described the value and curiosity of environments, solitude, and looking to nature for spiritual truths.

1830s–1840s   Hudson River School: This decade saw a series of artists focusing on nature, landscapes, and vistas as their subjects rather than human subjects. Artistic notions of light versus dark or civilization versus wilderness defined their expressions.

1844   George Catlin: Artist of the Great Plains with special focus on American Indians. Catlin's work reflected the persistent and problematic U.S. cultural view of a disappearing wilderness as well as the "noble savage," idea toward American Indians.

1854   Henry David Thoreau, *Walden*: Thoreau is perhaps best known for his cabin at Walden Pond, near Concord, Massachusetts. He "escaped" there for solitude to know an alive nature where "in Wildness is the preservation of the World." Thoreau became one of the well-known authors of Transcendentalism.

1861–1865   Civil War: During the Civil War, farm boys continued to serve; families continued to farm; demand for agricultural commodities grew; the development of technology advanced; and production of agricultural machinery increased.

1862   Homestead Act: The act extended the system of public land sales authorized by the Preemption Act of 1841 to the West (Nebraska being the state where a "homesteader" first filed a claim on public land under the 1862 act). The law (and those following it) required a three-step procedure: file an application, improve the land, and file for deed of title. Any head of household, twenty-one years of age and older could file an application to claim a federal land grant (except those who had taken up arms against the U.S. government). The occupant had to reside on the land for five years and show evidence of improvement.

1862   Morrill Land Grant Act: The legislation granted each eligible state 30,000 acres of public land for each state representative and senator. States used the proceeds to establish a land-grant college to offer training in agricultural and industrial sciences.

1864   George Perkins Marsh, *Man and Nature; or, Physical Geography as Modified by Human Condition*: As a scholar and diplomat, Marsh contemplated the benefits and challenges of natural resources. He argued in *Man and Nature* that societal decline is a central consequence of exploitation. His warnings about deforestation, soil fertility, and general wasting of resources found many adherents in the United States, inspiring early ideas about conservation and preservation of natural landscapes.

1870   Weather Bureau of the United States created within the U.S. Department of War to document meteorological observations and anticipate storms in the northern (Great) Lakes: The Bureau moved to the U.S. Department of Agriculture in 1890 and was renamed the U.S. Weather Bureau. It became a branch of the U.S. Department of Commerce in 1940 and was renamed the National Weather Service in 1970.

1872   Yellowstone Park Act: This Act established the "tract of land lying near the headwaters of the Yellowstone River as a public park." This designation created the first national park in the United States.

1873   Timber Culture Act: In an effort to "bring" vegetation to the grasslands, the naitonal government authorized the sale of 160 acres of land to anyone who planted 40 acres of trees and maintained the land for at least a decade.

1875   Chicago Meat Packer Swift and Company Establishes the Swift Refrigerator Line: Butchering an animal as large as a beef critter generated more meat than most families could consume quickly. Butchers corned beef to preserve and tenderize less popular cuts. The demand for fresh beef in places far removed from the prairie pastures of the Midwest or the ranges of the Southwest resulted in creation of refrigerated rail cars. Meat butchered in Chicago could reach Eastern markets unspoiled, even if less palatable than fresh meat.

1878   Free Timber Act: This act encouraged westward settlement by giving residents free access to timber reserves on public mineral lands.

1878   Timber and Stone Act: Another effort to encourage westward settlement, the federal government offered 160-acre allotments of "unfit" farmland in California, Oregon, and Washington for tree and stone harvesting.

1878   John Wesley Powell, *Report on the Arid Lands of the United States*: After returning from serving on the Union side during the Civil War, Powell served as the director of U.S. Geological Survey. The report declared land west of the 100th meridian as the arid west or territory that received less than twenty inches per year.

1883   Veterinary Division, U.S. Department of Agriculture: The U.S. Department of Agriculture created the Veterinary Division in the Bureau of Animal Industry to research and propose policy to eradicate contagious animal diseases. **The Bureau of Animal Industry replaced it in 1884.**

1887   Dawes Severalty Act: The act was designed to hasten assimilation of Indians on reservations by allotting land to individual families with the expectation that they would adopt Euro-American farming practices. This plan did not take into account cultural identity, social resistance, or the local environment and climate that made family farming on 160 acres of allotment nearly impossible. American Indian nations lost reservation lands because a provision of the bill authorized sale of any reservation lands not claimed through allotments as public lands.

1887 **Desert Lands Act:** The federal government encouraged westward settlement of arid lands through the sale of 640 acres of land if the owner irrigated it within three years of purchase.

1887 **Interstate Commerce Commission (ICC):** The Interstate Commerce Act created the ICC to regulate trade across state lines, an authority vested in the national government by the U.S. Constitution, but it was not exercised before the ICC.

1887 **Hatch Act:** The federal government establish experiment stations to support agricultural science research for the public.

1892 **John Muir and the founding of The Sierra Club:** Founded by famed conservationist John Muir, the Sierra Club worked to protect the environment and encourage interest in the conservation of natural resources and outdoor exploration, especially in the American West.

1892 **Ellen Swallow, *oekology:*** Swallow was one of the scientific pioneers of environmental chemistry as well as an industrial health advocate and safety engineer. Equally well-known for her efforts in domestic science (what became known as home economics), her idea *oekology* or studying the earth as "a household" ultimately became *ecology*.

1894 **Division of Agricultural Soil** created within the U.S. Department of Agriculture. The division hired geographers and chemists to survey soil (i.e., tobacco-growing areas of Connecticut and Maryland and irrigated soils in Utah and New Mexico). The Soil Conservation Service became responsible for soil surveys in 1952. The scope of the National Cooperative Soil Survey increased in 1970 to include urban as well as rural agricultural soils. The Natural Resources Conservation Service assumed responsibility for soil surveys when created in 1994.

1893–1939 **Good Roads Movement:** National interest in road improvement began in 1893 when the U.S. Secretary of Agriculture created the Office of Road Inquiry (Office of Public Roads Inquiries) as specified in the Agricultural Appropriation Act of 1893. It was renamed the Office of Public Roads (1905) and then the Bureau of Public Roads (1918). In 1939, the Bureau became the Public Roads Administration in the Federal Works Agency, and then in 1949, it was renamed the Bureau of Public Roads and placed as a division of the U.S. Department of Commerce. In 1966, the U.S. Congress established the U.S. Department of Transportation, and in 1967, responsibility for public roads fell to the Federal Highway Administration.

1897 **U.S. Animal Health Association (USAHA):** Concerned officials at the state and national level, along with industrialists formed the USAHA to regulate, eradicate animal disease, ensure shipment of healthy animals across state lines, and to plan disease prevention.

1900 **Lacey Act:** As a response to growing concerns by conservationists about the decimation of bird species for the millinery trade, Iowa Congressman John Fletcher Lacey introduced legislation to prohibit any trade of wildlife illegally killed for profit.

1900–1920 Golden Age: Many farmers prospered during the early twentieth century as the market price for commodities (i.e., crop and stock that farmers produced) increased faster than the cost of production. The prices of this era became the basis for agricultural parity, which is the concept that market regulation should prevent market prices from dipping below Golden Age prices.

1901 Right of Way Act: The U.S. Secretary of the Interior has the authority to issue rights of way through public lands.

1902 Reclamation Act: Established the Bureau of Reclamation to administer western water rights and technological developments. Also funded federal irrigation projects through selling public land.

1906 American Antiquities Act: Congress authorized the president of the United States to establish national monuments and preserve federal lands with historic or prehistoric structures. President Theodore Roosevelt designated Devils Tower, Wyoming, as the first national monument in the same year.

1906 Federal Meat Inspection Act: The act gave the U.S. Secretary of Agriculture the authority to deploy meat inspectors to visit slaughter houses, inspect live animals, monitor processing, and inspect finished meat products to determine what was fit for human consumption and what was not. It reflected national interest in retaining European markets for U.S. meat and responded to the pressure from Progressive reformers who called for regulation of food production. The demand for meat inspectors kept veterinary diagnostic laboratories on Illinois campuses busy.

1906 Pure Food and Drug Act: The act was written to protect consumers from tainted foods by increasing regulation on the "manufacture, sale, or transportation of adulterated or misbranded or poisonous or deleterious foods, drugs, medicines, and liquors, and for regulating traffic" of same.

1908 Country Life Commission: President Theodore Roosevelt appointed members to this commission to research rural conditions and propose solutions to improve rural life.

1908 Winters Doctrine: The U.S. Supreme Court ruled that American Indians had tribal rights to water in western states.

1909–1913 National Conservation Congresses: Building on President Theodore Roosevelt's conservation speech to the 1908 Conference of Governors, five national congresses were held in the early twentieth century to allow Americans to gather and discuss strategies for conserving natural resources.

1910 Federal Insecticide Act: The first legislation regulating pesticides. The law did not regulate applications, but the production and marketing of pesticides to protect consumers from fraudulent products.

1911 4-H origins: By 1911, the four-leaf clover represented head, heart, hands, and health. The funding from the Smith-Lever Act supported the creation of 4-H club agents employed through the Agricultural Extension Service at land-grant colleges to work with farm youth.

1914 Smith-Lever Act: President Woodrow Wilson signed this act that formalized the relationship between state land-grant colleges and the USDA's Federal Extension Service. It reduced private funding of African American extension agents in former Confederate states and led to the formation of Negro Divisions at 1890 institutions, administered by the administrators who directed Agricultural Extension Service offerings at 1862 land-grant colleges.

1916 Federal Aid Road Act (also called the Bankhead-Shackleford Act): This legislation authorized each state to form a highway agency and employ engineering professionals to implement federal-aid projects. The act emphasized improvement of farm-to-market roads and rural post roads.

1917 U.S. National War Garden Commission: This agency administered the war garden program, with the U.S. entry into World War I. The youth movement took the form of the U.S. School Garden Army, administered through the U.S. Bureau of Education. Although people in the cities contributed to the War Garden movement, women from the city went to the country as volunteers in the Women's Land Army to help meet labor needs on the farm.

1917 National Vocational Education Act (or Smith-Hughes Act): This legislation provided national funds on a matching basis to high schools that organized and conducted classes in agriculture over a twelve-month period and hired a qualified teacher to conduct these classes on a "learn-by-doing" basis.

1917 Tuberculosis Eradication Division of the Bureau of Animal Industry: Testing conducted between 1917 and 1940 resulted in the destruction of 3.8 million cattle.

1921 Farm Bloc: U.S. congressmen representing Southern, Midwestern, and Plains states continued to support agrarian legislation. During the 1920s, five powerful organizations, The National Cooperative Milk Producers' Federation, the National Council of Farmers Cooperatives, the Grange, the American Farm Bureau Federation, and the National Farmers Union, established strong lobbies in Washington, D.C., and worked with these congressmen to create the bipartisan Farm Bloc.

1921 Packers and Stockyards Act: National legislation protected farmers and ranchers from unscrupulous meatpacking companies by ensuring a fair price for livestock and poultry and regulating sanitary conditions to protect consumers. It did not address the hazards workers experienced on the job.

1926 Hi-Bred Corn Company: Henry A. Wallace founded the seed corn company. The company was renamed Pioneer Hi-Bred Corn Company in 1935, and it grew into the largest hybrid seed company in the United States. Wallace's name recognition likely elevated the company's visibility, if not its credibility. He held major posts with the national government including serving as U.S. Secretary of Agriculture (1933–1940), as vice president (1941–1945) during Franklin D. Roosevelt's fourth term, and as U.S. Secretary of Commerce (1945–1946).

1929   Stock Market Crash and the Great Depression: The New York Stock Exchange crashed, ending the speculative boom of the 1920s. This event marked the start of the Great Depression, an economic collapse that affected all western industrial nations and that lasted until military mobilization invigorated the economy after 1939. Farmers struggled to pay bills because of plummeting commodity prices, and many lost farms because they could not meet mortgage payments.

1931   Cow War: Violent disputes erupted in Iowa over testing cattle for tuberculosis. Farmers failed to repeal the testing program, so they resisted by blocking tests. Some confrontations turned violent. Dan Turner, the Republican Iowa governor, declared martial law and called out the Iowa National Guard to restore peace and to assist in capturing perpetrators.

1933–1938   New Deal: The New Deal began with Franklin D. Roosevelt's inauguration on March 4, 1933. Through executive action and legislation passed by a majority Democrat Congress, the national government began regulating the banking system, reducing unemployment through public work projects, and stabilizing processing and production industries, including agriculture. Historians tend to divide the New Deal into a first (1933–1934) and second phase (1935–1937). The following bills responded to crises in the agricultural economy:

> **1933   Reforestation Relief Act:** This act established the Civilian Conservation Corps (CCC), a relief program for unemployed men that provided vocational training through jobs in environmental conservation and public building projects. Initially created for young men ages 18–24, the CCC boys received five dollars per month and the remaining twenty-five dollars of their salary went home to their parents.

> **1933   Federal Emergency Relief Act:** More than one-quarter of the nation's work force (14 million people) were out of work. The act authorized immediate grants to states for relief projects that took the form of projects for writers, artists, actors, and musicians; construction projects on roads and pools and other public services; and production of consumer goods. It also operated workers' education projects, projects for women, and food-relief projects.

> **1933   Agricultural Adjustment Administration (AAA; Farm Relief Bill):** The AAA was created "to relieve the existing national economic emergency by increasing agricultural purchasing power, to raise revenue for extraordinary expenses incurred by reason of such emergency, to provide emergency relief with respect to agricultural indebtedness, to provide for the orderly liquidation of joint-stock land banks, and for other purposes" (H.R. 3935 Public No. 10). The most controversial strategy involved stabilizing the farm economy by reducing production and recompensing farmers for their lost earnings through subsidies. Different basic commodities became the focus of production reduction in different regions of the country: cotton in the South, field corn and hog reduction in the Midwest, wheat reduction in the Great Plains, and tobacco reduction in

the Chesapeake Bay-Carolina Piedmont. The Supreme Court ruled the AAA unconstitutional in the *United States* v *Butler* early in 1936. Other legislation replaced it in 1936 and 1938, although they established the precedent for US government policy focused on commercial agricultural production.

1933   Tennessee Valley Authority (TVA): Congress created this federally owned corporation to develop the Tennessee River Valley, a region devastated by unemployment and rural poverty. The TVA built flood control projects, recreation areas, and electric generating plants.

1933   Farm Credit Act: The act established the Farm Credit System as a group of cooperative lending institutions to provide short-, intermediate-, and long-term loans for agricultural purposes. Specifically, it authorized the Farm Credit Administration to create twelve Production Credit Associations and twelve Banks for Cooperatives alongside the twelve established Federal Land Banks, as well as a Central Bank for Cooperatives.

1933   Federal Surplus Relief Corporation: The government responded to public criticism of the Hog Reduction program by creating this agency to purchase, process, and distribute basic commodities such as pork, beef, and dairy products, for use in public relief during the Great Depression. The name changed in 1935 to the Federal Surplus Commodities Corporation. By March 1937, it was distributing commodities to school lunch programs.

1933   Soil Erosion Service: The U.S. Congress responded to interest in using New Deal funding for soil-conservation projects by creating the Soil Erosion Service in the U.S. Department of the Interior. The first director, Hugh Hammond Bennett, gained his expertise in soil erosion by working on soil surveys as an employee of the U.S. Department of Agriculture's Bureau of Soils established in 1901. President Franklin D. Roosevelt moved the Service to the U.S. Department of Agriculture, and Congress reauthorized it as a permanent agency, the Soil Conservation Service, in 1935.

1934   Crop Loan Act: This law funded $40 million to continue the Farm Credit Administration, so it could extend credit to farmers for planting and harvesting. Farmers used about 95 percent of the money to produce the 1934 crop.

1934   Jones-Connally Farm Relief Act: The list of basic commodities over which the 1933 Agricultural Adjustment Act had authority included wheat, cotton, field corn, hogs, rice, tobacco, and milk. The Jones-Connally Act added beef cattle to that list; the Jones-Costigan Act (the Sugar Act of 1934) added sugar crops to the list (cane sugar and sugar beets); and the list grew more to include rye, flax, barley, grain sorghum, peanuts, and potatoes. Various factors prompted the expansion of basic commodities. Farmers and ranchers lobbied for the inclusion of beef cattle, a designation they had previously resisted because they could no longer afford to feed cattle to keep them alive during the Dust Bowl. Sugar producers sought government intervention in the form of tariffs and subsidies to shore up a failing sugar industry. Acreage allotments applied only to wheat, cotton, field corn, peanuts, rice, sugar, and most kinds of tobacco.

1934–1940 Dust Bowl: Severe heat and drought during 1934, 1936, and 1939–1940 dried up the Great Plains. The extreme weather, combined with large-scale arable agriculture and not dryland farming, left the soil prone to wind erosion. The environmental crisis forced farm families to abandon their lands and relocate further west.

1935 The Second New Deal: Policies addressed the needs of laborers, the elderly, and the environment.

1935 Social Security Act: This legislation provided old-age insurance to working-class Americans, but less attention has been paid to who did not receive the benefits. Civil servants and public school teachers were excluded from the benefit. Theoretically, they received pensions from their state pension system. Agricultural laborers and domestic servants were also excluded and, thus, did not qualify for social security benefits.

1935 Emergency Relief Appropriation Act: The act authorized almost $5 billion for immediate relief and increased employment on "useful projects," one of which was the Works Progress Administration (WPA). The WPA put people to work constructing tourist destinations across the rural United States, including lodges and other features in state parks and recreation areas. Other projects included infrastructure such as bridges and roads.

1935 Rural Electrification Administration (REA): By 1935, cities and towns had installed power plants, but farm families depended on Delco plants and other independent means of generating electricity. President Franklin D. Roosevelt established the REA through Executive Order 7037. It provided federal loans to rural electric cooperatives. Farm families in the area served paid dues to the cooperative and received the benefit of power provided at a reasonable rate through the cooperative's electric power company. Once formed, the cooperatives received the loans to install poles, lines, and transformers in the rural area served. Electrification created a frenzy of purchasing to secure electric motors, water pumps, washing machines, stoves, and refrigerators to fully modernize the farm home. Investing in the cooperative generated additional economic stimulation to the economy, and the low-interest short-term loans available through other New Deal agencies facilitated these purchases.

1936 Soil Conservation and Domestic Allotment Act: The U.S. Congress responded to the *United States v Butler* decision by revising agricultural policy to address an interstate issue: soil conservation. This act made the Soil Conservation Service central to agricultural policy, appropriating funds to pay farmers to reduce the potential of soil erosion by removing marginal land from production and rehabilitating depleted soils.

1937 Bankhead-Jones Farm Security Act: This act established a credit system that helped tenant farmers purchase land and helped owners to rehabilitate their property. Farmers could also use the low-interest rate loans to purchase livestock, feed, seed, and machinery. The funds also helped the government purchase abandoned lands and reha-bilitate them into forests or grasslands.

1938   Agricultural Adjustment Act (AAA): The second AAA conceptualized soil as a national resource. Instead of compensating farmers for reducing production by reducing acreage in cultivation, it compensated farmers for soil-conservation practices, which, theoretically, reduced production. Farmers cooperated by planting alternative crops on marginal land, terracing to reduce erosion, and rejuvenating soils. Ironically, farmers also planted new varieties that increased yields on fewer acres, so realizing the goals of reduc-tion proved challenging. The policy also sought to ensure a steady supply of and steady market prices for basic agricultural commodities, an "ever-normal granary" as Henry A. Wallace, Secretary of Agriculture, labeled it. The second AAA also provided crop loans through the Commodity Credit Corporation and crop insurance through the Federal Crop Insurance Corporation.

1938   Food, Drug, and Cosmetic Act: The U.S. Food and Drug Administration, as a result of this act bears responsibility for ensuring the safety of food, drugs, and cos-metics. The Delaney Clause, added in 1958, prohibited the use of known carcinogens in food additives.

1941   War Food Administration and Victory Gardens: Agricultural policies during World War II balanced the need to grow food and ration consumption, which volun-teers embraced, with the need to manage basic commodity supplies needed by allies and U.S. troops.

1942   Emergency Price Control Act: This wartime legislation responded to consumer concerns about increasing prices on basic commodities (e.g., corn, wheat, rice, cotton, and tobacco) because of wartime demand. It set the limit on commodity price increases at 110 percent of parity (the Golden Age prices). Congress then passed the Steagall Amendment to protect farmers from the anticipated postwar commodity price decline. The Amendment required the U.S. Congress to sustain commodity prices at 90 per-cent of parity and to continue the support for two years after the war ended. Protected commodities included "hogs, eggs, chickens (with certain exceptions), turkeys, milk, butterfat, certain dry peas, certain dry edible beans, soybeans, flaxseed and peanuts for oil, American-Egyptian (ELS) cotton, potatoes, and sweet potatoes."

1942   Bracero Program: The United States signed the Mexican Farm Labor Agree-ment to provide needed manual labor to producers of fruits, vegetables, sugar beets, and other commodities during World War II. The agreement was extended through the Mi-grant Labor Agreement of 1951. It continued to 1964. Laborers were issued temporary work permits, provided room and board, and earned thirty cents per hour. Criticism of the program included exploitation of laborers, slow payments, and no procedure for extending permanent residence or citizenship to laborers intent on migrating to the United States.

1944   First Meeting of the North Central Weed Control Conference: The inaugural gathering of agricultural scientists, farmers, ranchers, and agricultural spray pilots in the

Great Plains region to discuss the hazards and possibilities of wartime insecticides and herbicides being used in agricultural production.

1945 Trinity Test (Manhattan Project): The first detonation of a nuclear weapon launched the atomic age, which some argue also launched the age in which human influences on the environment ushered in a new epoch, the Anthropocene.

1947 Federal Insecticide, Fungicide, and Rodenticide Act: The U.S. Department of Agriculture bore responsibility for synthetic chemical applications in the postwar United States. It recognized the potential risks of chemical applications to the environment, to the farmer using the chemicals, and to the consumers needing protection from residue on foodstuffs.

1949 Aldo Leopold, *A Sand County Almanac and Sketches Here and There*: In his book, Leopold established one of the fundamental principles of environmental science and activist politics: The Land Ethic: "A thing is right when it tends to preserve the integrity, stability, and beauty of the biotic community. It is wrong when it tends otherwise."

1949 Point Four Program: President Harry S. Truman's fourth point of his inaugural address emphasized the role that agriculture technical experts would play in international Cold War diplomacy.

1950s–1960s Air Applicator Information Series Spraying Handbooks: One of many private agricultural aviation spraying schools, the Air Applicator Institute published handbooks to train aerial spray pilots on different facets of aerial spraying. Experts in entomology, plant pathology, and chemistry consulted on the booklets. The series was one tool in providing additional training to those involved in agricultural aviation.

1953–1961 Ezra Taft Benson: Served as U.S. Secretary of Agriculture during the Eisenhower administration. Benson opposed production controls during the production revolution after World War II when farmers used synthetic herbicides, pesticides, and fertilizers and hybrid seeds to increase yields exponentially. He urged farmers to "get better or get out."

1954 Agriculture Act: The act established a flexible price support system for basic commodities. In his statement, Eisenhower wrote:

> At last our farmers are enabled gradually to redirect our agriculture toward better balanced production—and, at last, our farmers are assured of greater freedom instead of the rapidly increasing regimentation and Federal domination they were sure to suffer under a continuation of the present system of rigid price supports. Those who share my deep feeling about the great importance to our country of preserving the proud independence and initiative of our farming people will share my pleasure in this new law, and will also share my hope that in time nearly all production adjustments can be accomplished through flexible supports instead of direct government controls.

1956   Soil Bank Program: The Agricultural Act of 1956 created the Soil Bank Program, among its other provisions. The program encouraged farmers to take land out of production for short- and long-term intervals. In exchange for the acreage they banked, farmers received annual rent payments from the Soil Bank appropriation.

1957   Poultry Products Inspection Act: This act required inspection of all poultry slaughtered and processed into food for human consumption.

1960   Occupational Safety and Health Act (OSHA): The act provided for comprehensive oversight of working conditions to ensure the safety and health of laborers. Farmers received exemptions if employees were family members and if farmers employed fewer than ten laborers over the previous twelve months. OSHA regulations applied to equipment manufacturers who had to provide tractor roll bars and shields on farm equipment and to employers of temporary, seasonal, and migrant laborers who had to ensure sanitary conditions in fields and in labor camps.

1962   Rachel Carson, *Silent Spring*: Carson's book became the fundamental primer for environmental health and activist politics of the 1960s. She stated that the prodigious use of pesticides, especially DDT, had dire ecological consequences that could harm entire food chains.

1970   Environmental Protection Agency (EPA): President Richard Nixon created the EPA by executive order during a period of intense concern about the natural environment in the wake of Rachel Carson's *Silent Spring* and eight months after the first Earth Day. The EPA consolidated research, planning, and regulatory bodies on major natural resources (e.g., air, water, land, endangered species, hazardous waste, and agricultural chemical use).

1970   Clean Air Act: This act regulated emissions and set industry standards for air pollution control through the EPA. It also established the National Ambient Air Quality Standards (NAAQS) for human and environmental protection.

1971-1976   Earl Butz: U.S. Secretary of Agriculture during Richard Nixon's and Gerald Ford's administrations. Butz advised farmers to "get bigger, get better, or get out" and to plant "from fence row to fence row." Butz had served as assistant secretary for Marketing and Foreign Agriculture (1954–1957) during the Eisenhower administration and as the chairman of the U.S. Delegation to the Food and Agricultural Organization of the United Nations (1954–1957). Butz advocated for minimal regulations and international trade to market excess agricultural commodities.

1972   Banning of Insecticide DDT: Building on Rachel Carson's book *Silent Spring* in 1962 and the protests of Earth Day in 1970, the environmental movement helped shape the policymaking that ultimately saw the banning of DDT.

1972   Federal Water Pollution Control Act: This act amended existing law to increase national authority "to restore and maintain the chemical, physical, and biological integrity of the nation's waters" (PL 92-500). Amendments in 1977 resulted in the Clean Water Act (PL 95-217).

1973 Endangered Species Act (ESA): The act issued federal protections to threatened and endangered species as well as their habitats. The ESA could also prohibit resource development in these protected habitats.

1973 Agriculture and Consumer Protection Act: Before this farm bill, the U.S. Congress passed separate bills to authorize public land sales, create farm credit policy, protect rural and farm cooperatives from anti-trust legislation, or identify basic commodities eligible for price supports. This act consolidated several bills into one omnibus bill and set a trend for omnibus farm bills every five years that combined policies for consumers and producers.

1979 Farm Crisis: Between 1971 and 1980, land values increased more than 220 percent. Agricultural economists such as Folke Dovring at the University of Illinois encouraged farmers who owned the highest-valued land to use their land equity to purchase more land and new machinery and to funnel their incomes from higher yields into more land. Lenders profited from high interest rates paid by farmers with high debt loads. This contributed to an economic crisis that began in 1979 and intensified through 1981. Increasing interest rates cooled land speculation; a grain embargo closed trade with the Soviets in retaliation for the Soviet invasion of Afghanistan; and a tax cut created budget deficits and preserved high interest rates. Grain prices fell. Farmers defaulted on mortgages, lost their farms, became morose, and some took their own lives. The consumer perspective became critical to agricultural policy as their interest in low food prices trumped the strong agricultural lobbyists seeking pro-active policy to ensure stable agricultural supply and demand.

1980 Federal Crop Insurance Reform Act: This replaced the Federal Crop Insurance Corporation of 1938. Subsequent ad hoc legislation authorized reimbursement of a percentage of production losses resulting from emergencies (especially floods and droughts).

1981 Farmland Protection Policy Act, subtitle I of Title XV, section 1539–1549 of the Agriculture and Food Act of 1981 (Public Law 97-98): This act responded to the loss of arable land acreage because of urban sprawl. It, in conjunction with state-based farmland preservation program, helped reduce the loss of farmland through federal land purchases and cooperative agreements with farm families to continue farming the land. This expanded in 2004 to include farm and ranch lands.

1986 Coordinated Framework for Regulation of Biotechnology: Satisfied the goal of supporting the growing biotechnology industry without restrictive regulation while protecting consumer health. The framework focused on the product of genetic modification (GM) not the process, based regulation on documented risks, and used only existing policy to assess whether or not a GM product was "generally recognized as safe" (GRAS).

1990 Organic Food Production Act: Title 21 of the Food, Agriculture, Conservation and Trade (FACT) Act, established the National Organic Program to apply standards and lists of organic farming practices and acceptable production inputs. It established a certification process and prohibited the practice of labeling products as organic in the absence of certification. It allowed for flexibility if state standards differed from national standards, pending U.S. Department of Agriculture review.

1994 Natural Resources Conservation Service (NRCS): The Soil Conservation Service was renamed the Natural Resources Conservation Service as part of the reorganization of the U.S. Department of Agriculture. In addition to name changes, the goals of agencies expanded. The NRCS had authority to coordinate efforts of private landowners, local and state governments, and federal agencies to conserve and maintain healthy and productive agricultural and rural landscapes.

1996 Food Quality Protection Act: Increased the Environmental Protection Agency's responsibilities for defining safety standards relative to pesticide use on foodstuffs, reviewing those standards, and determine risk of exposure to pesticides over time. It resulted from amendments to the Federal Insecticide, Fungicide, and Rodenticide Act and the Food, Drug, and Cosmetic Act.

1997 Genetically Modified Organism (GMO): The U.S. Department of Agriculture's (USDA's) glossary of biotechnology terms defines "genetic engineering" as the "manipulation of an organism's genes by introducing, eliminating, or rearranging specific genes using the methods of modern molecular biology, particularly those techniques referred to as recombinant DNA techniques." The USDA defines "genetic modification" as "the production of heritable improvements in plants or animals for specific uses, via either genetic engineering or other more traditional methods." Organisms can be produced using either genetic engineering (GE) or genetic modification (GM). Scientists have engineered crops to be herbicide tolerant and bug resistant. USDA statistics indicate increases in acreage of herbicide-tolerant varieties since the 1990s.

2000 Population Statistics: The world's population reached six billion people (6,082,966,429), a growth rate of 12.6 percent from the 1990 statistic. In 2000, the U.S. population reached 281 million (281,421,906), a growth rate of 13.2 percent from the 1990 statistic.

2010 Population Statistics: The world's population reached 6.8 billion people (6,848,932,929), a 10.7 percent increase over the 2000 statistic. The rate of increase has slowed, and projections indicate that the slowdown will continue in future decades. The U.S. population reached 309 million (308,745,538), a growth rate of 9.7 percent from the 2000 statistic.

Index

Page references for figures are italicized.
The Bibliographic Essay is indexed by subject rather than by author or title. See "selected readings."

agriculture, xii, 14, 50, 66, 69, 90, 108, 158,
167, 173; agricultural extension agents/
service, 43n16, 48, 170; agricultural
science, 15–16, 34, 43n16, 147, 168, 176;
assarting, 65; changing the environment,
32, 58, 86, 103, 125, 158; cultivation,
34, 70, 103; cultural practice, 7, 34;
education in, 167, 171; Golden Age, 107,
169, 175; land use, xiii, 17, 64, 65, 132;
regulation (price supports, production),
169, 172, 174, 175, 176; parity, 169, 175;
producer organizations, 171; production
revolution, 104, 176; purchasing power,
172; reversing injustice, 69–71; slash-and-
burn, 64; statistics, 100, 179; yields, 34,
43n16, 80, 174, 176, 178; *See also* aerial
spraying, agricultural mechanization,
biotechnology, chemicals, cooperatives,
economics, farming/to farm, fertilizer,
food, interpretation, legislation, New
Deal agricultural agencies, organic (food),
organic (living organism), pesticides,
production, US Department of Agriculture
AHS. *See* Agricultural History Society
air, 17, 30, 177; air conditioning, 124; airways,
120; and Earth Day, 17; quality, 65, 177; *See
also* clean air
Alabama, 33–34
Alberta [Canada], 36; Edmonton, *40, 41*
Albright, Horace, 7
Alderson, William T. and Shirley Payne Low,
Interpretation of Historic Sites (1976), 46,
151–152
ALHFAM. *See* Association for Living History,
Farm and Agricultural Museums
almanac, 50, 87, 90–91; See also, Leopold,
Aldo (*Sand County Almanac*)
American Alliance of Museums (previously
American Association of Museums), xv, 57,
149, 150
American Association for State and Local
History (AASLH), xv, xix, 149, 150–151,
153
American bison. *See Bison bison*

American Farm Bureau Federation, 171; *See
also* Farm Bureau (county offices)
American Historical Association, 149, 150
American Indian(s): Agaidŭka Shoshone,
37; Comanche Empire, xvii; Crow, 38;
Eastern Shoshone, 37, 38, *39*; Flathead, 37;
land management (fire), 64–65; *Nakodabi/
Assiniboine*, 37; Navajos, 104, 106; Plains,
32, 36, *38;* relation to *Bison bison*, 36–39,
40; Trail of Tears, 33, 167; tribal rights to
water (Winters Doctrine), 170; Washakie,
37–38, *39*; Woodland/Eastern Woodland,
165
American Indians affected by: allotments/
assimilation, 168; Bureau of Indian Affairs,
154; conquest/"discovery," 11, 166; contact/
relations with, 148, 154, 166; dispossession/
removal/destruction of ecosystem, 11, 18,
75, 103, 114, 167; reservations, and loss
of, 168; Shoshoni and Bannock Indian
Agency, 38; stereotype(s), 11, 32, 39, 167;
subject of art, 32, 39, 167; treaties, 38; *See
also* legislation
American Revolution, 82–84; British navy/
Royal Navy, 83–84
American Society of Environmental History
(ASEH), xiii, xv, xix, 149; *Environmental
History*, xv, 149
Anasazi, 165
Anderson, J. L.: *Industrializing the Corn Belt*
(2009), 108, 161
animals, xvi, xviiin2, 3, 4, 11, 168, 169; *See also
Bison bison*, livestock
Anthropocene, xiv, 148, 165, 175
appliances, 92, 96–97, 100; cream separator,
93; electric iron, 94; electric range, 89,
94, 96, 97; electric refrigerator, 89, 95,99;
Frigidaire, 97, 99; gas range/stove, 93–94,
95–96, 97; hot water heater, 94; kerosene
stoves, 92; radio, 89, *98*, 99; skillet, electric,
97; wringer washing machine (gas or
electric tub), 94
archaeology, 36, 45, 46; archaeo-botanists, 36;
historic archaeology, 46, 59n1, 59n2

coast. *See* Carson, ecosystem, lighthouses, water

Colby Branch Agricultural Experiment Station, Kansas, 86

cold storage. *See* locker plant

Cold War, xiii, xx, 176

collection (museum). *See* archives, artifacts, collection development

collection development, 50, 51–53; cataloging, xii, xvii, 51–52

College of the Atlantic, 138

colonies/colonists, 166

colonization. *See* conquest

Colorado, 17, 103, 166; Denver, 17; Pikes Peak area, 72

commercialization/commodification of parks, 7, 11; *See also* tourism

commodities, 159, 167, 169, 172, 174; consumer protection, 178; markets, 171; prices, 171, 175, 176; production reduction, 172, 176; *See also* agriculture, crops, dairy, livestock, poultry

compost/composting, xiv

Comstock, Anna Botsford, *Handbook of Nature Study* (1911), 18

Conard, Rebecca, 11

Confederacy (Confederate States of America, CSA), 66, 170; former Confederate states, 170

Connecticut, 169

conservation, xiv, 6, 11, 156, 160–161, 169; Civilian Conservation Corps, 172; compared to preservation, 11; early ideas about, 167; harmony with opposite, 13; National Conservation Congresses, 170; values of being "conservation-minded," 6; *See also* environment, legislation; Muir, John; The Sierra Club, soil

conservation area(s)/district(s), xi, xiv, xv, xvi

conservationist, xii

Continental Congress, 166

Continental Divide, 166

controversy, xiv, xvi, 3, 160–161; private access versus public good, xii, xiv, 17; *See*

also agriculture, climate, natural resources, plastic, pollution, public land

cooking, 59, 80, 91–97, 110; farm-to-fork/field-to-table, 59, 170; fireplace/hearth, 59, 94, 145; fuel, 91–97; stoves, 91–97

Cooper, Susan Fenimore, *Rural Hours* (1850), 18

cooperatives, 171, 172, 177, 178; Banks for Cooperatives, 172; Central Bank for Cooperatives, 172; National Cooperative Milk Producers' Federation, 171; National Council of Farmers Cooperatives, 171; *See also* rural, Rural Electrification Administration

Corson, Barbara, 30–31

Country Life Commission, 170

Courtwright, Julia, *Prairie Fire* (2011), 65

Covert, Bertha, 134

Cronon, William, 5, 157; *Nature's Metropolis*, xvi; "A Place for Stories: Nature, History, and Narrative" (1992), xvi; "The Trouble with Wilderness; or, Getting Back to the Wrong Nature," 7; *Uncommon Ground: Rethinking the Human Place in Nature* (1996), 7, 149; "The Uses of Environmental History" (1993), xiii

crop(s), 33–34, 59, 67–69, 72, 79, 103, 106, 107, 111, 169; barley, 173; beans (dried), 175; corn (field and seed), 32, 43n16, 58–59, 65, 72, 80, 93, 104, 108, 124, 171, 172, 173, 175; cotton, 33–34, 65, 66, 70–71, 172, 173, 175; drought-tolerant, 36, 158; famine, 80; flax/flaxseed, 173, 175; grain sorghum, 173; indigo, 67; moon phase, 90; nutrient needs, 34, 58; peanuts, 33–34, 58, 173–174, 175; peas (dried), 175; residue, 65; rice, 66–67, 173, 175; rye, 173; saving endangered plants, 151; soybeans, 33–34, 65, 67, 80, 93, 175; sugar beets/sugar cane, 173; sweet potatoes, 33–34, 58, 175; tobacco, 169, 172–173, 175; wheat, 172, 173–174, 175; *See also* agriculture, aerial spraying, commodities, irrigation, legislation, vegetables crop insurance: Federal Crop Insurance Corporation (1938), 175, 178

cultural heritage/cultural patrimony, xiv, xv

Daggett, Hallie, 133

dairy (milk, butter, butterfat), 107, 171, 173, 175

Daniel, Pete, 15; *Toxic Drift* (2005), 108, 161

Darwin, Charles, *On the Origin of Species by Means of Natural Selection* (1859) xi, 32

Davis, Frederick Rowe, *Banned* (2014), 15

Davis, William Morris, 139

debate. *See* controversy/controversial

Deetz, James, 45, 46; *In Small Things Forgotten* (1977), 46, 59n2

Delco-Light Farm Electric Plant, 93, 174; *See also* energy

democracy, 16

Durkee, Alfred, 97

desert, 77n15, 80, 168

digital humanities, 5; crowd sourcing, 5; makerspaces, 5; telepresence technologies, 5; visualization, 5

disaster (environmental, natural), ix, 50, 80, 87, 162; earthquake, 50; eco-disaster, 26n37; *See also* fire

domestication, 165

Dorr, George, 141

Dovring, Folke, 178

Dust Bowl, xvii, 14, 18, 162–165, 173; storms, 13, 15–16

Earhart, Amelia, 73

Earth, xvi, xviiin2, 6–7, 14, 17, 32, 33, 41n2, 79, 89, 162, 169

Earth Day. *See* activism/advocacy

Eastern. *See* regions

eclipse (solar, lunar), 91

ecocriticism. *See* humanities

ecofeminism, xvii, 18–19; *See also* gender

ecology/ecological, xi, xii, 3, 5, 155; ecological change, 165; ecological methods, 166; Swallow, Ellen, and study of Earth as "a household," *oekology*, 169

economics: of agriculture/farming (collateral, costs, credit, debt, equity, financing, loans, market prices), 98, 172, 174, 178; domestic science (home economics), 169

ecosystem, 34, 35, 46, 85, 136, 152, 162; coast, marsh, xiii, 65, 75, 79, 138–141; concept, 13, 159; destruction of, xiii, 91, 103; ecotourism as threat to, 21; management of, 64–65

ecotourism/nature-based tourism, xi, 13, 21, 136

Eiker & Son, 94

Eisenhower, Dwight D., 176, 177

Electromaster Factory, 97

Eliot, Charles, 138–141

Eliot, Charles William, 141

Emerson, Ralph Waldo, 167; *Nature* (1836), 167

Emporia State University, 87endangered species, 136, 151, 177, 178energy; firewood, 91; Fresnel lights, 128; generating and harnessing power, xvi, 89–101; Hornsby-Akroyd engine, 128; hydroelectric plants, 89, 172; PurOPane Bottled Gas heating fuel, 94; renewable, xvii, 80, 91; solar, xvii, *99*, 100, 128, 143; sources, 89, 100; thermonuclear power/reactor, 89, 91; wind/windmills, xvii, 82, 89, 100; *See also* fossil fuels, nonrenewable, renewable, rural, Rural Electrification Administration, Tennessee Valley Authority

engineers/engineering, xvi, 170

enslaved people, 49, *66*, 82–84; Bush, Adam, 83; Pluto, 83

entropy, xiv

environment: definition, xviiin2, xi, 3; human affects on, xi, xii–xiv, xvi, 13, 32, 57; largest artifact, 51–52, 63–64; natural, 7, 13; *See also* activism/advocacy, built environment, conservation, human-nature relationships, interpretation, natural resources, preservation, restoration

environmental/environmentalism, 6, 17, 19, 22, 64, 156–157

environmental chemistry, 169

environmental degradation, xii–xiv, xvi, 13, 19, 32–33, 143, 145–146; *See also* natural resources, toxicity

environmental education, xvi, xvii, 16, 30, 46, 55, 57, 143; Arbor Day, 159; Audubon Society, 136–137, 159; Environmental Protection Agency's Office of Environmental Education, 149; literacy, xvii, 46, 53–55, *56*, 57, 59, 107; *See also* North American Association for Environmental Education

environmental history, xiii, xv, xvi, xix, 3–5, 11, 13, 29, 63, 148–149, 155–162; *See also* American Society for Environmental History

Environmental History. See American Society of Environmental History

environmental humanities. *See* humanities

environmental justice, 6, 18–21, 31, 69–70, 143, 144, 148; equality, 17; issues, xiv, xv, xvi–xvii, 4, 48–49, 70–71, 80–82, 110, 143, 147–148, 155, 157, 159; inequality, xvii, 17; People of Color Environmental Leadership Summit, 19–21; Principles of, *20; See also* activism/advocacy, class, ecofeminism, environmental degradation, gender, natural resources, race

environmental literacy. *See* environmental education

environmental movement, xii, xvii, 14, 18, 153, 155, 156, 160, 177

Environmental Protection Agency, 46, 49, 149, 160, 177, 179; *See also* legislation, regulation

environmental sites of conscience, 69–71

environmental stewardship. *See* steward/stewardship

environmental thinking, xv, 11, 14, 17, 19, 21, 22; *See also* thinking historically

EPA. *See* Environmental Protection Agency

erosion, 173

ethic(s), 145, 149, 156; Earth Day and new American standard, 17; ecofeminism as

new environmental ethic, 19; humanities discipline, 30, 42n4; and museum standards, 75n2; *See also* land ethic, Leopold, Aldo, activism/advocacy

ethnic/ethnicity, xiv, 10–12, 13, 69, 85

Eudora Area Historical Society, Kansas, 86

evolution, xi

exhibit(s), 3

Farm Bloc, 171

Farm Bureau (county offices), 48, 87

Farm Crisis, 178

farmers/agriculturalists, 166, 171; economic hardship, 171; farm families, 79, 82, 92–96, *95*, 167, 178; farm women, 94, 95, 99; mortgage payments, 171; planters, 66, 69–70; tenant, 70, *95*, 97, 166, 174; yeoman, 167; *See also* commodities

farms/farming/to farm, xi, 34, 96, 167; domestic life on, 59, 82, 92, 94; farm loss, 171, 178; improving farms, 49; percent living on, 96; power on farms, 91–100; protection of farmland, 178; *Silent Spring* influence on, 73; suitability of environment, 85, 168; *See also* rural, interpretation

fauna, xii, xiv, xvii, 165

Favretti, Rudy J. and Joy Putnam Favretti, *Landscapes and Gardens for Historic Buildings* (2nd ed., 2017), xv

fee simple, 166

fertilizer, 34, 39, 44n23, 107, 161, 176; bone-meal, 39, 44n23; nutrient experiments, 43n16; *See also* agriculture, chemicals, livestock

Fiege, Mark: *Irrigated Eden*, 80

field study(ies), 166

fire, 80, 87, 91, 132–135, 145, 162; anthropogenic, 64–65; controlled burns, 64–65, 162; fire finder, Osborne (alidade), 134; lookouts/watchers, 133–136; prairie fires, 36; fuel source, 65, 104

fire an engine or fire-up (idiom), 92, 129

Firestone Farm. *See* The Henry Ford

firewood, 91

First National People of Color Environmental Leadership Summit (1991). *See* People of Color Environmental Leadership Summit

Fitzgerald, Deborah, 107

Flint Hills, 72, 86

flood(s), ix, 36, 50, 80, 86, 87, 162, 173, 178; control, 172; floodplain, 79; Johnstown, Pennsylvania, ix

flora, xii, xiv, xvii, 165

Follin, Mike, 82

food, xi, 16; artificial, 34; growing, xvi, 103–111; policy to ensure low prices, 178; *See also* agriculture, chemicals, legislation, garden, organic

Ford, Clara, 67

Ford, Gerald R., 177

Ford, Henry, 58, 67–69, *68*, 79

forest, 13, 36, 45, 65, 70, 80, 132; conversion to farmland, 70; deforestation, xii, 70, 80, 167; experimental forest, 100n1; fire finders; foresters, 6, 64, 133; gender, 132–134; reforestation, 70; rangers, 132–136; *See also* forest preserve, legislation, lumber, US Forest Service, woodland

Forest History Society, 149

forest preserve, xi, xiv, xv, xvi, 131,

forest rangers: female, 132–136

fossil fuels, xiv, xvii, 52, 59, 91, 100, 142, 143; coal, 41n2, 49, 50, 59, 91, 114, 116, 145; coal oil, 94; "Flex fuel" precedence for tractors, 92–93; kerosene, 91–94, 100, 128; oil/petroleum, 15, 91, 92, 129, 162; 4–H, 110, 170

Fournier, Maureen, 137–141

Foy, Charles R., 82–84

Frazier, Jim, 96, 97

free blacks, 83–84; Ranger, Joseph, 83; Spriggs, Abel, 83

freedom: waterways as freedom trails, 83–84

Freeman, Dorothy, 74

Frehner, Brian, *Finding Oil: The Future of the Petroleum Geology, 1859–1920* (2011), 15

frontier, xiii

fruit, 79, 103, 106; citrus, 69; grapefruit, 69; grapes, 103–104; oranges, 69, 103, *104*

fuel. *See* energy, fossil fuel

Garner, Margaret, 82

garden(s)/gardening, xv, 72, 80, 91, 153, 155; growing food, 16, 39, 50, 58–59, 67, 103; family/home/kitchen garden, 39, 58–59, 67, 110; market, 39, 50, 58; South as, 166; urban/suburban, 16, 39; US School Garden Army, 103, *105*, 170–171; Victory Gardens, 175

Garrity, Tim, 137–141gender, xiv, 13, 18, 69, 71–74, 110, 133–134, 148; *See also* ecofeminism

genetic engineering (GE). *See* biotechnology

genetic modification (GM). *See* biotechnology

genetic modified organism (GMO). *See* biotechnology

geographical information systems (GIS), 87, 107

geography, xii; cultural, xix, xx; historical, xix; uses of to secure environmental justice, 42n10

Georgia: Bryan County, 67; Chatham County, 67; Cherry Hill Plantation, 67; Georgia Humanities, 75; Providence Canyon, 70; Richmond Hill Plantation, 67–69; Savannah, 67

Gershenfeld, Neil, Center for Bits and Atoms, Massachusetts Institute of Technology, 5

Gilbert, George and John, 86

GIS. *See* geographical information systems

Glassberg, David: *Public History and the Environment* (2004), 11

Glassie, Henry, 123

global positioning system (GPS), 87

globe/global, xiii–xiv; 21, 52, 149; warming, xiv, 59; *See also* climate

Good Roads Movement, 169; *See also* government agencies; legislation

government: Conference of Governors, 170; federal/national, 166, 168, 169, 171; parties/

architectural, xix; discipline, xi, xii, xvi, 29, 30–35; facts via Google and Wikipedia, 33; local, 150–151; of landscape architecture, xix; of wilderness as cultural construct, 7, 63; regional, xvi, 157; relation to science, xi, xvii, 30–31, 35; relevance, 31, 33; state history, xv, xvi, 157; uses of to secure environmental justice, 31; *See also* environmental history, historical, local history, natural history, research, thinking historically

History Relevance, 31, 33; "Value of History Statement," 31, 42n10; *See also* Cronon

Hodges, Claire Marie, 135

Holland, Francis Ross, *America's Lighthouses* (1972), 127

Hollis, Aaron, 108, 109–111Holmes, Julia Archibald, 72–73

Holocene, 165

homestead/homesteader, 167; *See also* legislation

Hornberger, Patrick and Linda Turbyville, *Forgotten Beacons* (1997), 127

human-nature/environment relations, xii, xiv, 4, 11, 45; affects on, xvi, xviiin2; boundary between nature and culture, 4; continuum, xiii, 7; cost of survival, xii; feelings toward, 167; inseparable companions, xiii; manipulation, xvi; study of as local history, xvii, 157; Understanding the Local Environment, *56; See also* agriculture, environment

humanities, xvii, 30, 32–33, 35, 42n3, 84–87, 136–137; adding to STEM, STEAM, STEMIE, xi, 13, 33; compared to science, xi, xvi–xvii, 29–42n3, 42n4; compared to social science, xvii, 42n3, 42n4; ecocriticism, 18; environmental humanities, 18; *See also* digital humanities, history, humanities council

humanities council (state), xix, 22, 75, 84, 85–86humanist/humanist thinking. *See* activism/advocacy

Humboldt, Alexander von, xii

hunter(s)/hunting, 13, 18, 36–39, 50, 79, 153, 158; mushroom, 111

ice (cooling), 79, 97, 99; ice box/refrigerator, 96

Ice Age(s), 165

Idaho, 37, 80

identity: construction in museums, 17; in relation to environment, xiii, 13, 17–18, 79, 148, 168; insular "home feeling," 17, 18; native soil (as place of origin), 17; transfer through conquest, 18; IE Toolkit, xiv, 3–5, 29, 45, 63–64

Illinois, xix, 43n16, 74, 94–99, 170; Byron Forest Preserve District, 74; Chester, 96–99; Chicago, xvi, 96, *106*, 119, 157, 168; Crawford County, 99; Eden, 94; Illinois Country, xvi; Jackson County, 96; Marseilles, *95;* Perry County, 96; Randolph County, 96; Red Bud, 95; Rockwood, 94, 97; Sparta, 95–99; St. Clair County, 96; University of Illinois, 43n16, 178; Washington County, 96

Illinois-Iowa Power Company, 97

Indian Head Nickel, 39–40

Indian Territory, 167

insecticide. *See* legislation, pesticides, regulation

International Coalition of Sites of Conscience, 69

International Union for Conservation of Nature and Natural Resources (formerly World Conservation Union), 21

International Shoe Factory (Chester, Illinois), 99

interpretation, x, 147–162; "a" whole, not "the" whole, 45–46, 57; Bloom's taxonomy (hierarchy of cognitive skills), 35, 54–55; first-person, 72–73, 119; guided inquiry, 33; interactive/participatory, 3; living history farm, *12*, 13, 64, 151, 152–153; of agriculture, 13, 58–60, 69–71, 103, 107, 108, 110–111, 151, 165; of the environment,

175; Emergency Relief Appropriation Act (1935), 174; Endangered Species Act (1973), 178; Farm Credit Act (1933), 172; Farmland Protection Policy Act (1981), 178; Federal Aid Road Act (Bankhead-Shackleford Act) (1916), 170; Federal Crop Insurance Reform Act (1980), 178; Federal Emergency Relief Act (1933), 172; Federal Insecticide Act (1910), 170; Federal Insecticide, Fungicide, and Rodenticide Act (1947), 175, 179; Federal Meat Inspection Act (1906), 170; Federal Water Pollution Control Act (1948), 177; Federal Water Pollution Control Act (1972), 177; Food, Agriculture, Conservation, and Trade Act (1990), 178; Food, Drug, and Cosmetic Act (1938), 174, 179; Food Quality Protection Act (1996), 179; Free Timber Act (1878), 168; Hatch Act (1887), 169; Historic Sites Act (1935), 7; Homestead Act (1862), 167; Indian Removal Act (1830), 167; Interstate Commerce Act (1887), 168; Jones-Connally Farm Relief Act (1934), 173; Jones-Costigan Act (Sugar Act) (1934), 173; Lacey Act (1900), 169; Land Ordinance (1785), 166; Lighthouse Act (1789), 125, 127; Louisiana Purchase (1803), 166; Morrill Land Grant Act (1862), 167; National Historic Preservation Act (1966), 7; National Vocational Education Act/Smith-Hughes Act (1917), 171; Northwest Ordinance (1787), 166; Occupational Safety and Health Act (1960), 177; Organic Act (1916), 6; Organic Food Production Act (1990), 178; Packers and Stockyards Act (1921), 171; Poultry Products Inspection Act (1957), 177; Preemption Act (1801), 166; Preemption Act (1841), 167; Pure Food and Drug Act (1906), 170; Reclamation Act (1902), 169; Reforestation Relief Act (1933), 172; Right of Way Act (1901), 169; Social Security Act (1935), 173; Soil Conservation and Domestic Allotment Act

(1936), 174; Smith-Hughes Act/National Vocational Education Act (1917), 171; Smith-Lever Act (1914), 170; Timber and Stone Act (1878), 168; Timber Culture Act (1873), 168; Wilderness Act (1964), 6–7; Yellowstone Park Act (1872), 168; *See also* New Deal, New Deal agricultural agencies

Leopold, Aldo, 6, 13, 17; land ethic, xiiin5, 22, 175; *Round River: From the Journals of Aldo Leopold* (1972), 13; *A Sand County Almanac* (1949), xiii, 14, 155, 175

Lewis, Pierce F., 64

Lewis and Clark Expedition, 11, 166

lighthouses, 123–129

Lindbergh, Anne and Charles, 92

Lindsley, Marguerite, 136

livestock, 93, 106–107, 168, 169, 171; cattle (beef and dairy), xx, 59, 65, 85, 168, 171, 173; Cow War, 171; disease eradication/prevention, 168, 169, 171; economics (financing, market price), 171, 174; feed/pasture and water, 59, 79, 93, 104, 111, 124, 158; hogs/pork, 67, 79, 98, 110, 172, 173, 175; interstate transport, 169; manure, 43n16, 34 64, 104, 106–107; open-range, 34, 124; saving endangered breeds, 151; slaughter and processing, 104, 169, 171; stock farming, 34; tuberculosis, 171; *See also* buildings/structures, legislation, New Deal agricultural agencies, organic, poultry, regulation, U.S. Animal Health Association

lobby groups, 170, 171

local environment, *56*

local history, xii, xv, xvi, 157; natural world as co-actor and co-determinate, xvii

locker plant, 98

Long, Leslie: *The Henry Ford Era at Richmond Hill, Georgia* (1998), 67

Louisiana, 166

Louisiana Territory, 166

Low, Shirley Payne and William T. Alderson, *Interpretation of Historic Sites* (1976), 46, 151–152

xii; gravitas, 5, 6–7, 18, 42n10, 71, 103, 127; natural, xi, 134, 140, 144; relation to space as a concept, xi, 34, 46–49, 52–53, 63, 131, 160; sense of place, xii, 17, 74, 160–161; setting, xi, xviii, 36, 69, 119, 134, 140; understanding for interpretation, xv–xvii, 3, 5, 11, 13, 31, 32, 45–46, 73, 84, 119

planet. *See* globe/global

plants, xvi, xviiin2, 11; plant disease, 16

plains. *See* grassland

plastic(s), xiv

Pleistocene, 165; *See also* Ice Age(s)

Point Four Program, 176

policy. *See* legislation

Pollan, Michael, *The Omnivore's Dilemma* (2006)

pollution, xiii, xiv, 6, 17, 49, 65, 145, 177; *See also* water

Popper, Karl, 31; *Logik der Forschung* (1934), 31; *The Logic of Scientific Discovery* (1959), 31

population, 96, 126, 179; low density, 120; removal of indigenous, 37–38, 75

potassium [K], 34, 107

poultry, 43n16, 104, 171, 177; chickens/geese/turkeys, 59, 86, 175; eggs, 59, 175; feathers, 34

Powell, John Wesley, 168; *Report on the Arid Lands of the United States* (1878), 168

power. *See* energy

prairie. *See* grassland

Prairie Museum of Art and History, Colby, Kansas, 86

presentism. *See* thinking historically

preservation, xii, xiv, 6, 7, 13, 30, 156, 169; briefs, 3; compared to conservation, 7; costs, 12–13; early ideas about, 167; Secretary of Interior Standards (protect, preserve, restore, rehabilitate), 11, 30, 42n4, 152; *See also* environment, monuments; Muir, John

Progressive reform, 170

protein, 34, 67; nonmeat, 34

provocation. *See* interpretation

public domain, 166

public history of the environmental movement, xvii; *See also* National Council on Public History

public land, 154–155, 158, 166; public land sales, 167, 169, 178; public mineral lands, 168; right to use/right of way, 17, 169; *See also* controversy/controversial

public works projects, 171, 172; Federal Art Project, *8;* Works Progress Administration (WPA), *8,* 174; *See also* legislation, New Deal

Pyne, Stephen, 65

race, xiv, 13, 18–19, 69, 85, 153, 157, 167; *See also* ethnic/ethnicity

railcars: refrigerated, 168; Swift Refrigerator Line, 168

railroad, 15, 37, 57, 135–136; reclaiming railways, xv

ranchers, 171

Rand, Edward, 140–141; with John C. Redfield, *Flora of Mt. Desert Island Maine* (1894), 140

range: cattle grazing, 168; range lines (surveying), 166

REA. *See* Rural Electrification Administration

Reconstruction, 4, 11, 13, 30, 152; Lost Cause myth, 69, 77n16

recreation areas/recreational spaces, xi, xv, 3, 158, 172

recycle/recycling; Reduce, Reuse, Recycle, xiv

regions (United States): East/Eastern, 37, 67, 168; Great Plains, 21, 65, 80, 85, 108, 136–137, 167, 171, 172, 173, 175; Midwest, *16,* 96, 103, 108, 168, 171, 172; Southeast/Southeastern, 70, 71, 103, 115, 125, 167; Southwest, 108, 165, 168; South/Southern, 66–67, *68,* 69–75, 108, 157, 161, 166, 171, 172; West/Western, 7, 15, 80, 153, 154, 155, 156, 157, 158, 161, 162, 166, 167, 169, 170, 171, 173

regulation, 160, 168, 170; agricultural markets, 169; of banking, 171; consumer protection,

South Dakota, *41*, 166

Southeast. *See* regions

Southwest. *See* regions

space(s), x

Spence, Mark David, *Dispossessing the Wilderness* (1998), 11, 75

sprawl (urban, suburban, exurban), 125, 131, 159, 178

squatters, 166

Standard Oil, 92

Stanton, Cathy, *Public History and the Food Movement* (2017), 104

STEALTH. *See* Science, Technology, Engineering, and Math to the power of H (History and the Humanities)

STEAM. *See* Science, Technology, Engineering, the Arts, and Math

Stegner, Wallace, *Angle of Repose* (1971), 7

Steinberg, Ted, *Down to Earth* (2002), 63,

STEM. *See* Science, Technology, Engineering, and Math

Sternberg, George, 65

steward/stewardship, xiv, xv, xvi, xx, 7, 11, 52–53, 64

Stoll, Stephen, *Larding the Lean Earth* (2002), 106

stone, 168

Stone, Joel, *Interpreting Maritime History in Museums and Historic Sites*, 82, 87

Stoutamire, William, 13

Stramm, Henry E., 37–38

Stratton Porter, Gene, née Geneva Stratton, 73

suburb/suburban, 39, 41n2, 85, 131, 158, 159

superfund sites, 6

Surman, Francis, 97

surveying, 166

sustainable/sustainability, xiv, xvii, 21, 42n4, 55, 69; agricultural methods reversing injustice, 69–71; museum practices, xv, xvi, 64, 153

Sutter, Paul, 70; *Driven Wild* (2002), 7

Sutton, Sarah, *Environmental Sustainability at Historic Sites and Museums* (2015), xv

Swallow, Ellen. *See* ecology

Taylor, Nikki, *Driven Toward Madness* (2017), 82

Tennessee Valley Authority (TVA) (1933), 89, 172

tension. *See* controversy/controversial

Texas, 36, 166

Thayer, Rufus H., *History, Organization, and Functions of the Office of the Supervising Architect of the Treasury Department* (1886),

Thayer, Sylvanus, 116

Thierer, Joyce M., 71–74, 119–120

thinking historically (historical thinking), xvii, 3, 29–44, 63; about the environment, xvi, 55, 148; avoid presentism, xvii, 4, 32, 33, 50, 87, 108; cause and effect, 3, 32, 63; change over time, 3, 18, 82; chronological, 63; sequence of events, 63; thematic/topical, 63; symbolic/cultural construction, 63

Thoreau, Henry David, 167; *Walden* (1854), 167

Tilden, Freeman, xii–xv, 7, 11, 45–46, 143; *The Fifth Essence* (no date), xii; *Interpreting Our Heritage* (1957), xiii, 45–46, 57, 141, 151; *The National Parks: What They Mean to You and Me* (1951), xii–xiii; *See also* interpretation

timber. *See* trees

timeline/chronology/sequence of events, xvii, 165–179

Tompkins, Adam, *Ghostworkers and Greens* (2016), 108

topography, 51, 52, 103, 113, 165

Tourism/tourism destination, xi, 7, 11; agritourism, 13; *See also* ecotourism/nature tourism

township(s), 166; thirty-six square miles, 166; township lines (surveying), 166

toxic/toxicity, 13, 15, 18, 19, 24–25n24, 108, *109*, 161

tractors, 92–93

trade, xi, xvi, 113–121

trail(s); hiking, 3; nature, xv; metaphorical, 3–4

Transcendentalism, 16

transportation: canals, 116–118; infrastructure, 114–116, 125–128, 169; mode, 53, 103–104, 113–114, 115; systems, 50, 115, 125; transport and trade, 113–121, 129, 170; *See also* lighthouses, travel, railcars, railroads, roads, US Department of Transportation

travel, xi, xvi, 113–121

trees: Arbor Day, 159; policy to encourage planting, 168; timber, 169; *See also* legislation

Truman, Harry S., 176

Trustees of Public Reservations, 141

Tuan, Yi-Fu,

Topophilia (1974), 42n10

Turner, Dan, 171

TVA. *See* Tennessee Valley Authority

Twin Lights Historical Society, 127–128; Twin Lights power station, *128*

United Nations (UN): Food and Agriculture Organization (FOA), 177; Sustainable Development Goals, 143, *144;* Nature Reserves, 100n1

United Nations Educational, Scientific, and Cultural Organization (UNESCO), 36, 89; Biosphere Program, 89, 100n1; World Heritage Sites, 36

urban, 41, 50, 148, 158, 159, 169, 178; gardens, 16, 39; markets, 67, 79

Utah, 37, 169

U.S. Animal Health Association (USAHA), 169

U.S. Congress, 166, 169, 170, 171, 173; *See also* Farm Bloc, legislation

U.S. Constitution, 168

U.S. Department of Agriculture, 15, 168, 175, 179; agricultural experiment stations, 169; Agricultural Extension Service, 170; Bureau of Animal Industry [1884], 168, 171; Bureau of Soils [1901], 173; Division of Agricultural Soil (1894), 169; Federal Extension Service (1914), 170; Secretary of Agriculture, 169, 170, 171, 174, 176,

177; Soil Conservation Service (1935), 169, 173, 174, 179; Tuberculosis Eradication Division (1917), 171; U.S. Weather Bureau (1890), 168; Veterinary Division (1883), 168; *Yearbook of Agriculture*, 15–16; *See also* agriculture, livestock, disease eradication, disease prevention, regulation, Weather Bureau

U.S. Department of Commerce, 168

U.S. Department of the Interior, *8,* 154, 169, 173; General Land Office, 154; Secretary of the Interior, 30, 42n4, 152, 169; US Geological Survey, 154, 168; *See also* National Park Service

U.S. Department of War, 168; US Army Corps of Engineers, 53, 115, 154

U.S. Forest Service, 7, 70, 100n1, 132–136, 155

U.S. Geological Survey, 37, *39,* 154, 168

U.S. National War Garden Commission, 170–171; *See also* garden(s), school(s), Women's Land Army

U.S. Supreme Court, 170; *United States* v *Butler* (1936), 172

U.S. Weather Bureau. *See* Weather Bureau

VAF. *See* Vernacular Architecture Forum

Vachon, John, 99

Vail, David D., ix–x, xix–xx, *9,* 15, *47,* 107–108; *Chemical Lands* (2018), 15

vegetable(s), 58, 67, 79, 86, 175; biomass, 34; collards, 67, *68,* 69; greens, 67, 69, 79, 111; iceberg lettuce, 67–69; *See also* crop(s)

Vermont, 33; Marsh-Billings-Rockefeller National Historical Park, 33

Venezuela, xii

vernacular architecture. *See* buildings/ structures

Vernacular Architecture Forum (VAF), xix, 150

Vetter, Jeremy, *Field Life* (2016), 15

Virginia, 83, 104, 123, 166

vocational education, 171

About the Contributors

Ann E. Birney, PhD, is managing partner of Ride into History, a historical performance touring troupe with Joyce M. Thierer, PhD. Birney is co-author with Thierer of *Performing History: How to Research, Write, Act, and Coach Historical Performance* (2018) and *Telling History: A Manual for Performers and Presenters of First Person Narratives.*

Maureen Fournier is a seasonal National Park ranger at Acadia National Park, Mount Desert, Maine, and a volunteer researcher at the Mount Desert Island Historical Society.

Dr. Charles R. Foy is associate professor, Early American and Atlantic History at Eastern Illinois University. His scholarship focuses on eighteenth-century black maritime culture. A former fellow at the National Maritime Museum and Mystic Seaport, Dr. Foy has published more than a dozen articles on black mariners and is the creator of the *Black Mariner Database,* a dataset of more than 27,000 eighteenth-century black Atlantic mariners. He is completing a book manuscript, *Liberty's Labyrinth: Freedom in the 18th Century Black Atlantic,* that details the nature of freedom in the eighteenth century through an analysis of the lives of black mariners.

Tim Garrity is executive director of the Mount Desert Island Historical Society in Maine.

Al Hester is Historic Sites coordinator with the South Carolina State Park Service where he provides technical support for interpretation, historic preservation, and museum collections management. He received his MA in Public History from the University of South Carolina.

Aaron Hollis is director of Education at West Overton Museums. He studied anthropology at the University of Pittsburgh and earned his MA in Public History at West Virginia University.

John C. F. Luzader is principal of Living Museums of the West, specializing in costumed historic programming, historic interpretive training, and presentations. He is a National Association for Interpretation (NAI) Master and an NAI Fellow.

Caitlin McDonough MacKenzie earned her PhD in biology from Boston University; she is currently a David H. Smith Conservation Research postdoctoral fellow at the University of Maine's Climate Change Institute. She likes to explore underused sources of historical ecology data, including herbarium specimens, field notebooks, photographs, and old floras, and likes to facilitate community-based participatory science in phenology research, as the project to document the Champlain Society and the Origins of Acadia National Park (undertaken with the Mount Desert Island Historical Society) indicates.

Julie Mulvihill is the executive director of Humanities Kansas, a nonprofit since 1972 pioneering a movement of ideas through programming, grants, and partnerships.

Debra A. Reid, PhD, is curator of agriculture and the environment at The Henry Ford Museum. She saw the landscape through new eyes after earning her minor in Historical Geography at Southeast Missouri State University, studying with Michael Roark. She completed a minor field in geography, studying with Peter Hugill, and her PhD in History at Texas A & M University. She taught in the Department of History at Eastern Illinois University from 1999 to 2016 before joining The Henry Ford Museum.

Catherine Schmitt is communications director for the Sea Grant program at the University of Maine. She is the author of *Historic Acadia National Park: The Stories behind One of America's Treasures* (2016); *The President's Salmon: Restoring the King of Fish and Its Home Waters* (2015); and *A Coastal Companion: A Year in the Gulf of Maine from Cape Cod to Canada* (2008 2015).

Nora Pat Small, professor emerita, Eastern Illinois University (EIU), served as coordinator of the Historical Administration Master's Program and as department chair during her tenure at EIU. She is an architectural historian and historian of the Early American Republic and is currently examining the history of historic preservation in New Harmony, Indiana, as well as the roles of unheralded women in shaping the culture and society of the Midwest in the late-nineteenth and early-twentieth centuries.

Chris Sommerich is executive director of Nebraska Humanities.

Joyce M. Thierer, PhD, Emporia State University in Emporia, Kansas, is a founding partner of Ride into History, a historical performance touring troupe. She is co-author with Ann Birney of *Performing History: How to Research, Write, Act, and Coach Historical Performance* (2018) and *Telling History: A Manual for Performers and Presenters of First Person Narratives*.

David D. Vail, PhD, has training in environmental history, agricultural history, and science and technology, and earned a PhD at Kansas State University. He is associate professor in the Department of History at the University of Nebraska at Kearney. His book, *Chemical Lands: Pesticides, Aerial Spraying, and Health in North America's Grasslands since 1945* (2018) is part of the NEXUS Series: New Histories of Science, Technology, the Environment, Agriculture, and Medicine. He is book review editor for *The Public Historian* (National Council on Public History) and a member of the editorial committee for *Agricultural History*.